THE POLITICS OF PERVERTS

LGBTQ POLITICS SERIES
General Editors: Susan Burgess and Heath Fogg Davis

LGBTQ Politics: A Critical Reader
Edited by Marla Brettschneider, Susan Burgess and Christine Keating

Beyond Trans: Does Gender Matter?
Heath Fogg Davis

Disrupting Dignity: Rethinking Power and Progress in LGBTQ Lives
Stephen M. Engel and Timothy S. Lyle

With Honor and Integrity: Transgender Troops in Their Own Words
Edited by Máel Embser-Herbert and Bree Fram

LGBT Inclusion in American Life: Pop Culture, Political Imagination, and Civil Rights
Susan Burgess

The Politics of Perverts: The Political Attitudes and Actions of Non-Traditional Sexual Minorities
Charles Anthony Smith, Shawn R. Schulenberg, and Connor B. S. Strobel

The Politics of Perverts

The Political Attitudes and Actions of Non-Traditional Sexual Minorities

Charles Anthony Smith,
Shawn R. Schulenberg, *and*
Connor B. S. Strobel

NEW YORK UNIVERSITY PRESS
New York

NEW YORK UNIVERSITY PRESS
New York
www.nyupress.org

© 2024 by New York University
All rights reserved

Please contact the Library of Congress for Cataloging-in-Publication data.

ISBN: 9781479822737 (hardback)
ISBN: 9781479822744 (paperback)
ISBN: 9781479822768 (library ebook)
ISBN: 9781479822751 (consumer ebook)

This book is printed on acid-free paper, and its binding materials are chosen for strength and durability. We strive to use environmentally responsible suppliers and materials to the greatest extent possible in publishing our books.

Manufactured in the United States of America

10 9 8 7 6 5 4 3 2 1

Also available as an ebook

To all those members and allies of sexual minority communities, past, present, and future, who fought and fight daily for our human rights.

CONTENTS

Preface ix

1. Introducing the "Perverts": Non-Traditional Sexual Minorities 1
2. Three (Or More) Is Company: The Politics of Polyamory 27
3. Sticks and Stones Can Break My Bones, But Whips and Chains Excite Me: The Politics of the BDSM Community 68
4. The Naked Truth: The Politics of Nudists 105
5. Lions and Tigers and Bears, Oh My!: The Politics of Furries 149
6. All Bi Myself: Bisexuals in Non-Traditional Sexual Communities 186
7. A Passel of Perverts: A Comparison of These Non-Traditional Sexual Minorities 216
8. Conclusions, Implications, Paths Forward: Kink Coalitions 228

Acknowledgments 237

References 239

Index 255

About the Authors 261

PREFACE

The past four decades have seen a dramatic expansion of research on the political and social lives of lesbian, gay, and, more recently, transgender (LGT) people and issues. How politicians and voters who are straight react to the claims put forth by these sexual minority communities has produced even more research. One dimension of the growing research has specifically focused on the political attitudes and affiliations of LGT persons themselves. This research has revealed a lot about LGT people in the United States including not only their demographics but also their political identities, affiliations, and attitudes. Missing from this research is any systematic consideration of non-traditional sexual minorities. The academy and society as a whole seem to think of sexuality as a binomial distribution (straight or not). This naive understanding of sexuality leads other sexual minorities, who may be considered "sexual deviants" or "perverts" by mainstream society, to be understudied or completely ignored. We attempt to cure that ongoing omission through an examination of the political attitudes and activities of those who identify as members of or engage in the following groups: polyamory, BDSM, the furry fandom, and nudism. These groups face similar discrimination, stigma, shunning, and shame as what we refer to as "traditional sexual minorities." Indeed, there are no legal protections at either the state or federal level regarding employment law, family law, landlord-tenant law, healthcare law, or in any other dimension for individuals who identify with any of these communities. Generally speaking, both the academy and the culture know much less about the political attitudes and political activities of these people and their communities than the gay and lesbian community. We present our findings from our surveys, interviews, and ethnographic observations regarding the polyamory, BDSM, furry, and nudist communities. We also present our results from the large bisexual population among these communities. We demonstrate that sexuality and politics go hand in hand and the personal and the political are intertwined even (and perhaps especially) at the margins of society.

At the MidWest Political Science Association in 2015, authors Tony Smith and Shawn Schulenberg attended a large cocktail party hosted by the organization for the various minority group clusters based on gender, race, and sexuality. Our conversations with people at the reception time and again returned to excitement about the impending same-sex marriage and equality cases before the Supreme Court. On the heels of the 2013 *United States v. Windsor* case, the *Obergefell v. Hodges* and related cases seemed certain to finally deliver marriage equality to the gay and lesbian community in the summer of 2015. As we mingled among the attendees of the cocktail party, we heard the same excited optimism about the cases over and over again. We then began to talk among ourselves about the future of sexuality and politics research. Our first thoughts turned to polygamy and polyamory. Throughout the anti-marriage-equality campaigns over the years, polygamy and polyamory were routinely held up as the horrible and inevitable destination of the slippery slope of marriage equality. We began discussing the implications of the decisions for polygamists and polyamorists should the Court go the way of equality. We left the conference with a vague notion that sexuality and politics research was about to enter a new frontier. Marriage equality for the gay and lesbian community would no longer be the driving force behind so many of the research questions. But what would fill that void? What were the next set of pressing questions the academy should engage? Through the spring, we continued to consider the implications for the polygamy and polyamory community, but also began to think seriously about how the law inhibits or discriminates against those in the BDSM community. We had arrived at our first two groups to study based upon our consideration of cultural and legal disapproval of these identities and lifestyles.

Meanwhile, summer was upon us. In Orange County, California, there is a beach called West Street Beach that is known as "the gay beach." Our friends, Jaime and Jason, a gay male couple who had previously lived in Irvine, had returned and were hosting a party at West Street Beach to mark the beginning of summer. As we socialized with them, we described the polyamory aspect of the new project and Jason began to chuckle a little. He said, "I want to introduce you to someone," and he introduced us first to his boyfriend and then to Jaime's boyfriend. He then said, "We started a polyamory support group in Albuquerque [New Mexico]! If you want, you can come talk to us if it will help the research." While, at that point, we were thrilled with our luck, we immediately hit the jackpot a second time. When we said we were also thinking about the BDSM community as one of our groups, Jaime laughed and gestured to his swimsuit. He was wearing a small leather swimsuit with a metal zipper vertically across his protruding bulge. It turned out our experts on polyamory were also experts in BDSM.

As we went through the exercise of our research design, we frequently chatted with Jaime and Jason about the two communities. We familiarized ourselves with polyamory and BDSM to the greatest extent possible before we embarked on the research. As we built our background understanding of BDSM, we began to appreciate the role that gear and clothing play in that community and that realization led us both to the furry community and to nudists. The furry community relies on anthropomorphism for its aesthetic—and engages even more elaborate gear than BDSM—while nudists stripped away, literally and figuratively, the vestiges and symbolism of clothing. We felt that we had a solid set of groups to research, and we began to map out how we would gain access to these hard-to-find folks. We correctly anticipated that there would be some resistance to participating in the research and we would have to build trust as quickly as possible.

We also initiated the relatively challenging IRB (Institutional Review Board) process. While we did limit ourselves to only taking surveys from or interviewing adults, we were concerned that people in these communities could face personal and professional peril, even legal peril, in some instances, should we not be able to assure anonymity. Once we were certain we could credibly demonstrate anonymity and confidentiality, we began to arrange our field work. As we discuss in each chapter, we sought to establish trust in large part by interacting with these communities in their comfort zones. BDSM conventions, furry conventions, nudist facilities, and polyamory support groups were the locations of our first wave of data collection, followed by the utilization of a virtual snowball technique to gain entry to private and closed online communities. From the outset of the data gathering, we grew attached to each of these communities and fond of the people we met along the way. We left each encounter with respect and admiration for their commitment to living their authentic lives and for their collective and individual courage in dealing with the disapproving external world. While people outside these communities have had little experience with these groups as groups, many people have experienced the occasional light spanking or bondage during sex, a foray into skinny dipping or a nude beach, perhaps a sexual threesome or two, or a Halloween costume party that embraces an animal character. In other words, these groups are not quite as removed from the mainstream population as it might seem. We hope this work can begin to destigmatize these groups and encourage serious scholarship about them to flourish.

1

Introducing the "Perverts"

Non-Traditional Sexual Minorities

Despite the absence of empirical support of a bimodal or binary model of sexuality, political science tends to treat sexuality as if there are only two categories: straight and not straight. In practice, to speak of sexuality and sexual communities in the context of political science research, and frequently the political culture at large, means categorizing people as "heterosexual" or "not heterosexual." This categorization sets the foundation for heteronormativity, the term that conveys the idea that society not only sees heterosexuality as the default expectation, but that any deviation from that norm is improper and sanctionable—even perverse.

Although research about members of the transgender community has become much more common (see, e.g., Davis 2018; Taylor et al. 2018), bisexuals and other non-traditional sexual minorities are rarely the subject of political discourse or scholarly research in political science. As has been written elsewhere, "political science frames the world as straight or gay—heterosexual or not—a 1 or a 0" (Smith 2011, 35). Generally, the "heterosexual or not" model also rests on an assumption of heterosexual monogamy as the proper or best family structure. Although still understudied, the politics of sexuality and the intersection of sex and politics have emerged as serious avenues of research (see, e.g., Jakobsen 2020).

While the role of sex and sexuality in politics has moved into the mainstream, the study of identity politics has been mostly focused on racial, religious, and ethnic categories and a binomial or bimodal gender frame since its inception. Despite the fact that a wide variety of non-conforming sexual and social behavior—from polygamy to bestiality—is often presented by some social conservatives as the terrible and unavoidable consequence of marriage equality for the gay and lesbian community, political science has given no serious consideration to those who define themselves as members of an array of other sexual communities beyond the gay, lesbian, and trans communities. Certainly, the academy has yet to consider how these marginalized sexual communities may, or may not, be engaged in politics.

In this work, we focus on these four specific communities: polyamory, BDSM (bondage and discipline, dominance and submission, sadism and masochism), furry, and nudist communities. In each of these cases, members have strong, sometimes overlapping, sexual identities that translate into broader social identities, and the group members in each of these cases also form and participate in large and ostracized social communities. Because our research revealed that a large percentage of people in these four communities self-identify as bisexual, we also consider bisexuals within and across these communities as a group. We also then aggregate our data for a consideration of these groups as a collective of social groups at the periphery of society. We make an initial foray into filling the scholarly and discursive gap in our knowledge about the political identities, attitudes, and activities of these non-traditional sexual minorities with this study. We use the term non-traditional sexual minority for descriptive purposes and to differentiate these people, groups, and communities from the more thoroughly studied, and hence traditional, minority groups of gay men, lesbians, and members of the trans community. We chose the term "perverts" for framing the project because the elites (leaders) we interviewed for each group invariably reflected on the fact that the world at large thought of their community as perverts constantly engaged in perverted things. For those outside of these communities, deviant sex and sexuality define those inside the communities. We use the term with affection and respect in the same aesthetic vein it is used by members of these groups—that is, in order to gently mock those who do not understand these communities. We note that we asked each elite we interviewed if they objected to the title of the project, and without exception they enthusiastically supported the *perverts* nomenclature.

This introductory chapter proceeds with a discussion of the relevant literature from the study of sexuality and politics and identity politics. We then present our research questions, case selection process, and empirical strategy. Finally, we conclude with an overview of the book and a brief description of the chapters to follow.

Identity, Politics, and Sexuality: An Overview of the Literature

This project comes together at the intersection of various lines of scholarly inquiry including identity politics, contemporary lesbian, gay, bisexual, and transgender political analysis, and examinations of political behavior among minority groups. Group identities are social in nature and result from the interactions of society, culture, and a host of other individual and group variables (Schildkraut 2014). Some of the first forays into understanding political attitudes and the motivations behind voting relied on interpretations of identity (Key 1949; Berelson et al. 1954; Campbell et al. 1960). More recently, scholars have construed group identity as a direct predictor of political attitudes and therefore as an independent variable that can predict political behavior (see, e.g., Achen and Bartels 2016; Barreto and Pedraza 2009; Kinder and Kalmoe 2017, among many others). Although identity has often been construed as an antecedent to political attitudes, some religion and politics scholars have begun to challenge the supposition of stability, and hence exogeneity, of identity (Campbell et al. 2018; Djupe et al. 2018; Hout and Fischer 2014; Margolis 2018). Even more recent research suggests that, at least for some in the United States, a person will realign their identity to match their politics and therefore identity can be a dependent variable (Egan 2020). In short, the robust efforts to understand identity politics have continued unabated across the discipline and in popular discourse. This effort is the first to make an assessment about identity politics regarding these specific groups. As will be shown, the members of these groups identify as members of the group in an indistinguishable fashion from the more traditional identity groups such as race and religion.

Although many group-based memberships are not formed on the basis of a shared heritage, religion, or racial or ethnic category, these types of groups have not received the same level of scrutiny that those that might be thought of as organic affinity groups have received. For instance, research that considers group identity and partisan cohesion among African Americans, women, Jews, Catholics, white evangelicals, union members, and Hispanics among many other groups persistently demonstrate that social group identity is a major factor in election vote choices and political attitudes (see, e.g., Barreto and Pedraza 2009; Kinder and Kalmoe 2017; Margolis 2018; Bishin et al. 2020; 2021). Even political ideology has been thoroughly examined as a group identity (see, e.g., Huddy et al. 2015) Although sexuality is ubiquitous, if varied, across the human condition, and those who deviate from the narrow heterosexual, monogamistic conception of sexual orientation are found across every demographic category, little is known about the political attitudes and activities of these marginalized groups.

The individuals who participate in our four groups come from many different walks of life and their only shared trait is their participation in these communities. Of course, their participation in these communities also brings with it a shared stigma as these groups and their members are perceived as deviants by mainstream culture. Like many other types of identities, the members of these communities have constructed their identities through the interplay of complex processes including those clustered around social interaction, cognition, and affective responses which occur in their particular local and cultural contexts (Vignoles et al. 2006). As Sherry Jeansonne observes about members of the furry community, "although furries argue that being a furry is not something they do, it is something they are, sociologically we can say that becoming a furry is a social construction" (Jeansonne 2012, 74). That these groups are composed of people who have constructed their particular identities within a community of other like-minded constructed identities—that is, the nature of these are socially constructed identities—allows us to classify them as "essentially contested subjects" (Schulenberg 2013). That is, these are social groups with a fixed identity *label*, but no universal, objective, or unambiguous *definition* of who is and is not a member of the group (i.e., "contestable boundaries"). That a social identity group may be described as constructed is well established (see, e.g., Chandra 2006; 2012). Moreover, as members of a group create and construct their social identity, the psychological attachment they develop for their ideological in-group influences both their social and political behavior and attitudes (Devine 2015). These self-categorizing groups—where members choose to become affiliated and expend considerable time and energy in doing so—shape virtually every dimension of the members' lives in one way or another (Hogg and Terry 2000). Additionally, the commitment to the identity may be more intense than with some other identities because these identities carry with them the potential for social disapproval and a real risk of serious consequences arising out of that stigma. Family law, employment law, and fair housing—generally any nondiscrimination legal regime at any level of government—omit any protections for the members of these groups.

Just as in the case of members of the LGBT community—and sexuality generally—we have a difficult time pinning down exactly what the sexual aspect of the identity describes: A sexual desire? A sexual act? A sexual identity? A sexual culture? A sexual community? No one quality captures every LGBT person. Many people, for a variety of personal and societal circumstances, know what they find attractive and join fledgling LGBT youth communities before they have sex. Only focusing on sexual desires ignores the rich history of the nonsexual aspects of queer culture that nonetheless bring people together. Further, there is no essential cultural icon, practice, or custom that unites the millions of LGBT Americans. The groups we study share those distinctive experiences and features with the LGBT community.

The impact of a community holding an essentially contested identity is significant because it means that there is no objective definition of who is and who is not a member of the group. Moreover, we frequently see competing definitions used by different people within the groups. Some individuals may be more inclusive while others may be more exclusive as they conceptualize their communities and identities. Because there is no objective definition, we take our respondents at their word and generally focus on *identity* as a signifier of who is part of the community. In other words, we left it up to each subject to identify their membership in the group. If you said you were a furry, we accepted that as sufficient proof of membership. We can see within our cases that the sexualities within these communities variously encompass desires, acts, identities, and cultures at different times. Many individuals have an *identity* that centers on their sexual *desire* that leads to participation in sexual *acts* and engagement in these sexual *communities*. Accordingly, we refer to these identities as "chosen." That is, we are simply stating that the subjects in our studies chose to express their desires and identities and take part in these cultures and communities. Because these identities are constructed, and reconstructed over time, the complex relationship between individual identity and political socialization within these communities deserves further attention. Chosen sexual communities are overlooked by the scholarly analysis of groups that, generally speaking, are easier to define, such as those along lines such as race, ethnicity, or religion (Bobo and Gilliam 1990; Uslaner and Brown 2005; Barreto and Pedraza 2009).

These sexual minority communities possess a great deal of potential political power that currently evades the analysis of academic researchers, political practitioners, and policymakers because these communities operate at the periphery of society and away from the mainstream gaze. The essence of our project is an investigation of the political attitudes and political activities of these large but ignored non-traditional sexual communities. Within the past three decades, we have begun to learn a lot more about how sexual identity influences political attitudes as more polls add sexual identity demographic questions and social scientists focus more of their work on these questions. However, nearly all of this research focuses on LGT or heterosexual political attitudes and political behavior. Both the academy and the culture fail to consider the complex variations and categories of sexual identity that fall outside of this simple binary. We hope to broaden our understanding of how sexual identity beyond the "straight versus not straight," "gay versus not gay" dichotomy plays an important role in political socialization, identity, attitude, and behavior.

Research Question and Cases

We chose the polyamory, BDSM, furry, and nudist communities because each of these groups represents communities centered around a sexual identity that falls outside the binary of gay versus not gay. The responses to our open-ended questions revealed that a large number of members of these groups identify as bisexual, so we have also included a chapter devoted to the bisexuals of these chosen communities. Sexuality is a significant dimension of each of these groups although, similar to the gay, lesbian, and trans communities, there is much more to these identities than sex and sexuality. Again, like the gay, lesbian, and trans communities, each of these groups also suffers from an intense level of disapproval from the society at large. Unlike the current state of affairs for the gay, lesbian, and trans communities, these non-traditional sexual minority communities currently are faced with a complete absence of legal protections, either individually or as a class, from discrimination based on their identity as a member of the group. Recall these are also chosen communities/identities where members must opt in or choose to belong as a member. Sometimes membership is costly in terms of time commitment and effort, social ostracization, and actual monetary cost.

Moreover, membership in any of these communities is risky since they are well outside of the socially acceptable and mainstream of sexual identities, so the threat of social costs is ever present. These groups are largely invisible to the rest of society and are frequently marginalized and labeled as sexual deviants or perverts. Despite this marginalization, these communities may both be larger and more politically engaged than previously recognized. They represent vast and diverse demographic groupings and each has clear political ideas and affiliations. These groups possess an unrealized potential to influence the political system. We briefly define each group below, with a greater elaboration reserved for the specific group chapters. The length of the explanation varies depending on the group, because some of these communities are more easily explained than others.

Polyamory is often broadly understood as *consensual nonmonogamy*, a large umbrella term that encompasses a variety of emotional and sexual relationships and familial structures. Polyamory represents a sociosexual practice of engaging in an intimate and sexual relationship with multiple partners simultaneously. Although people have engaged in polyamorous relationships for as long as people have been recording history, the most common though not exclusive historical form was polygamy, where one male has multiple female partners. The modern polygamy community is not bound by the historical patriarchal format of one man as the head of the family with several obedient wives. Rather, these modern relationships may take a multitude of forms and include a wide range of numbers of participants. They vary in degree of emotional, physical, and financial commitment. Some polyamorous relationships are long-term with commitments along some or all of those dimensions while others entail nothing more than nonmonogamous sexual relations. Some involve raising children collectively and collaboratively while others do not involve raising children at all. Polyamory is a chosen identity, a sexual orientation, and a chosen community. Polyamory is chosen in that individuals have knowingly entered into relationships with multiple consenting partners. Polyamory is a sexual identity because sexual relations are a significant aspect of the core of polyamory identity. Polyamory is a chosen community because individuals socialize with polyamorists outside of their partners in a variety of informal and formal ways.

BDSM is an acronym for "Bondage and Discipline, Dominance and Submission, and Sadism and Masochism." People "in the life," as it is casually referred to by some of its adherents, are likely to go beyond mundane and casual experimentation and routinely partake in their preferred activities, attend organized BDSM conventions or gatherings, and interact regularly with other members of their community. BDSM involves various subgroups of sexual activity that frequently overlap and are sometimes practiced together. Bondage and Discipline refer to the desire to bind and restrict others, or be bound and restricted, by your sexual partner(s). Dominance and Submission refer to role play where the submissive partner gives all negotiated (play) power to the other, dominant player(s). Sadism and Masochism refer to the desire to inflict or receive erotic pain from a sexual partner.

Under the nomenclature of BDSM, we include two other closely related, often overlapping identities of sexual practice: the leather and the puppy play communities. These communities utilize the foundational premise of BDSM but carry out specific types of scenarios or scenes and have taken BDSM in a particularized direction. Leather constitutes the use of leather clothing and accessories and the fetishization of leather equipment used during dominant and submissive sexual roleplaying. The use of black leather carries connotations of masculinity, sexual power differentials, and may impose a degree of discomfort—caused by the tightly-bound leather clothing or accessories—that invokes themes of sadism and masochism. Puppy play is the execution of submissive and dominant sexual roleplaying specifically through the roles of puppy (submissive) and handler (dominant). Puppy play often includes the use of leather or latex clothing and plastic props to make the participants more closely resemble canines. They engage in canine-human and canine-canine interaction scenarios using the mannerisms and behaviors typically seen between humans and domesticated canines. Handlers are not always involved: sometimes puppy play involves just the puppies playing with one another, establishing dominant-submissive relationships with each other and among the "pack." We use the acronym BDSM to refer to the traditional bondage-discipline-dominance-submission-sadism-masochism practices in addition to the leather and puppy play activities. We feel confident doing this because the latter two are subcultures of BDSM. We note though, there are many other subcultures within BDSM. Like polyamory, BDSM is a chosen identity, a sexual orientation, and a chosen community. BDSM is chosen in that individuals have consensually entered into specific types of relationships with other members of the BDSM community. BDSM is a sexual identity because sexual relations are a significant aspect of the core of BDSM identity. BDSM is a chosen community because individuals socialize with other members of the BDSM community in a variety of informal and formal ways.

Nudists or naturists consists of people who lead clothing-optional lifestyles. This can manifest itself through casual and routine nudity around the house but, importantly, also encompasses some element of social nudity or nudity outside of the immediate family. One mainstay of nudism is the nudist resort. These resorts range from luxury spa type facilities to the much more common and modest campground- and cabin-style rural retreats. Nudity around others, social nudity, is a critical dimension of the identity of a nudist. Nudist community spaces range from those that are highly sexualized with widely available opportunities for seeking out casual sex partners to those facilities that are specifically marketed and operated as family-friendly, nonsexualized spaces which include children of all ages as well as adults. Like polyamory and BDSM, nudism represents both a chosen identity, arguably a sexual identity, and a chosen community. Nudists have practiced nudism and forged nudist communities in a variety of ways at least since the late 1800s in the United States. Nudism is chosen in that individuals have consensually entered into clothing-optional social spaces. Being a nudist may be a sexual identity because nudity and sexuality are often seen as intertwined. Nudism is a chosen community because individuals socialize with other nudists in a variety of informal and formal ways.

The furry community, or furry fandom, consists of a subset of cosplay or costume play, where anthropomorphic animal costumes are worn and animal-like identities are assumed. One critical dimension of the furry fandom is that, unlike other types of cosplay, there is no canonical parameters that must be recognized (Dunn 2021). That is, superhero, Star Wars,

Star Trek, and other cosplay communities follow the rules and strictures of their literary origins (Strike 2017). In contrast, members of the furry fandom or furry community are free to construct their own identities, communities, and culture. (Reyson et al. 2020; Dunn 2021). Not all furries own or wear fursuits, which are elaborate full-body costumes, or have "fursonas,"—a portmanteau of "fur" and "persona"—which are the assumed identities of the fursuit characters. However, all furries identify as fans of and participants in the activities of those who don the suits and assume the identities including attending the furry conventions (Patten 2017). Furry fandom is also highly engaged in the creation and dissemination of furry art and the creation of furry fiction, like comic books via online communities. Although erotica is a critical dimension of furry art and the fursuits can be and sometimes are designed to be functional during sexual activity, the conventions are generally expressly billed as family friendly. The organizers and attendees make sure that the adult and sexually explicit content is sequestered from the other content. The culture of the furry community is overtly and unambiguously protective of and friendly toward children. That said, not all furries engage in sexual activities as part of their furry identity, and the community itself struggles with the role that sexuality plays. Some in the community see sex as central to the identity and culture while others see it as a salacious but minimal aspect of the culture. Some go so far as to urge the exclusion of sexuality from furry culture in order to win respectability or at least diminish hostility from the nonfurry society. Like the previous groups, the furry fandom represents both a chosen identity, perhaps a sexual identity, and a chosen community where sexuality is often intertwined. Joining the furry community is chosen in that individuals have undertaken considerable time and effort to learn about and join the community. Being a furry may be a sexual identity because sexual relations are a significant aspect of the core identity for many members of the community. The furry fandom is a chosen community because individuals socialize with other furries in a variety of informal and formal ways.

Our data revealed a large number of people from these four communities who, in response to one of our open-ended questions, self-identified in some way as bisexual. Accordingly, we also provide our observations and data about the prevalence of bisexuality in these communities. In hindsight, we should not have been surprised that these communities that exist at the sexual frontier have very large populations of self-identifying bisexuals among their ranks. We perhaps were surprised by the numbers because we fell victim to the norms in the literature. The B in LGBT is frequently neglected in the investigation of sexual minorities (Smith 2011). In the bimodal or binary model of sexuality, assumed by much of the political science literature, bisexuals are categorized and incorporated within the larger LGBT community defined simply as "not straight." The goals, challenges, and rights claims of the bi community are assumed to be identical to, and therefore subsumed within, the broad roster taken by the literature to be shared by all sexual minorities. The academic literature reflects the reality of political discourse for bisexuals in the United States. They are often invisible both within LGBT communities and in our larger political system as a whole. Bisexual "issues," while overlapping in some areas with other sexual minorities, are distinct, as they face unique forms of discrimination—including biphobia and monosexism, to name two—from both other members of the gay, lesbian, and trans communities and more generally from heterosexuals. In the end, the agendas of the major national LGBT activist groups have been slow to incorporate the independent claims of the bisexual community.

Moreover, the broader public does not distinguish bisexuals as a marginalized group with specific concerns. Given this lack of visibility and power within the LGBT community and more generally in the public at large, some bisexuals have instead found themselves better incorporated into other sexual minority communities like those we study here. Here we discuss bisexuals in the polyamory, BDSM, furry, and nudist communities, which provide them with a venue for political action and interaction as well as a simpatico community in which to locate. In our analysis of bisexuality in these communities, we analyzed bisexuality separately and as an umbrella term that includes pansexuality, bicurious, heteroflexible, and related terms. This group varies somewhat from the others because while membership in each group represents both a chosen identity and a chosen community, the identity dimension of also being bisexual brings what may be an innate characteristic into an intersection with chosen identities.

The communities we have studied have generally not been the direct target of laws singling them out for sanction. Instead, each community has had to deal with real threats from laws that were not designed to regulate these communities and the activities of the community members. They are all victims of "latent illegality" which refers to how a cluster of laws are weaponized to regulate new groups and behaviors unconnected to the original intent of the regulation in question (Strobel 2022). While the criminal penalties stemming from this sort of legal-mission creep can be severe, the stigma of activity or even identity being seen as illegal, and other extralegal consequences, can be even more intense than the actual a legal sanction or the threat of actual legal sanction. A judge could dismiss charges with prejudice and these latently illegal individuals and groups could nonetheless lose everything they treasure. We discuss the latent illegality risks for each group below.

Furries are routinely forced to differentiate themselves from the concept of bestiality, the BDSM community from nonconsensual sexual violence, polyamory from polygamy, and nudists from indecent exposure. Prohibitions against bestiality predate Abrahamic law and were meant to prevent interspecies sex. The laws were never conceived for the purpose of regulating identity claims, like furries who might have fursonas (anthropomorphized animal personas). Laws against sexual violence like rape and molestation are thought to protect individuals who did not and/or could not consent to sexual activity, not to police the tastefulness of particular kinks and fetishes of consenting adults. As discussed in the BDSM chapter, many intimate interactions are illegal at the level of a felony, and no state currently recognizes consent as a defense to battery. When different governments outlawed polygamy, the state addressed its concern through legal contracts and benefits and did not venture to regulate the number of simultaneous intimate bonds people might sustain. Laws against nudity that arose in the nineteenth and early twentieth centuries in the United States sought to shield bystanders' eyes and limit the use of public spaces for nude bathing and hygiene, not regulate how people lived in private spaces. Indeed, even the bisexual community has been subjected to a host of prohibitory laws that specifically targeted gay men and lesbians.

People in these four communities have been evicted, fired, lost custody, and faced a host of extralegal tribulations as a result of either state action against them or the attribution of illegality to these communities and the associated stigma. This is on top of the experiences of ridicule, harassment, bullying, and shunning the individuals in these communities have faced despite their actions and identities not affecting anyone else. At a community level, the spectacle that latent illegality has created can stifle individual and group behavior in addition to new membership. The power of latent illegality is that the shadow of the law becomes enough to encourage social enforcement by influencing norms and moral intuitions to dramatically affect life course outcomes.

Methodology

In order to examine the political attitudes and political activities of these marginalized communities, we utilized a mixed-methods approach. We administered two types of in-person surveys, conducted live in-depth interviews, expanded our subject pool through a novel "virtual snowball" technique, engaged in participant observation, and utilized modified ethnographic approaches. For our first type of survey, we parroted a Pew Research Center survey on general political attitudes and political activities which we customized for each group. Each question had a series of multiple-choice answers from which the respondents could choose. This allows us to compare our groups to the general population. Our second type of survey contained a series of open-ended questions where the respondents could expand, expound, and explain as they wished. This allowed our respondents to speak in their own voice as well as raise any issues not included in the Pew Research Center survey. At every venue we held informal, unstructured interviews with organizers and other elites as well as attendees. By elites, we mean anyone who was in any position of leadership or formal influence. For instance, our elite interviews included presenters from panels or workshops, social activities organizers, directors of communication, logistics managers, and security personnel. We attended workshops, events, and social interactions for each group and participated where possible and appropriate. We discuss our efforts for each group in brief below and at length in each group-specific chapter. There were slight variations in how we approached our data gathering in part due to differences among the groups, and in part because as we learned more about the different groups, we simply got better at understanding what we needed to do to engage the group members.

We did not change the surveys throughout the data gathering process and it may be useful to expand on the content of the surveys at this point. As mentioned, to measure the political attitudes and activities of each community, we administered two sets of surveys. The first set consists of twenty-nine multiple-choice questions about our respondents' demographic characteristics and political attitudes and political behaviors. In order for us to have a metric of comparison, we drew these questions from the Pew Research Center for the People and the Press (various years) (see Appendix 1.1). We also asked a second set of eleven open-ended questions to allow our subjects to speak in their own voices and provide us with information that might not be captured by the multiple-choice survey (see Appendix 1.2). Both were administered by us through Survey Monkey, and all answers were recorded anonymously with full confidentiality for our respondents. While we administered many of the surveys in person, about two-thirds of our respondents were obtained and surveyed through our virtual snowball technique discussed below. The surveys were the same for both in-person and online respondents. Some participants were provided with a modest cash incentive to take the surveys or a chance at a drawing for a somewhat larger reward, depending on the logistics of our survey site. In the case of our fieldwork within the polyamory group, respondents were each paid five dollars. In other cases, respondents were entered into a drawing to win a larger cash prize of either $50 or $100. We had light snacks available for those who took the surveys in person. We used candy when we were inside at the BDSM and furry conventions and salty snacks when we were outside at the nudist camps because the candy would melt in the sun. We also had water bottles and small bottles of sunscreen to hand out at the nudist camps. While we explain our steps for gathering data in more depth in each chapter, we give a quick overview here of our immersion and approach for each group. For each group, we obtained our data first through a convenience sample and then through what can be called a "virtual snowball sampling" (Baltar and Brunet 2012). In short, to get our foot in the door, we contacted elites and group organizers representing each of our communities to see if we could attend their events to promote our survey and talk with attendees. Our initial forays into these communities included data collection at two polyamory support groups; data collection on BDSM (including leather and puppy play) at three BDSM conventions; data collection on nudism at three nudist resorts; and data collection about furries at four furry conventions. One BDSM convention we attended had significant overlap with furries and polyamorists and some lesser overlap with nudists. Another furry and anime convention we attended had some modest overlap with BDSM. We list all of our group-specific efforts in each group-specific chapter including the locations of the field work.

In addition to on-site interviews, we also increased our volume of responses and broadened our audience well beyond our initial "seeds" through a technique called "virtual snowball sampling." In brief, snowball sampling, a method that has been around for more than fifty years, entails interviewing some randomly selected individuals in a specific group or community and then asking those subjects to name other possible interview subjects (Goodman 1961). This technique is especially appropriate in cases such as ours because the communities are composed of hidden populations, which means the size and scope of the populations are unknown and the stigma of association with these groups makes random sampling difficult and perhaps unreliable (Heckathorn 1997). To increase our leverage from the snowball sample technique, we utilized a "virtual snowball sampling," process which we collected in two different ways (Baltar and Brunet 2012). First, at the end of our in-person interviews, we asked each respondent if they were part of any closed social media or other online communities dedicated to their sexuality community (e.g., a furry fan fiction website, a polyamory support group) and whether they would be willing to share our survey links with their group. Separately, we also independently found online groups dedicated to each group and asked the owners or moderators if they would share our surveys. In each case, we asked the group administrators for permission to post our surveys in their group before we moved forward. Ultimately, we were led to several closed social media groups for each community where our surveys were shared.

We anticipate that because we used a novel, digital snowball sampling strategy, that our sample is younger, perhaps more educated, and certainly more technologically sophisticated than the population as a whole. Moreover, because we were able to reach some otherwise more difficult to study sectors of these communities this way, some sectors may be represented more than others. We do not assert that any of our samples are fully representative of the groups, but rather, we view these as sophisticated convenience samples that are useful, even if not fully representative, given that this inquiry is the initial effort to understand the political attitudes and political behaviors of these groups.

We began with a polyamory support group located in Albuquerque, New Mexico. As we mentioned at the outset, we discovered this group wholly by chance at the very beginning of our research. We were casually talking about the project in concept with two friends, Jason and Jaime, at an informal beginning-of-summer beach party. As we described the project, they both started chuckling in a slightly amused way. Jason then introduced us to his boyfriend and explained that he and Jaime both had boyfriends in addition to the committed relationship they shared. We had fortuitously engaged two members of the polyamory community without realizing it. Moreover, Jason told us he had organized a polyamory support group that we were more than welcome to come meet with. Jaime then pointed out he was wearing a black leather speedo that zipped up the front over his genital area and said with a grin, "I can probably help you out with more than one of the groups." We stayed in contact as moved forward with the project, and eventually, we spent four consecutive days among them in Albuquerque. We attended one of the polyamory support group's monthly social events—a large potluck dinner with over seventy-five people in attendance. We explained our project and then as we passed iPads around for people to take the surveys, we also conducted semistructured interviews with anyone who was willing to talk to us. We also attended a smaller presentation about polyamory at an LGBT nonprofit and likewise conducted semistructured interviews and took survey responses there. We engaged in in-depth interviews over several days with the elites we initially contacted to set up the group meeting. After we were given access to closed social network polyamory groups by some of the in-person subjects, we were then able to electronically distribute the surveys to the members of those closed social network groups—this was our "virtual snowball" technique. We then had many online exchanges with people both asking questions and providing us with perspectives that were rich supplements to the survey instruments. Finally, we also assessed the polyamory group as if it was a standard identity group, like race or religion, and engaged in participant observation that we more fully discuss in the polyamory chapter.

For our study of BDSM, we first contacted the organizers for "Beyond Vanilla"—a large annual BDSM conference in Dallas, Texas. We purchased space in the Gear and Goods Marketplace Hall that was held within the conference space. The conference was held in a hotel. We stayed in the hotel as conference attendees in order to be exposed to the environment around the clock. We were there for four full days. We took surveys in the gear and goods hall and held semistructured interviews with anyone willing to talk to us. We talked at length with the organizers and many of the volunteers for the event as well as many of the attendees. We attended the social events, including observing and talking to attendees at the sex party gatherings in the dungeon in the evenings. We also attended some of the panel presentations. Again, the surveys were distributed electronically to closed social network groups, and we also had many interactions with those who were virtually contacted. We then also visited DomCon for two days in Los Angeles, California, and Frolicon in Atlanta, Georgia, for four days for participant observation, elite interviews, and ethnographic analysis.

For the Nudists, we took three field trips to two nudist resorts in Southern California and one in Pennsylvania. At our first location in California and our location in Pennsylvania, we set up a table by the pool and dining areas, and, after we disrobed per community norms, took surveys, engaged in semistructured interviews, talked in depth with the elites, and had additional interactions with those contacted through their social networks. Like all of our cases, we asked participants if they would share our surveys with their friends and if they knew of closed social networks we could access. For our final visit, the second California location, we conducted participant observation, elite interviews, and ethnographic analysis. Each of the three nudist facilities had campground areas that had provided ample space and the necessary infrastructure for recreational vehicles (RVs). Each also had traditional tent style camping areas and cabins for rent by the night, week, or month that ranged in size from one to three bedrooms. Two of the facilities had full-time residents who seemed to have long-term rentals on the premises. Each also had many members who resided nearby and who would routinely spend the day at the facilities. All three resorts had a restaurant, multiple pools, hiking trails, tennis courts, pétanque or bocci ball, tennis and pickleball courts, basketball courts, and a host of other indoor and outdoor recreational facilities. They all scheduled a variety of activities from knitting to poker and from painting to yoga. Each one also had saunas, spas, and hot tubs. They also routinely schedule special events like Halloween costume parties, Thanksgiving potlucks, Easter egg hunts, and Fourth of July 5k races. In short, if you were to design a summer camp type experience for adults and families, these facilities would be exactly what you would construct.

For the furries, we attended Anthrocon in Pittsburgh, Pennsylvania (the self-described largest furry convention in the world), Califur in Pomona, California, and Further Confusion in San Jose, California. We also attended Frolicon in Atlanta, Georgia, which is a blended event for BDSM and cosplay including furries. We also attended Sakura-Con in Seattle, Washington, at the very beginning of the project. For Anthrocon we were unable to book a table in their marketplace hall, so we simply walked around the convention area and asked people to take our surveys. We also set up in the lobby of our hotel—which was full of Anthrocon attendees—and took surveys and conducted interviews there. We were there for four days.

For Califur, we were able to secure a table in the marketplace hall so we were able to attract survey participants and conduct interviews using the same techniques we used at the BDSM conferences. We had candy to handout and had a large sign on the table that provided the information about how to enter our cash drawing. We attended the conference for four days and gave away $50 in a random draw on the last afternoon. Participants would take the surveys and, if they wanted to be in the cash draw, write their email or phone number on a slip of paper and drop it in a fishbowl for the drawing later. This helped assure them that their identities were not associated with their answers in anyway. For Further Confusion and Frolicon, we did not take new surveys but rather conducted elite interviews and participant observation and engaged in ethnographic analysis. Frolicon was notable because it included members from each of our categories with several educational panels and workshops on polyamory and the furry fandom in addition to BDSM. Frolicon also had nudists in attendance and multiple opportunities and events geared toward social nudism like a strip boardgame event, a "dance off with your pants off" event, and a "strip twister" event, among others. As with the other groups, we engaged in semistructured interviews, in-depth conversations with the elites, and had additional communications after the virtual snowballing.

We begin each chapter with an expanded definition of the group as well as a brief history of the group. We follow that with a discussion of the group-specific germane literature as well as a full explanation of our data gathering strategy and execution for each specific group. We include the data we collected as well as participant quotes, our observations, and some anecdotes from our field work. Whenever we quote a member of one of these communities by first name only or by a character name, we use a pseudonym. If we use a first and last name and identify that person's role, we have used their actual name with their permission. We are using pseudonyms for most of our quotes since all members of these communities face the risk of severe consequences if they are identified as a member of one of these communities because of the stigma associated with these groups. While we conducted essentially the same style of data gathering across these communities, each group presented a different experience for us in profound and interesting ways that we discuss briefly in the chapters and in more depth in the conclusion.

Accordingly, our approach to data gathering differed at the margins but not in significant ways. For example, some people were given a small amount of money to take the survey while others were offered a chance to be in a lottery for a larger (although still small) amount of money. Others, in particular those who took the surveys remotely, were not offered any incentive. One of the truly remarkable aspects of the project that surprised us is that the communities had much more in common with each other, and with almost any other affinity group, than we could possibly have anticipated. The communities were supportive and protective of their members while friendly to, if initially suspicious of, us. They were all welcoming of new members and eager to show the newbies the ropes. They are mindful and reverential of their histories and are acutely aware of the challenges the outside world presents because of stigma and bias. These groups also all seem to take a bit of pride in their status as outsiders and rebels. Without exception, we found the members of these communities to have a humorous attitude about how those outside of the community may react to them.

Although, from a demographic standpoint, we did manage to capture a wide range of respondents across all the groups, we were still struck by the fact that white people were overrepresented in our responses compared to who we saw in attendance at the various groups. We explore various reasons for this in the conclusion, but in brief, we believe this is a manifestation of white privilege more than an indication that people of color are less involved in these communities. The intersection of risk for communities of color may mean there is simply a lower percentage of people interested in proclaiming their status as a member of the group. White people may be less concerned because whatever stigma they may face is not also compounded by racism. We touch on this issue in each chapter as the racial makeup of our pool of respondents varied a bit group to group.

The Chapters

Chapter 2 is titled "Three (or More) Is Company: The Politics of Polyamory." We find those who identify as members of the polyamory community are very politically active—they routinely vote and donate to candidates. They are either very liberal or, to a lesser extent, libertarian but share core values about personal freedom and limited government. We found a wide range of polyamorists from an age perspective. We found broad variation in the size and structure of the family groups from three to many. At the first event we attended, we found it fascinating that, if you did not know the event was a polyamory event, you might have mistaken it for any neighborhood potluck. The only unusual thing at all was the romantic relationship configurations. That is, three or more people holding hands, resting with their arms intertwined, or otherwise showing physical affection in some way was the only clue that this was a special gathering. Relationships and constant communication among partners were both on full display and issues of sex and sexuality, beyond the casual physical affection like hand holding, were no more prevalent than at a shopping mall or a restaurant.

Chapter 3 is titled "Sticks and Stones Can Break My Bones, But Whips and Chains Excite Me: The Politics of the BDSM Community." Here, the group was more evenly divided between very liberal and very libertarian. Although, much like the polyamory community, they can also be described as primarily concerned with personal liberty and limited government. They too are very active politically. Unlike the polyamory community, there could be no question about the sex and sexuality aspects of the BDSM spaces. Indeed, sex and sexuality are the unifying thread of the community. Still, there is much more to BDSM and the BDSM community than the sex. Our respondents are passionate about politics. Betty—one of the elites we interviewed, jokingly said, "Well hell, of course we're into politics, we're a bunch of masochists and sadists after all!"

Chapter 4 is titled "The Naked Truth: The Politics of Nudists." The nudists were older, whiter, and more conservative than the other groups, but with a strong libertarian bent to their conservatism. Unlike the other groups, which are much more liberal than the general population, the distribution of the nudists' political attitudes maps closely to the public in general. Like the first two groups, the nudists are politically active—they routinely vote and donate to candidates or parties they support. For the nudists, there seems to be a persistent tension in the background between embracing a nonsexual culture and being naked around many other naked people in a social setting.

Chapter 5 is titled "Lions and Tigers and Bears, Oh My!: The Politics of Furries." Perhaps because their community partially exists virtually or perhaps because they were on average younger than the other groups, the members of the furry fandom were much less politically engaged than the other groups. While they had opinions and political preferences, they did not reveal themselves to be as politically active as the other groups. Still, while their youth might account for their relative lack of political activism, they are very liberal in their political attitudes. The furries who answered our surveys and talked with us in our interviews were very comfortable with sexual fluidity. They also uniformly saw sex and sexuality as a relatively narrow aspect of the community. Without question, some members of the furry fandom see it as a sexual identity, but in general, for most members of the community, sex and sexuality are just one part of their identity and community. An interesting difference between the furries and the other categories we surveyed and interviewed is that only among the furries did we have any respondents identify as asexual.

Chapter 6 is titled "All Bi Myself: Bisexuals in Non-Traditional Sexual Communities." As noted earlier, we were surprised to find that a range of

20 to 45 percent of individuals in these groups self-identified as bisexual. The idea for the chapter came from an interaction we had at the BDSM conference Beyond Vanilla. Three women approached our table to take the surveys. As they took their time responding carefully and thoroughly to the questions, they constantly snacked on the candy we had spread out on our table. They paused to chat about which of the candy bars they liked best and to talk about what candy they wished we also had. Once they were done with the surveys, they handed back the iPads and the largest woman—she was just over six feet tall and very big—thanked us in her thick Texas drawl. She said: "I appreciate y'all. I appreciate y'all taking our community seriously and I appreciate y'all treating us with dignity and respect. I also appreciate this here candy, cuz by and large, we're all bi and large!" All three women—and us—had a good-hearted laugh at her observation. Over time, once we began to see the prevalence of bi self-identification in the data, we revisited that conversation and decided that should be the lead anecdote for it. We also spend time in this chapter discussing why someone who identifies as bisexual might find a home in these communities in particular. We discuss the intersecting stigma members of the bi community face not only from heterosexuals but also from the gay and lesbian community.

Chapter 7 is titled "A Passel of Perverts: A Comparison of These Non-Traditional Sexual Minorities." Here, we collapse all the data and compare it to similar data from the general public. We discuss the ways in which these communities are similar and the ways in which they are different. This includes common stigmas associated with these groups like the notion the members are all sexual perverts. This also includes some commonalities like some broad political attitudes and some community norms.

Chapter 8 is the conclusion where we discuss what we learned from this endeavor as well as some of the things that we failed to figure out or could have done better or differently. We make some observations from this research about the challenges of field work among communities that are vulnerable, hidden, or prefer to not be the focus of attention. We discuss possible conflicts of interest between the elites who manage the events and places that are central to these communities and the members of the communities. We also address the notion of "coming out"—or disclosure of identity—for these communities and compare that experience to that of the gay and lesbian communities. Finally, we address avenues of additional inquiry and research and briefly touch on what might be thought of as a follow-up project.

Appendix 1.1

These questions were modeled on a series of Pew Research Center questions. We present the question with the multiple-choice answers that were available to the respondents.

Part 1: Demographic Questions
1. Sex: Male, Female, Other
2. Age: 18–29; 30–49; 50–64; 65+
3. Race: White, Non-Hispanic; Black, Non-Hispanic; Hispanic; Native American; Asian/Pacific Islander, Mixed, Other
4. Education: High School or Less, Some College, College Graduate, Graduate School
5. Income: More Than $75,000, $30,000–$74,900, $20,000–$29,000, Less Than $20,000, Prefer Not to Answer
6. Religion: Evangelical Christian, Protestant, Catholic, Islamic, Jewish, Other, None
7. Attendance of Religious Services: Weekly or More, Monthly, Yearly, Seldom or Never
8. Marital Status: Single, Never Married; Single, Divorced or Widowed; Married; Married More Than One Time
9. Employment Status: Employed Full-Time, Employed Part-Time, Not Employed, Not Employed But Searching For Work

Part 2: Political Attitudes and Participation
10. Which of these statements best describes you? Are you absolutely certain that you are registered to vote at your current address; are you probably registered, but there is a chance your registration has lapsed; or are you not registered to vote at your current address?
11. And how often would you say you vote in primary elections—that is, the elections in which a party selects their nominee to run in a general election. Would you say you vote in primary elections always, nearly always, part of the time, or seldom?

12. In politics today, do you consider yourself a Republican, Democrat, or Independent?
13. In politics today, do you consider yourself a Republican, Democrat, or Independent? If Independent/No preference/Other party/Don't know/Refused: As of today do you lean more to the Republican Party or more to the Democratic Party?
14. In general, would you describe your political views as very conservative, conservative, moderate, liberal, or very liberal?
15. Would you say news organizations . . . are liberal, or conservative?
16. Thinking about the Supreme Court . . . In your view, do you think the current Supreme Court is conservative, middle of the road, or liberal?
17. Would you like to see Republican leaders in Washington move in a more conservative direction or a more moderate direction?
18. Would you like to see Democratic leaders in Washington move in a more liberal direction or a more moderate direction?
19. Thinking about the Republican Party's position on some issues, do you think the Republican Party is too conservative, not conservative enough, or about right when it comes to . . . government spending?
20. Thinking about the Republican Party's position on some issues, do you think the Republican Party is too conservative, not conservative enough, or about right when it comes to . . . abortion?
21. Thinking about the Republican Party's position on some issues, do you think the Republican Party is too conservative, not conservative enough, or about right when it comes to . . . gay marriage?
22. Thinking about the Republican Party's position on some issues, do you think the Republican Party is too conservative, not conservative enough, or about right when it comes to . . . immigration?
23. Thinking about the Democratic Party's position on some issues, do you think the Democratic Party is too liberal, not liberal enough, or about right when it comes to . . . government spending?
24. Thinking about the Democratic Party's position on some issues, do you think the Democratic Party is too liberal, not liberal enough, or about right when it comes to . . . abortion?
25. Thinking about the Democratic Party's position on some issues, do you think the Democratic Party is too liberal, not liberal enough, or about right when it comes to . . . gay marriage?

26. Thinking about the Democratic Party's position on some issues, do you think the Democratic Party is too liberal, not liberal enough, or about right when it comes to . . . immigration?
27. How often do you discuss political issues with your friends and family? Daily, weekly, seldom, hardly ever?
28. Have you contributed more than $25 to a political campaign or cause in the last two years?
29. What state do you live in? (Open Response)

Appendix 1.2

The open-ended questions were not based on Pew Research Center questions. Instead, these were based on a focus group beta test we did with a small group of people who were aware of if not active in these groups. We asked that group what else we should ask and constructed these open-ended questions based on our own thoughts as well as those of the focus group.

Part 3: Open-Ended Questions
1. Do you identify as part of the (insert each community here) community? How do you identify sexually? Do you carry one identity or multiple? If you carry multiple, are some more dominant than others?
2. How did you learn about and become involved in [insert each community here]? Friends? Online?
3. Do you feel a sense of community with others involved in [insert each community here]? If so, how important is the "community" aspect of [insert each community here] to you?
4. Does being a member of the [insert each community here] have any impact on your attitudes about politics or political issues? Do you see any connecting underlying themes among the following issues: government spending, abortion, gay marriage, immigration? If so, how? If yes, what are they?
5. Do you discuss political issues with people in [insert each community here]? If yes, is it because you believe they share the same values? If no, are you afraid it will cause conflict? If sometimes, are you selective? What type of information do you share and with

whom? How often do you discuss political issues with the other people in [insert each community here]?
6. Are there any political issues that unite the [insert each community group here] community? If so, what are they?
7. As a follow up, in what forms of political activism (petitions, lobbying, fundraising) does the [insert each community here] community engage?
8. Do you think the [insert each community here] community should be more politically active, less active, or is it just right?
9. Do you think people who are not part of the [insert each community here] community know about or understand the [insert each community here] community?
10. What, if anything, do you think politicians think about the [insert each community here] community?
11. Is there anything else you think we should know or you would like to share?

2

Three (or More) Is Company

The Politics of Polyamory

Polyamory is often described as "consensual nonmonogamy," a large umbrella term that encompasses a variety of emotional and sexual relationships and family structures. The polyamory community exemplifies the complexities of sexuality and sexual identity a byproducts of the intersection of desire, acts or behavior, nonsexual identity, and community. Polyamory is a both a chosen identity and a chosen community, the parameters of which, generally, are bounded by the emotional and physical relationships with other members of the community. Accordingly, because polyamory is an essentially contested identity, it is an appropriate case for us.

Like our other cases, we seek to understand the political attitudes and the political activities of the members of the polyamory community. This includes an assessment of the role of polyamory identity and engagement in the polyamory community as a reliable indicators of political attitudes akin to other demographic characteristics like age, income, and race. We also consider whether the polyamory community is a social network which mediates the political discourse for its members.

Those who choose to become polyamorous and join the polyamory community do so despite the fact that nonpolyamorous sectors of society frequently have an extremely negative view of polyamory (Ferrer 2018, 817). In short, monogamy—in particular, the model of a sexually exclusive heterosexual couple—emerged over the last several centuries as the relational ideal for proper society (Herlihy 1995; MacDonald 1995). The term "mononormativity" has been proffered to represent the "dominant assumptions of normalcy and naturalness of monogamy" (Pieper and Bauer 2005). Mononormativity is essentially a refinement of heteronormativity that posits heterosexuality as the only proper and normal state of human sexuality (Barker and

Langdridge 2010). Scholars have variously termed this cultural insistence on monogamy as "socially imposed monogamy" (MacDonald 1995), "compulsory monogamy" (Emens 2004), "mononormativity" (Pieper and Bauer 2005), "heteronormative monogamy" (Noel 2006), and "monogamism" (Anderson 2012), among others. The privileging of heterosexual monogamy is enforced at societal and cultural levels through the institutions and structures of promotion and oppression that support heterosexual monogamy on the one hand and undermine the consideration or acceptance of polyamory on the other (see, e.g., Berstrand and Sinski 2010; Emens 2004).

Promoting the ideal of heterosexual monogamous coupling inherently demonizes alternatives like polyamory (Conley et al. 2013). Indeed, some scholarship even frames polyamory in terms being *negatively not monogamous* rather than *positively polyamorous*. For instance, a branch of the extant literature refers to polyamory as "consensual nonmonogamy" (see, e.g., Conley et al. 2012; Seguin 2019). Defining polyamory by clarifying that it is *not* monogamy suggests an ongoing stigmatization and moral approbation even in the scholarly community (Barker and Langdridge 2010; Conley et al. 2012; Young 2014). Generally speaking, it is inarguable that Western cultures have developed strong and broad-based negative views against polyamory (Anderson 2010; Barnett 2014).

The size of the polyamory community is not obvious or easily assessed. In part, the ambiguity surrounding a proper assessment arises from the amorphous definitional boundaries of what is meant by "polyamory" (Rubel and Burleigh 2020). Polyamory could be an identity, a cluster of beliefs about relationships, the actual status of a relationship, or the agreements among those in a relationship (Klesse 2014). The most thorough analysis we found concludes that there are a minimum of 1.44 million American adults who could be classified as polyamorous under the most narrow definition and as many as 12 million under the most inclusive definitions (Rubel and Burleigh 2020, 22–23).

Like our other cases, popular media generally portrays polyamorous relationships as some combination of unethical, immoral, pathological, sex-obsessed, and abusive (see, e.g., Seguin 2019; Slick 2010). Those who are part of the polyamory community face moral disapproval and stigmatization from many of the people in their lives who are not polyamorous (see, e.g., Weitzman 2006; Young 2014). If children are part of the polyamorous family, then the societal disapproval is more intense and more overt (see, e.g., Scheff 2014). This general stigmatization can be attributed at least in part to the societal norm of disapproval of sex with multiple partners and of casual sex (Hamilton and Armstrong 2009; Mint 2004). Some research also suggests there is a belief that jealousy ultimately dooms polyamorous relationships (see, e.g., Seguin 2019). Several of the polyamory elites we interviewed suggested a significant dimension of the societal hostility toward polyamory arises from the effort of the elites of Christianity to demonize other religions, like Islam and Mormonism, that have sects or branches that not only allow, but also encourage polygamy. Others suggested to us that a broad level of homophobia across the American culture was an inherent source of animosity toward those in polyamory. That is, the ubiquitous heteronormative slant of normative behavior means the notion of two women or two men engaged in intimacy—even with other men or women in the picture—is wholly unacceptable. Still others we interviewed suggested that the ownership dimension of the American version of patriarchy meant that sharing another person sexually was emasculating and therefore unacceptable. One woman told us that people fear what they secretly desire—she used the example of homophobic priests molesting the teenagers in their congregations. So, according to her, those who fantasize about the taboo of group sex or multiple partners lash out at anyone who engages in those behaviors from a place of self-loathing. We found each of these explanations to be persuasive, and we speculate they may all play a part in the societal animus toward polyamory. In other words, the hostility toward polyamory may arise from a variety of intersecting beliefs.

Of course, we should also recognize that elites play a substantial role in creating hostility toward marginalized groups so these sources of stigma may primarily trace back to conservative religious elites (Bishin et al. 2021). We leave a definitive resolution of the source or sources of the animus toward polyamory for other scholars to work out or perhaps for future projects for us. For our current purposes, that polyamory is held in low regard by outsiders demonstrates the associated costs for those who choose to join the community. One lawyer we spoke with suggested that anyone in polyamory faces an almost automatic loss of custody in divorce proceedings. We talked with a long-term trio that related how awkward office holiday parties always were. Each worked in a white-collar environment and heteronormative monogamy was the corporate expectation. As a family unit, they repeatedly had to decide whether to avoid corporate holiday get-togethers—and thus seem to be antisocial or hostile to the corporate culture—to be dishonest and exclude one member of the throuple in order to present as a "normal" couple, or to be honest and have all three of them attend and then be transparent and direct in the introductions. They reported that over the twenty-five or so years they had been together (there was some disagreement among them as to whether they had been a throuple for twenty-four or twenty-five years), they had tried each of these strategies and had never arrived at a strategy they deemed to be a complete success.

A Brief History of Polyamory

The practice of nonmonogamy has long been present in human societies across the world. Polygamy is legal and widespread in parts of West and Central Africa known as the "polygamy belt." Polygamy also remains legal in many parts of the Middle East and Asia, though it is rarely practiced in these regions. In virtually all of these cases, polygamy takes the form of polygyny, where a husband has more than one wife; polyandry, where a wife has more than one husband, is significantly rarer both in the present day and throughout human history (Kramer 2020). Despite the continued existence of polygamy across the world, *polyamory* in its modern form first emerged in the United States with the growth of nineteenth-century utopian communities and the free love movement of the mid-nineteenth and early twentieth centuries. Nonmonogamy gained a new prominence during the sexual revolution of the 1960s and 1970s, not just among youthful radicals but also in middle-class suburbs, where some three million Americans began taking part in the practice of swinging. Some of those most involved in the nonmonogamy movement in the 1960s and 1970s remained influential into the 1990s, during which much of the current vocabulary of the community, including the word polyamory itself, was first adopted. The advent of the internet has seen polyamory and related nonmonogamous lifestyles grow rapidly, first through message boards and subsequently via websites, social media, podcasts, and blogs, with some estimates putting the number of Americans in consensually nonmonogamous relationships at 4–5 percent of the population (Harvard Law Review 2022, 1444). As the community has grown, so have efforts to gain legal recognition and protection, with Somerville, Massachusetts, becoming the first US city to legalize polyamorous relationships in 2020.

In the late eighteenth and early nineteenth centuries, over one hundred utopian communities, some religious and some secular, were founded in the United States (Kern 1981, 3). One of the earliest and most well-known of these communities to engage in nonmonogamous practices was the Church of Jesus Christ of Latter-Day Saints, commonly known as the Mormon Church. While the practice of polygamy was not publicly acknowledged by the church until 1852, it was legitimized in a revelation to its founder, Joseph Smith, in 1832 and secretly put into practice prior to the community's resettlement in what would become the state of Utah (Chmielewski et al. 1993, 165). For the early Mormon church, what they termed "celestial marriage" served as a means to most efficiently carry out God's command to "be fruitful and multiply." This practical approach to marriage meant Mormon polygamy (technically polygyny, as it only involved men taking multiple wives, not vice versa) differs markedly from modern polyamory. Celestial marriage "robbed love of all the attractions—companionship, loyalty, mutual respect—that were not directly related to reproduction" (Kern 1981, 145). Mormon polygamy was also based on deeply patriarchal understanding of society; women were viewed as incapable of self-control, and plural marriage allowed male members of the church to constantly supervise female members and prevent their engagement in immoral sexual activities (153). Despite the widespread association of polygamy with Mormonism, only around 25 percent of the Mormon population practiced "celestial marriage" and, under pressure from antipolygamy laws and Utah's push for statehood, the church discountenanced the practice in 1890 (Chmielewski et al. 1993, 165).

Perhaps the most important long-term impact of early Mormon practices on polyamory in the United States was the social and legislative backlash against the church's activities. The Republicans' 1856 party platform placed polygamy alongside slavery as one of the "twin relics of barbarism" in the territories (Marquis 1993, 176). Antipolygamy fiction became a popular genre in the United States and United Kingdom during the mid to late nineteenth century, often with an explicit focus on

Mormonism; by the beginning of the twentieth century, almost eighty full-length novels had been published in the genre, including works by Sherlock Holmes author Sir Arthur Conan Doyle (Barringer Gordon 1996a, 296–97). Polygamy was first criminalized in the US territories by the Morrill Anti-Bigamy Act of 1862, though the law was not strictly enforced due to the pressures of the Civil War (Cummings and Turner 2019). However, continued pressure from groups such as the Anti-Polygamy Society and the Women's Christian Temperance Union—the latter of which in 1877 collected 250,000 signatures in support of revoking women's suffrage in Utah due to Utah women's defense of polygamy at the ballot box—culminated in the passage of the 1882 Edmunds Act, which made polygamy a felony, and the 1887 Edmunds-Tucker Act, which disincorporated the Mormon Church and seized its property (Barringer Gordon 1996b, 830; Cummings and Turner 2019). While the Edmunds Act and Edmunds-Tucker Act were repealed in 1983 and 1978 respectively, as of 2022, all fifty states and Washington, DC, still prohibit bigamy or polygamy in their statutes or constitutions (Vazquez 2001; Harvard Law Review 2022).

The most well-known of the nineteenth-century utopian communities to engage in polygamy, as opposed to polygyny, was the Oneida Community. Like the Mormon Church, the Oneida Community was similarly founded and presided over by a patriarchal figure in the form of John Humphrey Noyes. Throughout the community's history Noyes was known as "Father" and saw himself as the spiritual leader of his tribe of Bible Communists (Klee-Hartzell 1993, 182). The form of non-monogamy practiced at Oneida was known in the community as "complex marriage" and termed "free love" by Noyes.

The Oneida Community was founded in 1848 in Madison County, New York, by preacher John Humphrey Noyes following the forced abandonment of an earlier community in Putney, Vermont, as a result of local opposition to his fledgling group's religious and sexual activities (Kern 1981, 208). Noyes, who began developing his unconventional beliefs while studying for the ministry at Yale Divinity School, grounded Oneida in Bible Communism, where all members held property in common, and Christian perfectionism, the belief that each individual was able to rid themselves of sin in this lifetime. These two principles came together in the institution of complex marriage. Noyes railed against the conventional relationship between men and women in contemporary society, in 1850, likening a woman's life in marriage to a slave in the South's bondage (Wonderley 2017, 95). Complex marriage, whereby all adults in the community were considered married to each other, was possibly the most radical expression of the group's communitarian ideals. Noyes believed that sex was a way for individuals to unite with God (99). Thanks to the employment of "male continence" developed by Noyes, whereby men would refrain from ejaculation, members of the community could engage in sexual experiences with a lower likelihood of conception. Therefore, at Oneida, "each individual was to love all family members of the other sex as a spouse and without jealousy or selfishness. There was to be no exclusiveness in love that would encourage the formation of couples" (101).

The institution of complex marriage was aided by a broader attempt to break down barriers between men and women at Oneida. The communal horticulture, where members of the community would work in volunteer task groups called "bees," gave male and female members an opportunity to work together. As well as adopting new technology that reduced women's labor burden, such as sewing machines, the male community members also engaged in traditionally feminine tasks such as cooking and housework (Wonderley 2017, 95). It was nevertheless difficult to prevent individuals forming bonds of exclusive love with another, despite the implementation of punishments, such as forced separation, designed to prevent such behavior (Kern 1981, 253). This was made all the more challenging by the fact that most people who arrived at Oneida did so as a conventionally married couple (Wonderley 2017, 101). Faced with such difficulties, as well as the departure of John Humphrey Noyes, who was forced to flee to Ontario due to charges of statutory rape being brought against him, the decision was made in 1878 to abandon complex marriage, and the community itself ultimately dissolved in 1880 (DeMaria 1978, 213). While Oneida's system of polygamy only lasted a generation, its approach to community and the mitigation of jealousy continues to influence polyamorous communities into the twenty-first century (Anapol 2017, 46).

The writing of French philosopher Charles Fourier was also influential in the development of America's nineteenth-century utopian movement, though not in unadulterated form. In *The Theory of the Four Movements and of General Destinies*, first published in 1808, Fourier provided a framework for the proper organization of society based on the proposition that human "passions" dictate social interaction and the success of communities. Love was one of Fourier's twelve radical passions, which also encompassed the "luxurious" passions associated with each of the five senses and other aspects of social life such as friendship and ambition (Steadman Jones and Patterson 1996, xvii). One of Fourier's core propositions was that these passions could only be expressed collectively; Fourier's basic unit of analysis was the group, not the individual. Based on the number of passions and their relevant personality type, Fourier proposed that the ideal number of members for a community, representing a complete spectrum of personality types across both sexes, was 1,620 (xviii). Most radically, because the minimum group size was three, Fourier's framework represented an assault on the concept of the monogamous couple. The passions were also "inescapably libidinal" as they always leaned toward the pleasure of the senses (xx). Fourier therefore saw contemporary society's denigration of much sexual activity, particularly by unmarried women, as irrational prejudices: "All that is needed is a law that reunites nature and public opinion and treats sexual behaviour as a decent pleasure instead of absurdly declaring it a vice in women and regarding it as a gracious accomplishment in men" (Fourier 1996, 140). It was the practice of love, rather than organization of production, that Fourier identified as the most important aspect of historical change (Steadman Jones and Patterson 1996, xx).

Despite the centrality of sexual relations to Fourier's philosophy, Fourier's American publicist, Albert Brisbane, omitted any discussion of this subject—particularly the philosopher's critique of marriage—from works published in the United States out of fear that it would detract from Fourier's economic message (Passet 2003, 11). When these aspects of Fourier's philosophy began to surface in the United States, many American Fourierists either rejected this vision or tried to make assurances that these prescriptions would only be implemented in multiple generations' time. This sleight-of-hand was observed by John Humphrey Noyes, who noted that "it was always the policy of [. . .] all organs of Fourierism, to indignantly protest their innocence of any *present* disloyalty to marriage" (Spurlock 1988, 65). Before the Civil War, ten thousand people were involved in American Fourierism, with twenty-two Fourierist associations established between 1843 and 1845 alone (62–63). These associations, utilizing the Fourierist term "phalanxes," were primarily economic endeavors organized as joint-stock ventures. However, 1843 also marked the beginning of America's economic recovery and by 1847, all but two of the phalanxes had disbanded (63). The failure of these endeavors focused the remaining Fourierists' attention on the theoretical components of Fourier's writings. Fourierism's middle-class critics continued to focus on the subject of marriage and the movement's perceived immorality. However, some members of the movement also began to set aside their previous assurances that any changes in marriage would not take place for generations, instead embracing Fourier's critiques of marriage in the present.

One of those responsible for bringing Fourier's prescriptions for sexual relations to an American audience was author and theologian Henry James Sr., father of novelist Henry James. In the early 1840s, James developed an interest in the Swedish mystic and philosopher Emanuel Swedenborg. Swedenborg offered theories of spiritual affinities in which sexual love was viewed as the union of not only bodies but also souls (Passet 2003, 9). James began to incorporate Fourierist theories into his thought after interacting with former members of the Brook Farm utopian community, which had been influenced by Fourierism in its later years. In 1849, James anonymously translated *Love in the Phalanstery*, a tract written by Victor Hannequin, one of Fourier's French followers (Stoehr 1979, 17). Hannequin maintained the position that changes in marriage should be reserved for the distant future, but he nevertheless outlined Fourier's attitudes toward the institution as well as the full range of sexual behavior Fourier deemed acceptable and necessary in his vision (Spurlock 1988, 69). James's familiarity with Fourierism saw him chosen to review Marx Edgeworth Lazarus's *Love vs. Marriage* in 1852. Whereas James accepted the need to delay wholesale changes to the concept of marriage, instead advocating for stopgaps such as the liberalization of divorce laws, Lazarus was deeply critical of the institution and sparked a debate that drew in other advocates of what was beginning to be known as the "free love" movement.

The term "free love" was first coined by John Humphrey Noyes, but the midcentury free love movement was far removed from the Oneida perfectionists, instead being closely connected to America's emerging anarchist movement. Outside Oneida, free love could "mean anything from monogamous cohabitation outside of wedlock to old-fashioned promiscuity" (Stoehr 1979, 29). The first emergence of free love was in the Modern Times community, a ninety-acre plot on Long Island, founded by Josiah Warren and Stephen Pearl Andrews in 1850. Warren, one of the fathers of American anarchism, based Modern Times on the principle of individual sovereignty and denied the authority of both church and state (Spurlock 1988, 117). In 1852, Andrews entered the Love versus Marriage debate, advocating for the wholesale abolition of marriage (Passet 2003, 12). This combination of individual sovereignty and hostility toward marriage made Modern Times a symbol of free love radicalism. The community's numbers ranged from seventy to one hundred during its heyday in the 1850s (Stoehr 1979, 6). Despite the image of licentiousness painted by the New York press, Modern Times was not simply about sexual relationships. Indeed, while Warren recognized the individual sovereignty of other residents to pursue life as they saw fit, he disapproved of their sexual morality (14). Unlike many other utopian communities, Modern Times also had few communal living spaces. However, Modern Times, along with the community of Berlin Heights in Ohio, laid the groundwork for the free love community in the United States.

In the late nineteenth and early twentieth centuries, the concept of free love continued to be taken up by bohemian communities across the United States, particularly in New York City. For the female and male feminists in these communities, free love not only involved participating in sex but also talking and writing about these experiences. While they viewed contemporary monogamous marriage as an institution of subjugation for women, many of these early free love advocates did not condone what they called sexual varietism, or the practice of taking multiple partners (Schroer 2005, 71). Rather, they believed a greater openness toward sex would "lead to a nobler monogamy" (Stansell 2000, 276). However, these objections to varietism were not shared by all members of this community, particularly those arriving from Eastern Europe and strongly influenced by Russian revolutionary literature. The feminist anarchist Emma Goldman, for example, along with her friend and lover Alexander Berkman, were also sexually involved with the young man and woman with whom they shared their apartment (280). In 1905, when working on book documenting the labor movement in Chicago, journalist Hutchins Hapgood found that free love and nonmonogamy were perhaps even more prevalent among the Chicago anarchists (282).

Free love had by this stage moved away from Josiah Warren's principles of individual sovereignty, a concept too friendly to private property for the European radicals joining the scene (Spurlock 1988, 230). These activists firmly established the connections between idealism, feminism, and free love that would influence the growth of polyamory in the United States from the mid-twentieth century onwards.

While the bohemian feminists of New York and beyond were precursors to the sexual revolution of the 1920s, it was the second sexual revolution, declared by *Time* magazine in 1964, that led to a new wave of interest in polyamorous lifestyles (Anapol 2010, 53). The 1960s and 1970s saw rapid social change in the United States, not least in regard to sex and gender. Polyamory was therefore able to evolve within this context of increased activism and autonomy for women and sexual minorities. American utopian communities had been in decline since the end of the nineteenth century, but communes saw a rebirth in the 1960s and 1970s as individuals sought to implement the ideals of this revolution with other like-minded people. Despite many being founded to explore nonmainstream aspects of sexuality, nonmonogamy was not the norm among these communes (Sheff 2022). However, the polyamorous communes that were founded during the period were important for the community's development.

One of these communes was the Sandstone Retreat in Topanga Canyon outside Los Angeles, California, founded by married couple John and Barbara Williamson in 1968. John Williamson was perhaps an unlikely pioneer for a polyamorous commune, having previously trained as an electrical engineer in the Navy and worked on the Polaris missile project in Cape Canaveral in the late 1950s. After marrying in 1966, John and Barbara founded Sandstone based on the belief, in Barbara's own words, "that a traditional heterosexual marriage could not last, because two people could not give each other everything they need[. . . .] So we build a bigger marriage" (Yardley 2013). Like many utopian founders, John and Barbara were also disillusioned with contemporary society's assumptions about sex and sexuality, and John drew on his background in whole systems engineering to research how the alternative lifestyle offered at Sandstone could result in the improvement of the human condition. This principle was implemented in the form of what John and Barbara called "open sexuality," whereby individuals and couples could engage in sexual relations with members of the community openly and without jealousy (Cornell University Library, n.d.). The Williamsons sold Sandstone in 1973 and the retreat closed in 1976. They had hoped to develop an even larger "growth center" that could serve a thousand residents, but the project never came to fruition (Yardley 2013). However, even during its relatively short lifespan, Sandstone had a significant cultural impact. Writer Gay Talese, one of the pioneers of New Journalism, spent several months living at Sandstone while researching his book *Thy Neighbor's Wife*, a study of changing sexual culture in America released in 1980. Dr. Alex Comfort, whose 1972 book, *The Joy of Sex*, spent eleven weeks at the top of the *New York Times* bestsellers list, discussed the ideas of the Sandstone Retreat in his 1973 follow-up, *More Joy of Sex* (Cornell University Library, n.d.). Dr. Robert Francoeur, one of the "most prolific academic authors to advocate a greater range of sexual and marital choices," also wrote extensively about Sandstone in the influential 1974 book *Hot and Cool Sex*, co-authored with his wife Anna Francoeur (Anapol 2010, 53–54).

Longer-lived and arguably even more influential than Sandstone was another California-based community, Kerista. Beginning in the mid-1950s, Kerista took several forms before the establishment of the "New Tribe" in the Haight-Ashbury district of San Francisco in 1971. Kerista's founder, John Presmont (known in the community as "Brother Jud" or "Jud the Prophet") embarked on the project after experiencing a vision in which he was told that he would start the next great religion (Hamelin 2013, 59). Two key features of Kerista were economic communalism, with all property held in common, and "polyfidelity." The term polyfidelity, which has been retrospectively employed to describe the sexual structure of the Oneida Community, was coined at the Kerista commune and involved nonmonogamous sexual and romantic relations between a well-defined group of people (Anapol 2010, 57). In Kerista, this eventually took the form of three different group marriages, known as "best friend identity clusters" (57–58). At its height, the commune consisted of some thirty members living according to the doctrines laid out by Presmont. As well as polyfidelity, the term "compersion" was coined at the Kerista commune (Hamelin 2013, 63). Compersion, as defined by one of Kerista's core members, is "the positive emotion that comes from seeing one's partners enjoying themselves together, the antithesis of jealousy" (Even Eve 1985).

Compersion has since become a core principle for the polyamorous community (Theroux 2018). While the commune saw itself as drawing on the Israeli kibbutz movement, there are clear parallels between Kerista and Oneida in terms of both economic and sexual practices. Mirroring John Noyes's implementation of "male continence," Kerista required male residents to get a vasectomy before joining to prevent unwanted pregnancies (Anapol 2010, 57). Kerista disbanded in 1991 following Presmont's departure (58). Again, like Oneida, the community was ultimately unable to continue absent its highly dominant leader (Brumann 2000, 433).

Nonmonogamy during the sexual revolution of the 1960s and 1970s was not confined to communes in progressive West Coast cities. Swinging, the practice of swapping sexual partners either with another couple or in a group setting, also gained prominence during this period. The growth of swinging culture, often known at the time as wife-swapping, spouse-swapping or comarital sex, saw a very different demographic engaging in nonmonogamous activities. According to contemporary anthropologist Gilbert D. Bartell, who extensively studied swinging communities, most of the two to three million Americans engaging in swinging were from the suburban middle class. These individuals were generally antidrug and "antihippie," creating a clear distinction between those engaging in swinging and the broader free love movement. Bartell also found that these encounters were primarily focused on sex, with any deeper expressions of affection for a partner frowned upon (Samuel 2013). Unlike some other forms of nonmonogamy, swinging still relies on an adherence to the couple, and "remaining part of the couple is one of the strongest unspoken but universal rules of swinging" (McDonald 2010, 72–73). This has led some to differentiate between polyamory and swinging on the basis that swinging still demands an "emotional monogamy" of participants. However, many within the community resist this distinction, placing their lifestyle firmly in the category of polyamory (Anapol 2010, 14). Nena and George O'Neill's 1972 book, *Open Marriage*, was particularly influential and "helped spread the youthful sexual revolution of the 1960s to the middle-aged, middle-class Middle America of the 1970s." While distinctly promarriage, it was the book's short section on "elastic properties of marital fidelity" which entered the popular imagination, and more than thirty-five million copies have been sold worldwide (Fox 2006). As well as its discussion of the Sandstone retreat, Talese's *Thy Neighbor's Wife*, as the title suggests, provided readers a detailed account of the swinging community and its practices.

It was not only nonfiction accounts of alternative lifestyles which proved influential during this period; the mid-twentieth century also saw the publication of multiple novels popularizing the concept of polyamorous relationships. Robert Rimmer's 1966 book, *The Harrad Experiment*, which follows the lives of undergraduates at the fictional Harrad College where students are encouraged to think beyond monogamous norms of society, sold over three million copies and in 1973 was adapted into a film starring Tippi Hedren and Don Johnson. Rimmer's novel *Proposition 31* (1968), the title of which refers to a fictional ballot measure that would amend the California Constitution to recognize nonmonogamous relationships, also gained popularity among libertarians for drawing attention to antipolygamy laws and their creation of "crimes" without victims (Gross 1973). In his autobiographical writings, Rimmer explained how the Tantric teachings he was exposed to while serving in India during the Second World War influenced his beliefs on the importance of sexuality in human relationships. Rimmer and his wife also practiced polyamory themselves, having been in a long-term relationship with another couple that was only made public when the couple with whom they were involved passed away, and he remained engaged with the American polyamorous community throughout the rest of the twentieth century (Anapol 2010, 52).

Robert Heinlein's novels also proved influential in the development of polyamory, particularly in the founding of the Church of All Worlds. Heinlein's science fiction novel *Stranger in a Strange Land* (1961) told the story of Valentine Michael Smith, a human raised on Mars who came to Earth and found himself unfamiliar with many concepts he encountered, including jealousy and sexual possessiveness. *Stranger in a Strange Land* became the first science fiction book to appear on the "New York Times Best Sellers" list and was included in the Library of Congress's 2012 list of the "Books that Shaped America" (Vonnegut 1990; Dirda 2012). The book was particularly influential for the development of polyamory because it took nonmonogamy as a given, following the main character's attempts to understand and accept monogamy. The novel directly motivated Oberon Zell to found the neo-pagan Church of All Worlds, named after the church founded by Smith's character in the novel. As well as its promotion of pagan ritual, the Church of All Worlds saw polyamory as an accepted and even ideal approach to life. For many years, Zell, along with his wife Morning Glory Zell-Ravenheart, were in a polyamorous relationship with the editor of the Church of All Worlds's magazine, *Green Egg*, and eventually formed a group marriage with three others (Anapol 2010, 50). It was in this magazine that Morning Glory Zell-Ravenheart, in a 1990 article entitled "A Bouquet of Lovers," coined the term "poly-amorous" (Sunday Times 2014).

Support groups for polyamorous communities, such as Family Synergy in Los Angeles, California, and Family Tree in Boston, Massachusetts, began to emerge in the 1970s (Sheff 2022). In 1984, Ryam Nearing, who was a close friend of the Kerista residents, formed Polyfidelitous Educational Productions, an organization dedicated to nonmonogamy with a newsletter called *PEPtalk for the Polyfidelitous*. In the same year, Deborah Anapol, a clinical psychologist and relationship counselor, formed the IntiNet Resource Center (unaware that the word *internet* would soon become ubiquitous), which taught workshops on polyamory and published a long-running newsletter called *Floodtide* (Alan M., n.d.). However, the emergence of the HIV/AIDS epidemic in the 1980s and the awareness of sexually transmitted diseases drove subjects like swinging out of mainstream society and made the founding of new sexually permissive communes in the mold of Sandstone or Kerista an unlikely prospect. In 1984, *Time* magazine, which had declared the beginning of the sexual revolution in 1964, proclaimed the revolution's death (Anapol 2010, 53). While this marked the end of what sociologist Elisabeth Sheff has called the "second wave" of polyamory in America (the first being the utopian communities of the nineteenth century), many of the individuals and groups involved in this wave would continue to be influential during the "third wave," facilitated by the advent of the internet and the growth of online communities (Sheff 2012).

The utility of the internet was apparent to those seeking to develop a community of polyamorous people from the platform's earliest days. In 1992, Jennifer L. Wesp created the Usenet newsgroup "alt.polyamory." The Oxford English Dictionary credits this usage as the origin of the term "polyamory," and Wesp invented the word independently from Morning Glory Zell-Ravenheart's use of "poly-amorous" two years earlier (Alan M. 2007). The popularity of this group ultimately saw the consolidation of the term polyamory across the American nonmonogamous community. In late 1993, following a conference about sexuality and spirituality organized by Deborah Anapol and featuring speakers including Robert Rimmer, Deborah Anapol and Ryam Nearing decided to merge Polyfidelitous Educational Productions and the IntiNet Resource Center (Alan M., n.d.). The result of this merger was *Loving More* magazine, which began publication in 1995. As well as producing a quarterly magazine, the Loving More organization also held conferences and created a website, becoming one of the most prominent online resources for polyamorists. Since the establishment of these sites in the 1990s, innumerable polyamorous websites and online communities have emerged, transforming the way people interact and share thoughts, advice, and concerns. The dramatic growth in avenues for communication presented by the internet has increased the number of people engaging in alternate sexual lifestyles, including polyamory. The growth of crowdfunding sites like Patreon and Kickstarter has also allowed for an expansion of books, podcasts, and blogs engaging with the subject. Communication facilitated by the internet has also seen a growing interaction between polyamorists and members of other sexual minorities. Members of the polyamorous community often overlap with bisexuals and those who practice BDSM (Sheff 2012). Indeed, nonmonogamy is so prevalent in the BDSM community that "the monogamous minority at times feels peer-pressured to try out non-monogamy" (Bauer 2010, 142). The connection between bisexuality and polyamory is not a new one; bisexual women in particular were some of the earliest polyamory activists (Anapol 2010, 61). However, the scale of interaction taking place in the twenty-first century is certainly greater than any previous period.

The growing number and prominence of Americans in consensually nonmonogamous relationships since the turn of the twenty-first century has also seen a push for greater legal recognitions and protections for the community. Those practicing nonmonogamy have long faced legal barriers; the first federal legislation outlawing polygamy in the United States and its territories, the Morrill Anti-Bigamy Act, passed in 1862. In 1879 the Supreme Court upheld this criminalization in *Reynolds v. United States*, describing the practice of polygamy as "odious" (Harvard Law Review 2022, 1458). While most federal legislation targeting polygamy was aimed at the Mormon Church and repealed in the late twentieth century, antipolygamy and antibigamy statues still exist at a state level (1455). In some states the definitions of these practices can be broad, such as in Colorado, which classifies bigamy not only as entering into a second marriage but also as cohabiting with another person (1457). Yet a desire for legal reform has not always been present in polyamorous communities. Legal scholar Hadar Aviram, based on research conducted in the San Francisco Bay Area in the early 2000s, observed that the local polyamorous community's roots in spirituality and utopian thinking often saw them dismiss activism that specifically sought legal change, despite participation in other forms of social activism like conferences, publications, and Pride marches (Aviram 2010).

However, as the prominence of those pursuing consensually nonmonogamous lifestyles in America has increased, so has documentation of ongoing discrimination and legal barriers. Consensually nonmonogamous individuals face discrimination in housing law (which sometimes restricts who can cohabit), custody battles, and access to healthcare through a spouse (Harvard Law Review 2022, 1455). In 2020, prompted by the COVID-19 pandemic and issues of access to spousal healthcare, the city of Somerville, Massachusetts, adopted a multiple-partner domestic partnership ordinance, the first of its kind in the United States, thus legally recognizing polyamory (Aspegren 2020). In 2021, the city of Cambridge, Massachusetts, also passed an ordinance aimed at recognizing and protecting people in multipartner families and relationships (Polyamory Legal Advocacy Coalition 2021). Cambridge's ordinance was developed with the input of the Polyamory Legal Advocacy Coalition (PLAC), a group formed to build on the legal success in Somerville. According to its website, the PLAC "seeks to advance the civil and human rights of polyamorous individuals, communities, and families through legislative advocacy, public policy, and public education" (PLAC, n.d.). The passage of such ordinances does not clear residents in consensually nonmonogamous relationships of all legal threats; though unlikely, groups recognized in Somerville or Cambridge could still face prosecution in another city or state where bigamy remains outlawed (Harvard Law Review 2022, 1456). However, with the precedents set in Massachusetts and the ongoing advocacy of groups like the PLAC, legal recognition of polyamory in further cities and states across the United States is a distinct possibility.

Data Collection

To measure the political attitudes and activities of the polyamory community, we administered polyamory-oriented versions of our two sets of questions. Like all of our surveys, one survey contains twenty-nine multiple-choice questions (Appendix 1.1) and the other contains eleven open-ended questions (Appendix 1.2). As with the other cases, we first collected answers to the surveys in person through a convenience sample and then collected additional responses through the virtual snowball technique discussed earlier. As recounted in the opening chapter and preface, by happenstance we knew people who had started a polyamory support group. We contacted these founders of this large polyamory support group, whose members live in and around Albuquerque, New Mexico, to arrange our field work. We attended two separate social events in New Mexico where participants responded to our surveys in person. Our first forty-eight responses were obtained in person. We paid each person who completed the surveys a modest sum of five dollars. We also asked those who participated in person to share the links to the questionnaires through their closed social media polyamory networks and with anyone else they knew who identified as a member of the polyamory community. We also conducted semistructured interviews with the elites as well as roughly thirty people there who were willing to talk to us after filling out the surveys. We also engaged in participant observation and ethnographic analysis.

The first event was a monthly potluck dinner and activity that had been scheduled before we arranged to visit with the group. Members of the group take turns hosting a variety of different activities. These range from picnics in the park to movie nights or game nights. They have held wine tastings, softball games, bowling events, art walks, and virtually any other activity you might think of to entertain a large group of friends. There were more than eighty adults at the event ranging in age from late teens to late eighties. There were also a perhaps as many as twenty children ranging in age from infant to early teens. (We did not interview or allow surveys from anyone under the age of eighteen.)

At first glance, the potluck was indistinguishable from any number of neighborhood or community events throughout the United States. One long folding table was set up with a variety of soft drinks, wine, and beer as well as cups and ice. The informal dining room table was a very large indoor picnic table and it was overflowing with a variety of homemade dishes from macaroni and cheese and potato salad to spaghetti and meatballs, chicken wings, and a sliced ham. The extraordinary thing about the potluck was the complete and absolute normalcy of it all. The potluck took place in a sprawling and beautiful upscale home just north of Albuquerque. After the event, out of curiosity, we entered the address in the property information site Zillow and it suggested the value of the home was over 1.5 million dollars. The host, Clyde, was gracious and had a soft sense of humor. He was dressed casually in khaki shorts a golf shirt, and Birkenstock sandals and told us to make ourselves at home. He admonished us to be respectful and leave anyone alone who did not want to participate.

We also should note that not all of those in the group were as financially well off despite the obvious economic comfort of the host. We spoke with people who lived in apartments, trailers, self-identified "cottages," and several people mentioned they really enjoyed the times Clyde hosted because the house was so nice. One family group of four adults told us they have a two-bedroom apartment with two very small bedrooms. They made the main room their bedroom with a king size bed and use one of the two bedrooms as an office and the other as a television room or den. If someone mentioned their living situation was more modest than Clyde's, we asked how they managed to host this large of a group. Invariably, the events hosted by those with smaller houses, apartments, cottages, or trailers were held in more public locations like parks or bowling alleys or in the community center of an apartment complex. The mix of economic status was notable not only because of the sheer variation, but also because we detected no emotional dynamic driven by class. There seemed to be no guilt or condescending attitudes from the well off or resentment or envy from the less wealthy. Perhaps outside of the group setting we might find those sorts of attitudes or dynamics, but they were not on display that night.

After some time, perhaps a bit over an hour, the organizers urged everyone to finish up their meals so the entertainment activity could begin. The group watched the 2013 movie *Her* starring Joaquin Phoenix. The plot of the film revolves around a romantic relationship that develops initially between Joaquin Phoenix's character and an artificial intelligence (AI) assistance platform—like Siri or Alexa—that understands and responds to the protagonist more thoroughly and in better ways than other humans. As Joaquin Phoenix's character grows more reliant on the AI, he also becomes more emotionally connected to it. Eventually, he develops a sexual relationship with the AI where he masturbates while engaging in conversation with the AI. Eventually, he completes the process of distancing himself from the actual humans in his life and is almost completely reliant on the AI for his emotional and physical interactions. As the movie begins the final act, it is revealed that in fact the program has engaged in this same in-depth emotional and physical relationship with every other human on the planet as well. Just as the characters begin to navigate the challenges and the opportunities of the ubiquitous poly-love—among multiple humans and the program—and they begin to resolve their feelings of betrayal and jealousy that are intertwined with their intense feelings of love for the AI, the artificial intelligence abandons everyone. The movie ends as the characters try to navigate their way through the loss of their closest emotional companion.

As the group watched the movie, we were struck that they were entertained by and understood the humor of some of the subtext that might have eluded nonpolyamorous audiences. The recurring references to having all parties talk through their feelings and manage their emotional responses with transparency and integrity never failed to draw a laugh. Once the movie was over, the organizers facilitated a long group conversation about the movie, the lessons from the movie, how the nonpolygamous world might interpret the movie, as well as a host of smaller topics. Once the roughly forty-five-minute discussion of the movie ended, we were allowed to give our short presentation about our research project, answer any questions, and then pass around the iPads to administer the surveys. After Clyde, our host, took the surveys and we handed him a $5 bill, he looked at it puzzled and asked "Why are you paying us just to talk about ourselves?" We told him it was in order to show respect and appreciation to the people who participated and he shrugged and said, "If you say so, it just seems weird to me, but you know, whatever." This was typical of the reaction from many members of the group. That is, they were puzzled as to why anyone would think about them and slightly amused by the formality of our process. One woman said, "You know we tend to not pay a lot of attention to a lot of the rules, so it's a little funny that you guys are so formal." While we listened to many stories and anecdotes wholly unrelated to polygamy, most of our conversations were about specific instances of funny or difficult situations arising because of the story teller's polygamous status. For instance, one "throuple" of a man and two women, all white-collar workers, told us about the difficulties they had with business events like Christmas parties. They struggled to keep their stories straight about which woman was the "wife" and which was the "sister-in-law" or "cousin" or "college friend." They had decided early on in their relationship that it would be more fun for them if they did not have one set lie to stick with over time. Although they laughed about the situation, at one point during the story, one of the women said "It is critical that neither one of us is relegated to being the 'second wife,' so this is a fun way for us to keep in mind we are a triad of equals and we're limber enough—at least so far—that we haven't caused ourselves any real problem with this game we play with others." We talked with another family group made up of three women and two men with several young children. Polyamorous families are not immune from the ubiquitous demands of youth soccer and they told us about causing confusion among the other parents as they cheer on one of their sons and one of their daughters at soccer matches. One of the men told us, "I assume people force us into their heteronormative and patriarchal framing so they see us as perhaps aunts and uncles instead of a cluster of parents because they can't easily interpret a parental grouping of five."

As soon as anyone completed the surveys, we engaged those who were willing to talk in semistructured interviews. Almost everyone spent a few minutes with us and several spent as much as fifteen minutes with us. Many continued our conversations via email for several weeks after we left. Typically, those emails were expanding a previously mentioned idea or clarifying something. We ended each of the semistructured interviews by raising the idea of passing along the survey links to their closed social networks or other individuals they might know who identify as part of the polyamory community. As discussed earlier, by virtual snowball technique, we mean that we asked our subjects to share the surveys with others in the community via Facebook, social networking, and email. That is, we asked those who participated in person to share the links to the questionnaires with anyone else they knew who identified as a member of the polyamory community. As might be expected, we were often directed to the same network by different people. Ultimately, we were led to several closed Facebook groups for polyamory communities where our surveys were shared by the administrators of those groups. In each case, we asked the group administers for permission to post our survey in their group before we moved forward. Within three weeks, we obtained 565 responses for the multiple-choice survey and 188 responses for the open-ended questions. As a caveat, we do not assert this is a representative sample of all members of the polyamory community. Rather, because we are using this novel approach of a virtual snowball sample, we anticipate that our sample is younger, perhaps more educated, and certainly more technologically sophisticated than the population as a whole. Moreover, because we were able to reach some people from otherwise more difficult to study sectors of the polyamory community this way, some sectors may be overrepresented. In particular, we may have more lesbian identifying members of the community than would be true of the full population because we were able to virtually access an exclusively lesbian polyamory network.

Our second event was also in New Mexico but involved a completely different group. We attended a presentation and workshop about polyamory in the LGBT community at an LGBTQ resource center. This was a smaller event with about twenty-five total attendees. The panelists talked about issues like communication between people in a polyamorous relationship, coming out as polyamorous, and navigating your workspace as a member of the polyamory community. Once the panelist finished up their presentation, we were able to again present our project, take survey responses, do semistructured interviews, and pursue more responses through the virtual snowball technique. Like the first event, we paid each respondent $5 dollars to take the survey.

Unfortunately, although we were also scheduled to attend a polyamory conference in Denver in the Spring of 2020, it was canceled because of COVID-19. We were able to attend a virtual meet up of a polyamory group based in upstate New York in the fall of 2021 as observers. The virtual meet up was not as informative as the other events and was akin to a quick corporate check in. We suspect the somewhat moribund discussion and brevity of the virtual event can be attributed to Zoom fatigue and general exhaustion of the challenges of engaging in your community during the pandemic. Several people in the zoom event did talk about the fact that the pandemic isolation was less severe for them because they inherently had a larger number of people in their households.

Results

For a number of the demographic characteristics, our sample is not perfectly representative of the US population. However, given that polyamory is a chosen identity, it is highly unlikely that those who identify as polyamorous are evenly distributed among the US population generally. Indeed, there is no particular reason we should expect polyamory to closely map over every demographic. For instance, we expect the polyamory community to be younger than the population as a whole because, in general, evolving social norms may be less inhibitory than in the past. We also expect the active members of the polyamory community to be younger than the population as a whole because of the role of social media in organizing the community. What this unfortunately means is that we have no way of knowing how closely our sample aligns with the actual demographics of the entire polyamorous-identified population in the United States. Without further data allowing us to weight our results based on population demographics, we will make the uneasy assumption that our data is, more or less, representative of those most active in the polyamory community. Given all of this, we can make some observations about the community to the extent respondents in our sample are a somewhat representative cluster of polyamorists. Note that we have included some charts of the answers to the questions throughout the chapter, but frequently simply report the numbers discursively. We have decided to present the data conversationally rather than through any econometric presentation because the information is very straightforward, and we are not making causal claims with the data. We have included charts and graphs but the presentation of the data is limited to counting.

More of our respondents identified as women than the general US population. In our sample, 60.07 percent are women (n = 337), 34.76 percent identify as men (n = 195), and 5.17 percent identify as other (n = 29). By contrast, in the population as a whole, since 2013, women have accounted for just over 51 percent of the population (Statista.com 2021). This finding is consistent with our in-person interactions and observations with the two polyamory groups in New Mexico and the one in New York. While the proportion of women is greater in our sample than the general United States population, the notable difference is suggestive of several characteristics of the community which we will discuss later in this chapter.

We did have several elites tell us that it was not uncommon to see one person, frequently a male, be the primary income earner while multiple women, often but not always of different age brackets, manage the household and take primary responsibility for raising the children. For some in polyamory, this dynamic allows for a pregnant woman or a new mother to take more downtime and shed more responsibilities during and immediately after a pregnancy. In other words, as Carol, a woman at the potluck, put it, "There are some organic reasons it is easier to have another woman around when I'm pregnant or have just given birth." When we asked her whether another man would also make it easier, she said "Well, I suppose so, but another man still doesn't get what it is to be pregnant or breastfeed." We also cannot discount the possibility that for some men, there may be some reasons that they prefer to interact only with women in their relationship. These reasons might include stigma attached to having sex or even just the perception of having sex with another male or another male having sex with the women in the relationship. In other words, some manifestation of embedded patriarchy and heteronormativity could account for this pattern. We also certainly have more women respondents as a proportion because one of our online networks was expressly for lesbian polyamorists. Although we found several family clusters that had more than one male in the group, we did not find any poly-family in our sample that consisted of one woman and multiple men, although that likely has to do with our data not reality.

Our sample skews young with a nearly equal proportion of 18–29 year olds and 30–49 year olds accounting for 92.06 percent of our respondents. In the general population, this age bracket is closer to 50 percent of the adult population and those who are 50 years old and over account for the other half. We believe one of the downsides to our virtual snowball data collection is that we did not reach older people as easily as we reached younger people. There may also be some arcs of polyamory as a process. That is, it could be that as people age, they are less likely to seek out new partners to replace those who have left the relationships or passed away as part of the normal familial evolution (Sheff 2013). We also cannot discount the idea that some people may lie about their age by choosing a younger category. Indeed, we are certain at least some people were older than they claimed. In any event, the reported ages of the polyamorists we took surveys from included 262 people in the 18–29 year range, 260 people in the 30–49 year range, 41 people in the 50–64 range, and 4 people in the 65 and over range.

The parity between the first two age groups suggests that polyamory is not actually bounded by age. That is, if people came to polyamory later in life, we might see greater variation between the first two age groups with the second bracket, 30–49 years old, larger as more people move into the lifestyle. Since our data collection happened online and through live nighttime social events, we believe we have dramatically under sampled the older polyamorist population. One implication, if we are correct that polyamory is not a particularly age-bounded community, is that there may be a constant level of those who seek out polyamory. In other words, if the age brackets generally contain the same numbers of people across the range of ages, then those who claim polyamory is an organic sexual identity akin to being straight or gay, may have some suggestive evidence to support the claim. An alternative idea is that, given the prevalence of bisexuality among the polyamory community, the notion that some percentage of the population is bisexual and those people are more likely to seek out polyamory is a compelling argument.

Our sample skews young and it also skews non-Hispanic White (figure 2.1). Non-Hispanic Whites make up 83 percent of our sample—much larger than the US population generally—perhaps indicating that the polyamory community is racially homogenous or the polyamory communities are racially segregated. It is also possible that there are intersectional pressures which may make involvement in the polyamory community more costly for people of color. In other words, if people of color face an additional layer of challenges as members of the polyamory community because of structural racism, they may simply choose to be less active or visible and keep their polyamory to themselves in order to avoid additional challenges beyond what they already face. We also observed a much more racially diverse population than our surveys revealed. In addition to the greater consequences of nonconformity that people of color face, it is possible, perhaps even likely, that because we, the authors, are all non-Hispanic White, we were not able to establish the same level of trust with those in attendance who were African American, Latino, or Asian.

While we were at the Beyond Vanilla conference in Dallas, we had a conversation with a multiracial polyamorous "open throuple" that suggests the community is neither racially homogenous nor racially

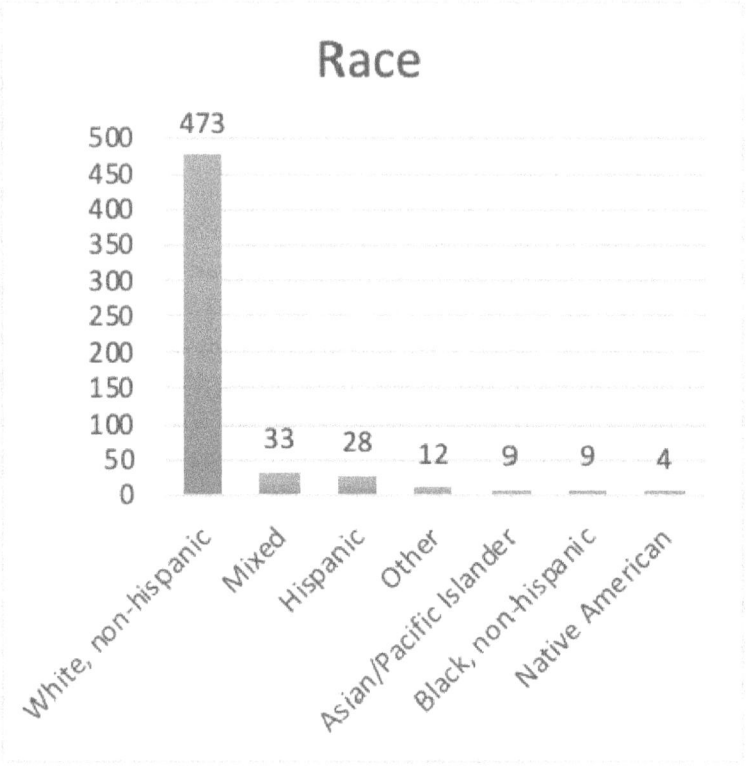

Figure 2.1. Polyamorists by Race

segregated. While Beyond Vanilla is primarily a BDSM conference, there was also a significant amount of polyamory programming there and the polyamory community attended in force. The group had three main members of the family—an African American woman, Jesse; a non-Hispanic white male, Jason; and a Latina woman, Adriana. Each had a boyfriend or girlfriend on the side who were more casual members of their family unit. Jesse had a girlfriend who was Latina. Jason had a boyfriend who identified as "blasian" because his mother was African American and his father was Chinese American. Adriana's boyfriend was non-Hispanic white. We spent close to a half hour with them and asked a variety of questions. We asked them how they managed a range of things in their lives like sex and the division of labor. Invariably, like every other elite member of the polyamory community we interviewed, the answer was simply a commitment to communication, honesty, transparency, and empathy. When we asked if the racial makeup of their group was remarkable or problematic to others in the polyamory community, both Jesse and Jason actually laughed at the question and Adriana furrowed her brows and was playfully disapproving of it being asked. Collectively they thought it was a strange question. Jason put it succinctly, "Are you kidding? That is the least shocking taboo we break." We believe it is more likely that the racial homogeneity we find in our sample is merely an artifact of our sampling and data gathering approaches. Because the events we sampled were local in nature or online as compared to the national conventions that we visited for the other groups, geographic constraints on the samples might also account for some of the underrepresentation.

Without more research, we cannot be certain about why our sample skewed so heavily to non-Hispanic whites. However, some of our elite interviews and the scattering across other demographics of our survey responses does suggest the polyamory group is more racially diverse than our sample captured.

We found those in the polyamory community to be highly educated with more than 57.27 percent of our respondents reporting either a college or postgraduate degree. This compares to a bit over 35 percent for the general public (Statista.com 2021). We had 564 respondents answer our question about educational attainment. Of those, 200 reported some college, 196 reported they were college graduates, and 127 reported attending graduate school. Only 41 reported they had attended high school or less. Given the age blocks, we think many of the "some college" group are likely to graduate as the 18–25 age group might still be enrolled or pursuing their degrees. That is, given the high proportion of respondents in the 18–29 age bracket, many of the "some college" respondents are likely in the process of adding to the percent of the community with a college degree.

We cannot tell if members of the polyamory community are more educated because they are polyamorous or if they are polyamorous because they are more educated. Given that college is often a time for people to decide who they are and how they choose to live, it is possible that the privilege of higher education allows a more critical assessment of the societal and cultural constraints on relationships. There may be a correlation between discovering polyamory and the freedom associated with attending college. That is, the freedom that comes with the college experience, perhaps in conjunction with the distance from familial control, might lead to a greater likelihood of consideration of polyamory as a viable alternative. It is also possible, of course, that these things are not causally connected or are connected in some unobvious ways that go beyond our speculation. Many students live in group settings as undergraduates and as graduates. This may foster an appreciation for and understanding of a group familial setting that goes beyond two romantic partners. Many young people try new experiences, sexually and otherwise, as part of their growth in college. In New Mexico, we talked with Kelly, a man in his thirties, about how he became a member of the polyamory community. He said his openness to it began in college. He had a roommate in a small dorm room, and as they became more comfortable with each other over the first year, their barriers began to drop. The first big barrier was when they decided they did not need to masturbate in secret anymore. This led first to voyeurism and exhibitionism then to mutual masturbation and then eventually oral sex. They both also had girlfriends with whom they were sexually active. Kelly could not recall exactly how—he thought there might have been alcohol involved—but eventually, one night, all four of them had group sex and then that became a common, but not exclusive, occurrence. That is, each couple was also sexually active apart from the other couple, but any combination of the four people involved might engage sexually at times. He saw the four of them as a family. While the group did not survive college as a family, he realized that was the sort of set up where he was happiest and most fulfilled. Kelly is still friends with his former roommate, who is still married to his girlfriend from college. While Kelly defines himself as bisexual and polyamorous, Kelly says his former roommate just thinks of those college days as his wild youth. Kelly is now in long-term relationship with two women and has a boyfriend, as does one of the women in the relationship.

Although our sample is highly educated, it makes less money than the general US population, with 44.25 percent saying that they make less than $30,000 per year (figure 2.2). However, accounting for the relative cost of living in the oversampling of respondents from New Mexico, there is a nontrivial likelihood that the poverty rate within the polyamory community might be lower than the raw income level might suggest. Both the average income and the cost of living are lower than average across the country. Moreover, many of the subjects we interviewed explained that there was a primary income earner in their family unit, so those with parttime jobs or those who do not work outside the household may be skewing the numbers downward. Given the large number of one full-time income earner households and the large number of "prefer not to answer," more might be learned from household incomes rather than individual incomes. We also had a fair number of people who declined to answer the income question. Also, from our in-person interaction with some people who declined to answer the income question, we suspect those nonresponders may be at the upper end of the income distribution. Indeed, one woman told us she had never had a job but had a high six figure income off inherited wealth

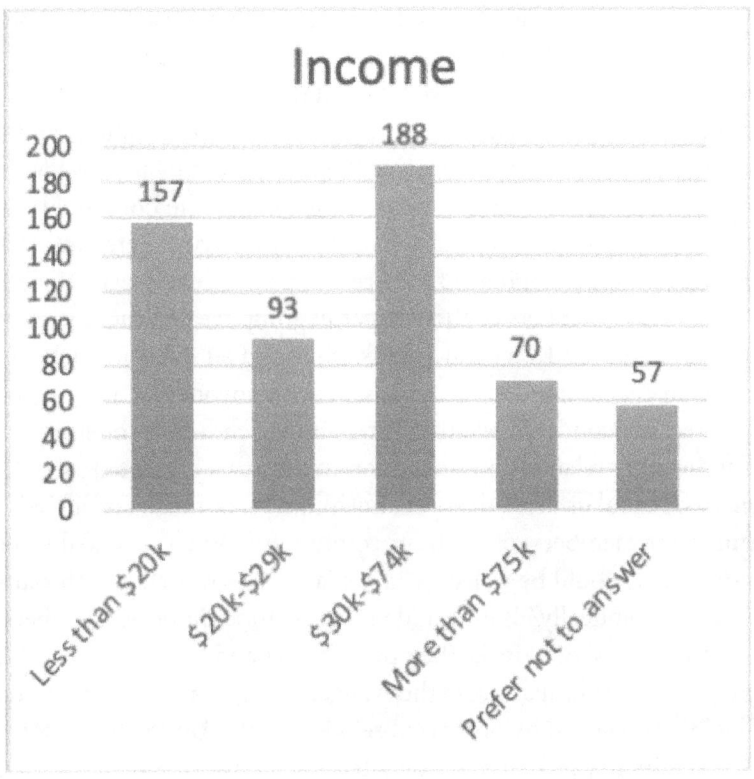

Figure 2.2. Income Distribution of Polyamorists

that kept her polyamorous family very comfortable. We noted that the three people at the first event that told us they would not reveal their income wore Rolex watches, two of which had diamonds surrounding the face of the watch. In any event, generally speaking, our sample suggests that polyamory does not have any particularly pronounced negative or clearly positive relationship to income.

Given the hostility of most organized religions toward any model of the family besides heterosexual and patriarchal monogamy, as might be expected, our sample does not reflect a high level of attendance at religious services. Almost 79 percent of our respondents chose "Seldom or Never" in response to our question about how frequently they attended religious services. Note though, we did have a small number of Evangelical Christians who attend services routinely. We talked in depth with an Evangelical Christian couple, Helen and Peter, who explained that they do not disclose their real status to their fellow parishioners. Rather, the other two women in the family unit, and the occasional third other woman, were introduced as cousins or sisters of Helen rather than as Peter's additional wives. We asked them if the women in the relationship could have outside romantic or sexual interests or encounters, and the answer was adamantly negative. For them, their family unit follows the Old Testament guidelines and Peter is the head of the household while the others serve his needs all in the name of the divine. Peter and Helen were outliers in the approach to the relationship in every way. Nonetheless, the other members of the polygamy group treated them with dignity and respect and very much took a live and let live approach. Peter and Helen also seemed to have no issue with anyone else in the group. Of course, we wondered whether Peter and Helen were as open-minded about the other relationships in the community that presented as gay, lesbian, or bisexual or those that were not all white, or those that included a member (or members) of the trans community. When we asked Peter if another male would be welcome in his family, he was clear: "Absolutely not, we live biblically." But he added that he thought other members of the community should make their own choices and he was in no position to judge them. Still, apart from the evangelicals, given the general disdain officially propagated by organized religion in the United States for sex and sexuality beyond the ideal of heteronormative monogamy, it is not surprising that religious services are not a priority for this community.

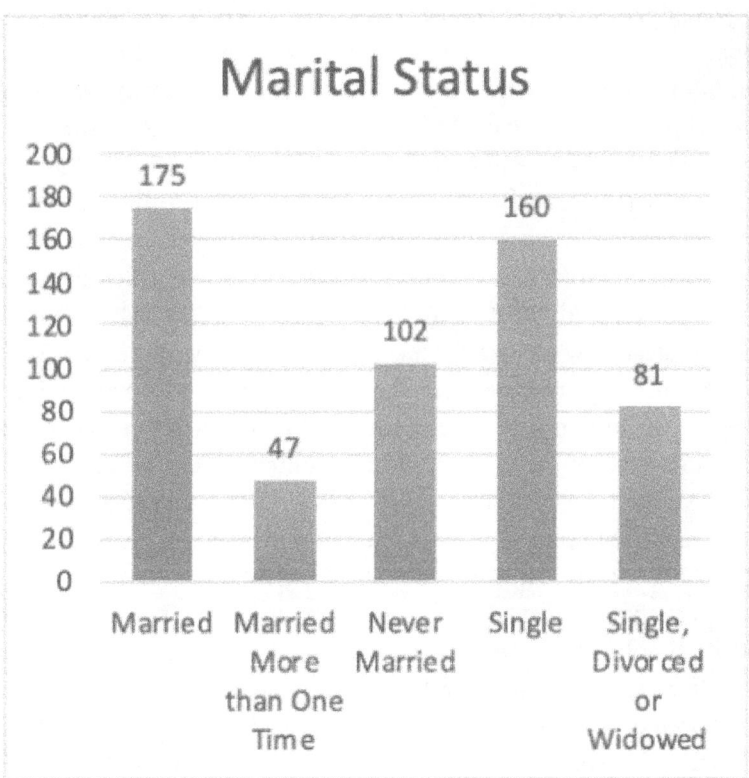

Figure 2.3. Polyamorists' Marital Status

Out of our sample of 559 respondents, only 26 attend religious services weekly or more often than weekly, 51 attend religious services monthly, and 41 attend yearly. An outsized 441 seldom or never attend religious services. Lane, a man in his midsixties, said his family would only attend church for weddings or funerals. Will, Nancy, and Tom said they go for Christmas services every year because they like the music but celebrate Kwanzaa at home because Tom is African American and, in Will's words, "It's a really cool celebration—we grow a lot of our own food so it really speaks to us—and it's a holiday that isn't controlled by some ancient and rigid religious order."

While formal religious attendance is not a priority, the community does not seem as hostile to formal marriage recognition. Nearly 1 in 3, about 31 percent, of our sample is married (figure 2.3). This number is somewhat deceptive though because there is no state that allows a third spouse. Accordingly, even if every respondent only had three people in their household union, the number who could be legally married would have a cap. Of course, many of these households consisted of more than three people, and sometimes many more than three people. If given the opportunity to marry, many more members of the community would certainly choose to do so. This high rate of marriage is particularly notable since the group skews young and young people generally are less likely to be married.

As suggested when we discussed income, only 57 percent of our respondents report being employed full-time. The proportion of college-aged students accounts for some of the difference between the polyamory community and the overall United States population. Also, recall that many of these households have one primary income earner, so the high rate of part time and not employed respondents is unsurprising in that context. While we had a smaller cluster of older people in the pool, perhaps as many as half of the "not employed" respondents are actually simply retired. In hindsight, we should have included a "retired" option for that question. Overall, the polyamory community looks to be industrious contributors to society as a whole in the context of working or looking for work. Of the 565 respondents to the question about employment status, 320 reported they were employed full-time and another 115 reported they were employed part time. Only 88 were not employed or looking for employment and, as mentioned, some of these were retirees. The remaining 42 were actively looking for employment.

We now move beyond demographics and look into the political attitudes and activities of those in the polyamory community. Although we cannot be sure that our sample is representative of the entire polyamorous community, we believe our data so far points to a several important conclusions. First, we should note that our sample reports registering to vote at a very high rate. Figure 2.4 shows the responses to the following question: "Which of these statements best describes you? Are you absolutely certain that you are registered to vote at your current address; are you probably registered, but there is a chance your registration has lapsed; or are you not registered to vote at your current address?"

People who self-identify as members of the polyamory community and who participate in the polyamory community are far more liberal than the general population. Only 4 percent of our respondents identify as Republican compared to 21 percent in the general population—a 17 percentage point gap—while the percentages of polyamorous independents and Democrats are 9 and 10 percent higher than the general population, respectively (figure 2.5). When we include leaners into our

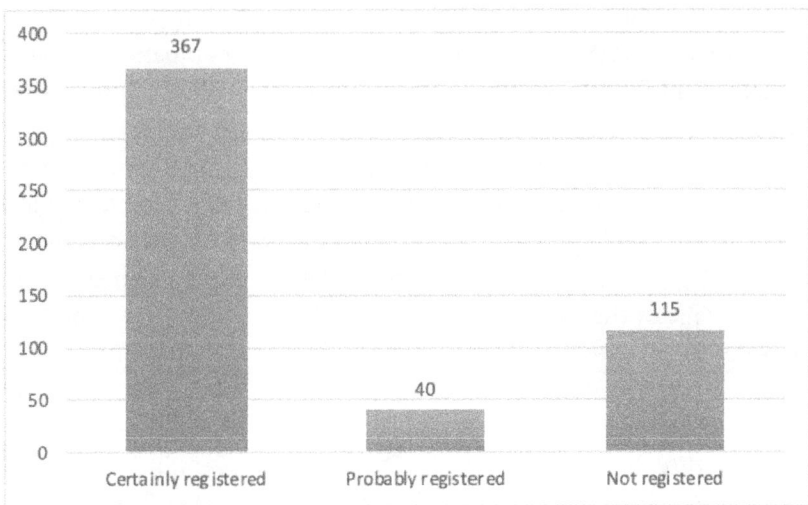

Figure 2.4. Polyamorists' Voter Registration

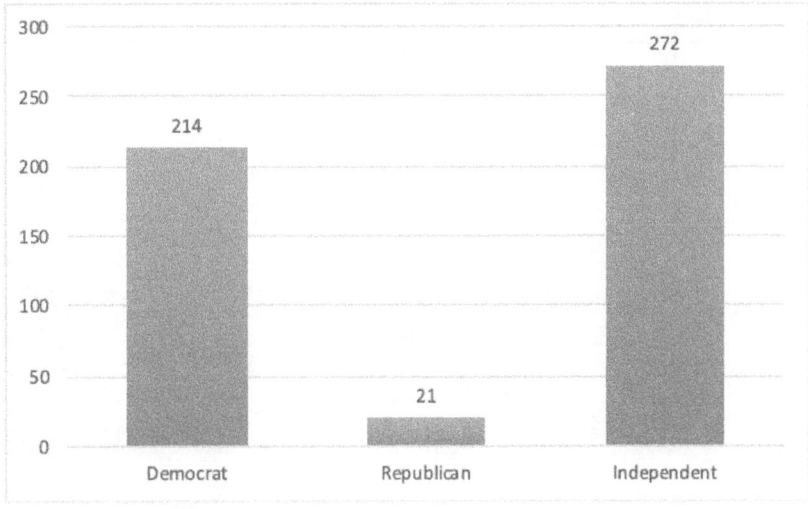

Figure 2.5. Polyamorists' Party Affiliation

numbers, the percentage of Republicans with leaners increases only to 8 percent compared to 31 percent of the US population. Given the share of non-Hispanic white vote that the Republican Party can generally count on, this very white community skewing very liberal is notable because this group is dramatically more liberal than expected based on race alone. We see the same trend when we look at ideology instead of party identification: only 1 percent of our respondents identify as "Very Conservative" compared to 9 percent of the general US population, while 37 percent identify as "Very Liberal" compared to 6 percent of the general population (figure 2.6).

This data indicates that although many in the polyamorous community prefer to identify as politically independent instead of as Democrats, they consider their political philosophy to be very liberal and consistently hold policy positions very far to the left of center. In other words, this may mean that many in the polyamorous community choose to consider themselves as politically independent, but not politically moderate, mainly because they are to the left of the Democratic Party. We can see this clearly from one of our questions. We asked our respondents in which direction they would like Democratic leaders in Washington to move, 63 percent responded a "More liberal direction" (figure 2.7). The Pew Research Center poll we modeled our questions after found 37

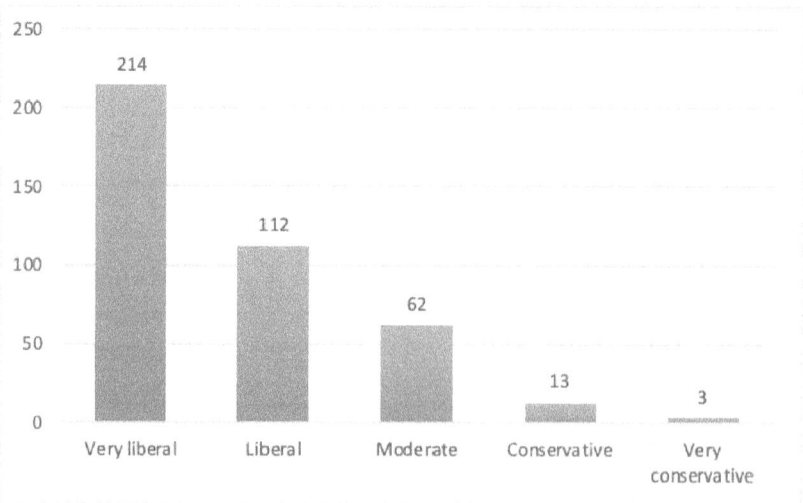

Figure 2.6. Polyamorist Ideology Ratings

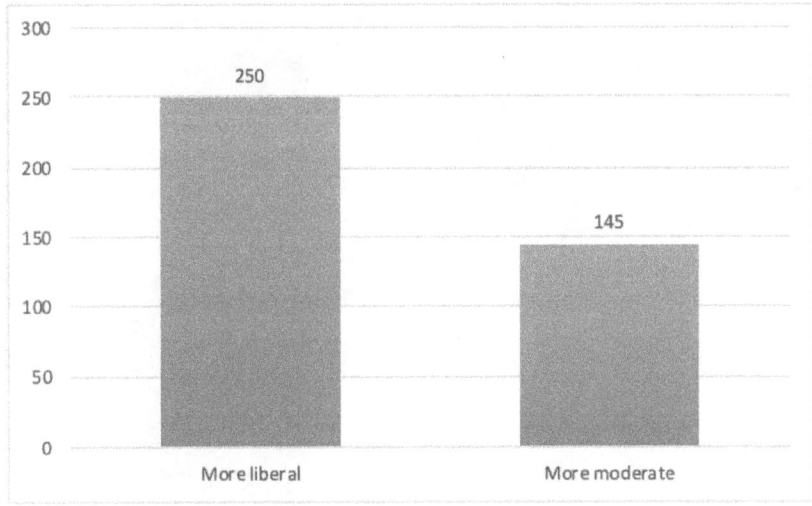

Figure 2.7. Polyamorists' Opinions on Democratic Leaders

percent of Democrats and leaners in the general population chose "more liberal direction" (Pew 2013). Conversely, 26 percent of our polyamorous sample answered a "more moderate direction" compared to 53 percent in the same Pew poll. This suggests that the Democratic Party might be able to pick up more support, money, and votes from the polyamory community if they were to speak more directly to political issues that affect the polyamory community and move further to the left on a range of policy positions or at least on the framing of those issues.

Conversely, when we asked about republican leaders, the overwhelming majority wanted to see Republican leadership move in a more moderate direction, as opposed to a more conservative position (figure 2.8).

Notably, issues that can be thought of as orbiting bodily or personal autonomy, in particular, abortion rights and same-sex marriage, were very revealing. For our questions about the policy position on abortion, 369 out of 395 respondents believe Republican leaders are too conservative, 16 thought Republicans leaders have it about right, and only 10 respondents thought republican leaders were not conservative enough. For Democratic leaders, 202 respondents thought they are not liberal enough, 154 respondents thought the Democrats have it about right, and only 35 thought Democrats leaders were too liberal. Likewise on the

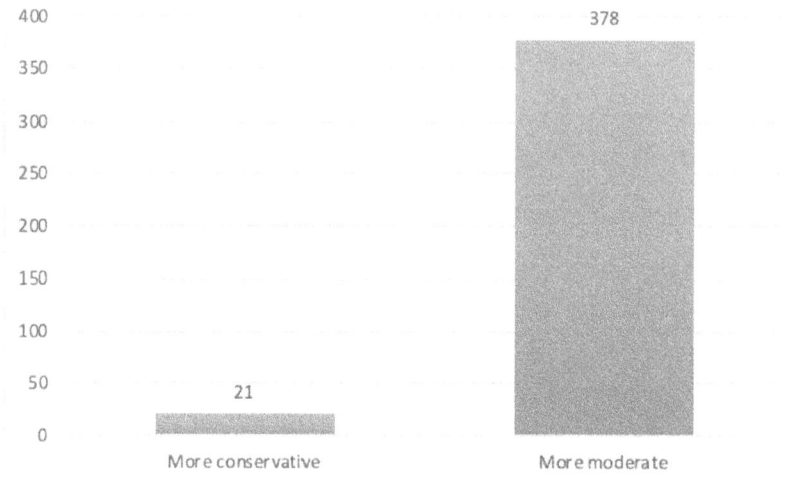

Figure 2.8. Polyamorists' Opinions on Republican Leaders

issue of same-sex marriage, 386 respondents reported that Republican leaders are too conservative, 11 respondents thought they have it about right, and not one single respondent thought that Republican leaders should be more conservative on the issue. Democratic leaders were not liberal enough for 262 of the respondents, they have it about right for 123 respondents, and they were too liberal for only 9 respondents. We can see a somewhat consistent ideology with issues of personal autonomy as, perhaps, a unifying thread through the community.

Not only are the members of the community left of center ideologically, but they are politically sophisticated. Our data also indicate that individuals in the polyamory community closely follow politics, they discuss political issues frequently, and they want the polyamory community to become more politically active (figure 2.9). A strong majority of the respondents in our survey, 70 percent, indicate that they frequently, either daily or weekly, discuss political issues with their family, friends, and other members of the polyamory community. In the open-ended questions, many respondents suggested they are comfortable discussing politics because they believe that most others in the polyamory community share their values. This supposition is correct if our data is accurate.

An interesting aside made to us by a woman at Frolicon was that because people in polyamorous relationships must continuously have open dialogue about very sensitive issues, there is no community barrier to a discussion of politics. As she commented, "Once you're scheduling sex and frankly discussing it more or less constantly, politics is easy."

In addition to being politically sophisticated, the community as a whole seems ready to become more politically active. Nearly 57 percent of our respondents believe that the polyamorous community should become more politically active in the future. In the open-ended responses, there were many references to the same-sex marriage ruling as creating an opportunity for greater and more effective political activism for the community.

Our data suggest that politics and the political world are frequent topics of conversation that are part and parcel of the polyamory community. About 55 percent of our respondents in our open-ended responses said that they discuss politics within the community, undeterred by the potential opinions of others in the group. One respondent provided us with a great insight on whether political discussion is open within the community that appears highly representative:

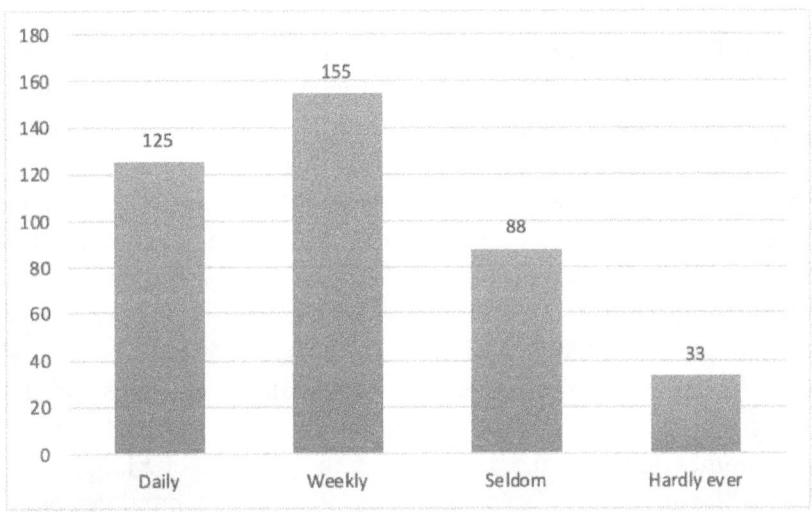

Figure 2.9. Polyamorists Discussing Politics

Yes, mostly because much of my closest circle of friends are of the poly community in one form or another. It is also because I expect and enjoy open and honest discussion on all topics with those that I spend time with. I respect their view and expect them to respect mine even if they are different. Most of my opinions are out in the open within most of my relationships romantic or not. Politics comes up in conversation with poly people as often as with anyone I feel comfortable talking politics with, that is anyone I respect that I feel is enlightened and mature enough to have a political discussion with.

As has been suggested above, in addition to identifying as poly/polyamorous, a very large number of polyamorous individuals also identify as bisexual. When respondents were asked open-ended questions to identify their sexual identities, 44 percent of the respondents also identified with some label approximating bisexuality. Some of the various descriptions that amounted to bisexuality include bicurious, heteroflexible, "mostly straight," or "mostly gay." Because almost half of the respondents identified as some type of bisexual, bisexuality is by far the largest identity that these people carry only after polyamorous and race. Following bisexual, 26 percent of the sample identified as straight/heterosexual, 11 percent identified as queer, and a sprinkle of the respondents carried other identities such as asexual (2 percent). Although some respondents have bimodal sexual identities, our data shows that sexuality in the polyamorous community generally is perhaps much more fluid and amorphous than the traditional labels of gay versus straight and without question is more nuanced. Although we further explore the idea of the communities as organic homes for those who identify within the bisexual umbrella in the chapter devoted to bisexuality, the intersection of bisexuality and polyamory merits some discussion here. The prominence of bisexuality in the polyamory community is notable for several reasons. First, research on gays and lesbians has often failed to reveal large bisexual populations and the B has sometimes seemed to be silent in the assessment of the LGBT community (Smith et al. 2017). Second, the presence of a large number of bisexual-identifying people in the polyamory community, often with partners of both genders in the family group, seems organic. That is, this is a family structure that avoids the imposed choice instituted by the heteronormative monogamist culture. Third, the number of self-identifying bisexuals in polyamory undercuts in profound ways a common biphobic argument frequently made in both straight and gay contexts: that being bisexual is just a phase before the individual either fully embraces their gayness or grows up and becomes straight.

Just as sexuality is often discovered slowly over time, and in particular when the sexuality in question defies societal norms, we found that members of the polyamorous community often entered the community slowly and were slow to realize they were indeed polyamorous. When we asked, "How did you learn about and become involved in polyamory?" 40 percent of respondents mentioned doing research, often reading books like *The Ethical Slut* (Hardy and Easton 2017), reading blogs, and attending informational talks. We also found that community played an important gatekeeping and guiding role for our respondents, with 41 percent of respondents saying that they became aware of polyamory through their involvement in other social, political, and work groups or through friends, lovers, and neighbors. One respondent concisely captured a common process, "A friend introduced me to the concept [polyamory] and I read *The Ethical Slut*, found myself in a few open/poly relationships, and got involved from there."

Having a sense of community with other polyamorists was very important for 65 percent of our respondents. One respondent described this well: "I feel we are a large and very close community but well-hidden, as it is still shamed. Having others like me to support me and understand me is a huge importance in my life and I doubt I would be able to function happily without the community." Respondents noted that being a part of the polyamory community was important for learning, growing, and sharing in a broader value system. It was common for respondents to say that they found a particular community like "Nerd Polys" or "Egalitarian Polys" in addition to finding meaning as a part of the broader polyamory community. That is, perhaps not surprisingly, there are many subcommunities within polyamory that also provide a deeper sense of community and belonging in a narrower fashion.

When we analyzed the open-ended responses, we found that respondents ascribed high levels of left-leaning libertarianism to the community that was not reflected as clearly in the replication of the Pew Research Center questionnaire. Respondents regularly noted that being a part of the polyamory community encourages open-mindedness to other people's identities while allowing for considerable variation in individual economic attitudes. There are many possible reasons why the community understands itself as having a larger libertarian element than our policy questions illustrate and warrants further study. While the issue of marriage rights was commonly identified as a unifying political issue for most respondents, they were mostly unsure about other types of issues that ought to be at the forefront of concern for the polyamory community. This suggests that the community may not have a cohesive issue alignment on highly salient issues. This would mean that should a potential mobilizing issue arise, it would not be competing with other commonly held priorities. Recent scholarship on elite-led mobilization suggests that the polyamory community could be activated and motivated if the elites chose the right messages and policy goals (Bishin et al. 2021). Interestingly, although most respondents claimed to be routinely engaged in political activity, they also thought that other polyamorists were not as engaged. While most generally detailed their regular participation in a host of different forms of civic activity, they believe other polyamorists are not as active as they are. It is of course possible that the disengaged members of the polyamory community simply did not answer our surveys. However, given our data, it seems possible, perhaps even likely, that there is a gap between the perception of engagement of others and the actual engagement of others.

Our respondents overwhelmingly want the polyamory community to be more politically active. The analysis shows that 60 percent of those surveyed want the community to become more politically active, particularly on issues related to the polyamory community like changing marriage laws and electing politicians who are members of the polyamory community. Many of the respondents were astute, noting the need to educate the broader public as an essential function of political activism to avoid misconceptions about polyamory and perhaps reduce the level of stigma. This is consistent with the commonly held belief from our respondents that people outside the polyamory community do not tend to have a strong understanding or acceptance of polyamory. On the other hand, while our respondents think the outside, or nonpoly, world does not understand them and thinks poorly of them, only 2 percent express any concern for social or political risks as a consequence of increased activism. As one mentioned, "It's not like the world could think much less of us."

Our data suggests that affiliation with the polyamory community acts as a primary identity for many of its members. Construing polyamory as a behavior, an identity, and a community sheds light on the connection between polyamory and political attitudes and political behaviors. One of the more interesting aspects of the data is the *B* in LGBT research may no longer be silent. We have revealed a community that relies heavily on those who identify as bisexual for its membership. It seems organic that in our research, unlike the heterosexual couple ideal embracing world and some sectors of the gay and lesbian communities, the polyamory community shows no evidence of hostility toward bisexuality. We know that the members of the polyamory group we surveyed are more liberal, more educated, and more active than the general population. We know that more self-identified bisexuals are in this group of polyamory people than in the general population by factors of magnitude. We believe this research presents a next step at the intersection of identity, sexuality, and politics.

3

Sticks and Stones Can Break My Bones, But Whips and Chains Excite Me

The Politics of the BDSM Community

"Everything we do is illegal." This comment by Sarah Steele, an attorney in Atlanta who specializes in representing members of the BDSM community in a host of legal arenas, parsimoniously explains one of the major challenges for members of the kink community. Steele made this opening observation during her presentation called *BDSM and the Law* at the Frolicon/Froliween convention in the fall of 2021. Her point succinctly framed the challenges inherent in embracing an identity and building or joining a community clustered around behavior that is expressly illegal. Not surprisingly, members of the BDSM community face social disapproval and discrimination like any other sexual minority (Moser and Kleinplatz 2006; Weiss 2006; Wright 2006; Yost 2010). But those "in the life," as it is casually referred to by many in the BDSM community, also face the added challenge of legal consequences for their preferred style of intimacy (Holt 2016; Moser and Kleinplatz 2006). Of course, this parallels an earlier era for gays and lesbians when they too faced strong antisodomy laws in addition to other mechanisms of legal discrimination (Smith 2007; Yost 2010.) Unlike the gay and lesbian community, legal prohibitions have not abated for the BDSM community (Damm et al. 2018). Also, the BDSM community has not, as a class, benefited from recent improvements in affirming mental health services and medical treatment for the gay and lesbian community. Instead, BDSM behavior and identity continues to be pathologized and labeled as deviant, which perpetuates shame, distress, and alienation (Herbert and Weaver 2015).

BDSM is the common acronym for *Bondage and Discipline, Dominance and Submission, and Sadism and Masochism*. At the most abstract level, this cluster of words represents specific types of behavior, identities, desires, and communities (Newmahr 2011; Weinberg et al. 1984; Weiss 2011). For any given member of the BDSM community it could mean some or all of these at any given time. One parsimonious description in the literature is that BDSM is the "eroticization of power" (Ortmann and Sprott 2013, 11). Estimates of how many people engage in BDSM vary widely. Some research has suggested 10 percent of adult Americans engages in BDSM in a routine manner (Moser and Kleiplatz 2006). Others estimate that as little as 4 percent of the population and as much as 65 percent of the population regularly engage in BDSM (Arndt et al. 1985; Janus and Janus 1993; New et al. 2021; Sprott and Randall 2017). Other research has found over 60 percent of college-age men and women fantasize about BDSM (Powls and Davies 2012). The larger numbers seem plausible given that the BDSM-oriented novel *Fifty Shades of Grey* sold over ten million copies in six weeks and over one hundred million copies in two years with over 80 percent of sales happening in the United States (Lewis 2014). Virtually every third person in the United States could own a copy of the book. Interestingly, without exception, whenever *Fifty Shades of Grey* was mentioned by elites in our field work, the audience listening to the elites' presentations would chuckle and the elite who brought it up would essentially apologize in a joking manner for referencing it or refer to it only in a comical fashion. More often than not, the book was mentioned by elites in relationship to its massive sales in order to make a larger point about the broad popularity of kink, even while dismissing the content of the book as what unimaginative "vanilla," or non-kink people, might suspect happens in BDSM. The point that underlies these mentions of the book, and occasionally the movies made from the book, was that the BDSM kink community is very large and, moreover, has the capacity to grow. During a session at Frolicon about ropes play, an audience member asked the session leader how to approach someone they were dating about their interest in BDSM. The speaker said, "You can always mention *Fifty Shades of Grey* and see how they react!" The audience laughed, as did the woman asking the question. The speaker then said "Seriously, just be honest—say something like 'Have you ever fantasized about being tied up or spanked?' and you'll know your answer in their immediate reaction."

At the most concrete level, BDSM refers to a sexual identity informed by a set of sexual practices that include explicit and negotiated power differentials (Yost and Hunter 2012, 245). Like our other cases, a BDSM identity is an essentially contested identity because the boundaries and even the status of the identity are not rigid and indisputable (Damm et al. 2018; Schulenberg 2013; Sheff and Hammers 2011). The process of continuous identity construction and reconstruction that is common among BDSM community members suggests an ongoing and persistent negotiation, internally and externally, about the parameters of the individual BDSM identity (Baldwin 1991). Concurrent with these internal dialogues, the community is also in a constant discussion about risk and safety (Bauer 2008). Because the consensual exchange of power is at the core of BDSM, in practice, the community creates a vocabulary and definable boundaries about the manifestation and negotiation of power that may be constantly evolving (Damm et al. 2018). The sexual transgression from the norm creates a tension between the essentially contested identity of being a member of the BDSM community and being a member of society at large (Connolly 2006; Ernulf and Innala 1995; Janus and Janus 1993; Langdridge 2006). This tension leads to a self-definition and societal definition of being the "other" which demarks but also may empower the community (Langdridge and Butt 2005). In other words, this boundary-making can create negative stigma and effects from outside the community while reifying their belief in the merits and joy that come from the BDSM community and BDSM activity.

Engaging in BDSM as an identity means to go beyond routine sexual interaction or casual experimentation with more exotic sexual behaviors. What ties a person to the BDSM community can include partaking in BDSM interactions or "scenes" as they are called, attending organized BDSM conventions, regularly socializing with other local members of their community, and participating in a variety of online forums (Weiss 2006). BDSM covers a wide range of sexual behavior and a variety of focused subgroups that frequently overlap and, on occasion or even sometimes frequently, are practiced together (Santilla et al. 2002). Bondage refers to roleplaying centered on the desire to bind and restrict (or be bound and restricted by) your sexual partner(s) (Thompson 1991). Discipline is simply what it sounds like—the eroticization of punishment. Discipline can manifest in a multitude of ways from spanking to sensory deprivation to male genital cages that inhibit arousal and orgasm.

Dominance and Submission refer to role play where the submissive partner gives power to the other dominant player to control the situation or scene within prenegotiated parameters (Weinberg et al. 1984). Sadism and Masochism refer to the desire to inflict or receive erotic pain from a sexual partner (Santilla et al. 2002; Yost and Hunter 2012). As may be obvious, these are broad categories that are not mutually exclusive—for instance, many Dominance and Submission scenes might involve Bondage and Discipline as well as the infliction of pain.

Under the nomenclature of BDSM, we include two other closely related, often overlapping identities of sexual practice: the *leather* and the *puppy play* communities. These communities utilize the foundational premise of BDSM but carry out specific types of scenarios and have taken BDSM in a particularized and narrower direction. *Leather* constitutes the use of leather clothing and accessories and the fetishization of leather equipment used during dominant and submissive sexual roleplaying (Baldwin 1991). The use of black leather carries connotations of masculinity, sexual power differentials, and may impose a degree of discomfort—caused by the tightly-bound leather clothing or accessories—that invokes themes of sadism and masochism. Activities might include "boot blacking" where the submissive player shines heavy black leather boots of the dominant. This may also include permutations of foot fetish behavior, boot licking, kicking or stomping, as well as other types of play. Some leather adherents also incorporate kink involving lit cigars including the eroticization of smoke and scenes involving lighting or extinguishing the cigar. For instance, one common scene includes the extinguishing cigar ash on the tongue of the submissive. Leather pants, vests, harnesses, whips, hoods, and restraints are all common accoutrements of the Leather scene.

Puppy play is the execution of submissive and dominant sexual roleplaying specifically through the roles of the puppy (submissive) and handler (dominant) but also may be played out exclusively among puppies (Midori 2005). Puppy play is an emerging kink community with sparse literature at this point. Our elite interviews were instrumental to our understanding of the puppy play community. Puppy play often includes the use of leather or latex clothing and plastic props to make the participants more closely resemble canines. These props include masks that cover all or part of the face and head. The masks usually have canine styled facial features and in particular, canine snouts, tongues, and ears. Many puppy play adherents utilize butt plugs which include an extension outside of the body that resembles canine tails. Some of these tails can wag due to a compression ball contained in the portion of the plug that is inside the body. The compression ball can be squeezed by the rectal muscles to create movement in the tail. Gloves that resemble dog paws are also a common prop. Some who engage in puppy play do so with only the mask, tail, and paw gear on without any other clothing. Other puppy play adherents wear wrestling singlets while some wear only jock straps, and others wear clothing that allows maximum physical flexibility and also provides the proper level of canine vulnerability for that particular person. Puppy play adherents engage in canine-human and canine-canine interaction scenarios using the mannerisms and behaviors typically seen between humans and domesticated canines or among domesticated canines. Handlers are not always involved: sometimes puppy play involves just the puppies playing with one another, meanwhile establishing dominant-submissive relationships with each other and among the "pack." As one adherent to puppy play, Pup Sparky, explained to us: "It's all about getting inside the headspace of a dog." Many but not all adherents of puppy play also bark, growl, and whimper like a dog. While puppy play also shares many similarities with aspects of the furry community that we discuss elsewhere, puppy play, with or without a handler, comes out of the domination and submission subculture, and its aesthetics and high use of leather illustrate its affinity in the BDSM community that would not otherwise be present in the furry community. While puppy play began in the gay male leather scene and continues to be primarily an activity among men, we have observed through the course of our research that more women have begun to be involved. When we attended our first BDSM conference, the puppy play arena was directly ahead of us, perhaps seventy-five feet away. There, no women engaged in puppy play at all throughout the conference. When we attended our last BDSM conference, when we visited the puppy play room, roughly 20 percent of the "puppies" were women.

As an aside, we originally conceptualized leather and puppy play as distinct groups outside of the BDSM community. As we learned about them, we realized they are subsets of BDSM, and like many other subsets of BDSM, could be included in our BDSM group without any issue.

Accordingly, we collapsed these two subsets into the larger grouping. We also verified the accuracy of this step with members of the BDSM community and we were met with universal confirmation that puppy play is seen by other members of the BDSM community as being a subgroup, and members of the puppy play subculture saw themselves as being within the broader BDSM umbrella. Importantly, we do not mean to suggest these are the only subgroups in BDSM. While the leather community is very large, puppy play is an emerging community that may still have a great deal of growth potential.

We use the acronym BDSM to refer to the traditional bondage-discipline-dominance-submission-sadism-masochism practices in addition to the leather and puppy play activities. We feel confident doing this because the latter two are subcultures of BDSM. Like Polyamory, BDSM is a chosen identity, a sexual orientation, and a chosen community. BDSM is chosen in that individuals have consensually entered into relationships with other members of the BDSM community. BDSM is a sexual identity because sexual relations are a significant aspect of the core of BDSM identity. BDSM is a chosen community because individuals form enduring commitments to the community and its members that extend beyond simply enjoying kink.

The history of the BDSM community makes it abundantly clear why it is a chosen community. The BDSM community in the United States arose out of a unique combination of war, religious attitudes, and forms of social stratification that are distinct from, say, the origins of Japan's deep BDSM community. Other BDSM communities around the world have variations in their histories which are beyond our scope here. Much has already been written about the role of authors like the Marquis de Sade in ushering in a nomenclature and allure to nominally BDSM themes and practices. Instead, we want to focus your attention on the history of the American BDSM community, whose segmented growth provides us tremendous insight into why power is the point of interest, how BDSM is related to sexual orientation and the LGBT community, and how the community became a recurring scapegoat during feminist and culture war debates.

The initial rise of BDSM culture in the United States dates back to the interwar period and the Roaring Twenties. BDSM's American birth coincided with the initial development of a broader interest in kinks.

This interest is generally attributed to experiences that veterans brought back with them after serving in Europe during World War I as well as the influx of German immigrants during and after the war. The Lost Generation, those who were young adults during and after World War I, became interested in kinks as a part of its consistent pattern of questioning conventional norms, a system of belief they held responsible for the purely unnecessary war. As Bienvenu notes, the development of BDSM culture was elite-led by entertainers, artists, and entrepreneurs seeking to unite the next generation of sexual and aesthetic tastes around their products (1998). BDSM and other kinks where not limited to the urban bohemians that inspired F. Scott Fitzgerald's Jay Gatsby. Kinky interests found their way into homes throughout America, beginning in cities, with the help of mass advertising and periodicals. Early kink culture was characterized as explicitly heterosexual—mild experimentation rather than overt transgression that would undermine accepted norms about sex. This is sometimes attributed to the first BDSM scenes having some similarity with sex games played in brothels.

Interest in BDSM grew during the Great Depression. Practically speaking, large unemployment numbers over an extended period of time put people in a position of wanting to satisfy their natural sexual appetites while lacking the economic means to support a growing family. Kinks that enabled heterosexual couples to find sexual pleasure without the need for or risk of insemination, like BDSM, were conducive to people's economic anxieties. As the stimulative effects of the New Deal, war effort, and GI Bill had taken full effect, leather bars, in particular, began popping up in cities around the country now that they could be patronized by a large, stably employed community no longer made fragile by the Great Depression.

The explicit heterosexuality of early American BDSM stands in stark contrast with its development in Europe. BDSM was most developed in Weimar Germany, benefiting from the comparatively progressive sexuality in Germany at the time, which was further supported by popular interests in different sexual kinks throughout many parts of continental Europe. German immigrants before and after World War II would import some aspects of European BDSM as well as being among the first wave of entrepreneurs in the early commercial aspects of the community. Some community historians have suggested that American service members brought back some of European practices, but there does not appear to be data to suggest that this had a general impact on BDSM in the United States if it did, in fact, occur.

The leather community as it is now recognized spun out of the first motorcycle clubs that were formed by veterans of the Second World War in the late 1940s. The popularity of motorcycling after the war was more than simply a product of having veterans who had used motorbikes or, more frequently, flew planes during their service. Motorcycles were marketed as the height of freedom, an extension of the attempts to instill a car culture into the American psyche. As Magister notes, these early biker groups were unified by "leather, Harley Davidson bikes, and painful memories of war" (1991). Postwar cinema frequently had leading men in leather jackets riding motorcycles, with actors such as Marlon Brando playing the new, ideal masculine man. Leather motorcycle jackets, like bomber jackets used in the military, were first a practical choice due to their ability to block the chills of the winds and the general durability of the material. The leather jacket quickly became a prominent masculine symbol for patriotic Americans and the growing counterculture movement alike. Leather in the 1950s was not simply for greasers like Danny Zuko from *Grease* or "The Fonz" from the television sitcom *Happy Days*. The term greaser referred to a working-class aesthetic of slick, sheeny hair that young men wore, not leather.

The growing number of veterans associations ballooned with large numbers of the public having served in at least one of the wars—World War I, World War II, or the Korean War, if not more than one of them. American veterans are commonly attributed as the originators of modern American BDSM. It was not, as reactionary groups like the New York Society for the Suppression of Vice claimed, because of the young men returning from Europe with bohemian and immoral sexual tastes and practices arising from the perversions and corruptions they were exposed to while on furloughs during their tours of duty. Instead, as many young veterans transitioned from the frontlines of war back into the mundanity and freedom of civilian life, they found themselves longing for the structure and the order of military life. Whether as the giver or recipient of commands, BDSM presented an analog to the military life that framed and structured their time at war. Being the recipient of domination from archetypally masculine commanding officers imbued leather with a new sexual power. While homoerotic, given that men yearned for domination by and of other men, BDSM expanded and became something also fueled by heterosexual interests. While there is less history on the motivations of women during this period, there is a belief by many people currently in the life that women in the early American BDSM scene may have also found assuming a domination role appealing as an extension of their growing economic and social independence. In other words, women's empowerment made power more sexually interesting because they began to enjoy exercising power in the labor force and at home.

Of course, gay service men also played a role in the development of BDSM in the United States. The term "Old Guard" is sometimes used in the BDSM community to refer to early BDSM community members, particularly gay men, with important cultural distinctions from today's BDSM community. The Old Guard is often thought of has having a higher emphasis on giving and receiving orders, hierarchy, and strictness as a personality feature in doms, with scenes playing out like erotic renditions of military relationships. These qualities are inextricably tied to the military service of these men and, therefore, also help us understand why BDSM culture has diversified and created a litany of subcultures since its inception—a person's elective communities need to be salient to who they are and what they are interested in. Biker clubs and enduring gay communities throughout the United States helped nurture the incipient gay leather communities in the United States (Weiss 2015).

Members of gay biker clubs have had a profound effect on America's imagination about sex, deviance, and masculinity. Thompson rightly observed that "it was the gay leathermen of the time who really cut the archetypal mold of a sexual outlaw" (1991, p. XV). In 1954, the first gay motorcycle club, the Satyrs, was founded in Los Angeles and was quickly followed by other West Coast gay biker clubs such as Oedipus in Los Angeles, the Warlocks in San Francisco, and the California Motorcycle Club in the Bay Area. These communities were difficult if not impossible to differentiate from straight bicycle clubs in California that catered to riders from a specific marginalized community. While many of the members did not have an express interest in BDSM, the clubs nonetheless created an enduring space for those who did. These clubs were key for the early dissemination of BDSM norms, preceding BDSM publications and the depiction of BDSM in mass media. Highly insulated in their early years, BDSM groups generally excluded the curious and potential onlookers or voyuers. Instead, those looking to join "the life" took on apprenticeship roles from experienced doms and subs, needing to demonstrate a commitment and understanding of the norms before being able to participating in BDSM scenes (Magister 1991).

By the early 1960s, interest in BDSM also developed into a niche commercial industry. By this time, Americans interested in BDSM no longer had to rely on a spattering of BDSM clubs or make-shift gear for home use. Instead, those interested in BDSM could learn about it through magazines, catalogs, and a variety of stores with gear and clothing in stock specifically designed for use in BDSM scenes and roleplaying. BDSM magazines are credited as the inspiration for several of Bettie Paige's famous pictorials and pinups. The "Queen of Pinups" expanded the American public's interest in BDSM, particularly by those interested in erotica. But it was not the case that only someone with the celebrity of Bettie Page could make BDSM mainstream. The mass marketing of BDSM during this period was concurrent with a rise of nudist entrepreneurs, pamphleteers around sexual and reproductive health, and a variety of sex and gender topics. As Chauncey notes, front page pictorials of drag shows donned the front of national newspapers like the *New York Times* repeatedly throughout the early portions of the twentieth century (1996). And, as detailed in chapter 4, nudist organizations advertised in front of major motion pictures. This constellation of entrepreneurs around sex, gender, and the body made the mainstreaming of BDSM less novel and helped create a primed consumer base. BDSM began to be widely understood, even if it was not mainstream.

The general public's exposure to BDSM rapidly expanded through normalization efforts in addition to the sensationalization of Bettie Page's pinups and the like. *Life Magazine* had a large, transatlantic readership and shared images of Chuck Arnett's BDSM murals outside bars in San Francisco that depicted gay men and BDSM with hypermasculine details, far from the effeminate, dandy stereotypes of gay men that were already commonplace. The magazine published Arnett's murals as a part of a broader campaign to break stereotypes through the visual arts. In addition to helping cement San Francisco's place as the gay capital of the world, this campaign also focused attention on the city as a center for stretching sexual boundaries and donned San Francisco with a reputation as one of the "leather capitals" of the world (Rubin 1991). Many historians find that the mass reach of that "issue of *Life* started the migration to San Francisco" (Fritscher 1991). While the magazine sought to primarily focus on gay men in San Francisco, they did describe a tolerating relationship between the BDSM community and the gay community in San Francisco as largely motivated by a shared aversion to the hostility the were facing by the straight public. Sexual outlaws were welcome and those who broke the norms of the heterosexual patriarchal boundaries would find a safe haven.

Major American cities, notably veteran-heavy San Francisco, Chicago, and New York City, began hosting explicitly gay BDSM events and contests like International Mr. Leather and Mr. Drummer (Laroque 2014). This coincided with the expansion of circulation of homoerotic magazines that were explicitly geared toward the BDSM community, like *Physique Pictorial*, as well as broader male erotica publications. *Drummer*, which purports to be the most-read gay BDSM magazine currently in circulation was founded in 1975. As Laroque notes, *Physique Pictorial* and other male BDSM periodicals were able to avoid censorship because the men would be scantily clad in leather gear and thongs and not entirely nude. More importantly, however, the articles and photographic spreads portrayed the models in strong, masculine ways. This combination avoided being seen as pornography and avoided challenging gender norms.

Yet, the mainstreaming of BDSM through economic means made the future of BDSM in the United States particularly vulnerable to the heightened use of antiobscenity laws, like the Comstock Act, and changes in federal rules around interstate mail and commerce. BDSM, a series of private interests and activities, became restricted on economic or commerce clause grounds and, as a result of shared oppression and disapprobation, BDSM leaders threw their lots in with nudists, gays, antiwar activists, and other marginalized groups that built the American Civil Liberties Union (Wheeler 2013). While these regulatory regimes were eventually repealed, struck down, narrowed, or restricted as the Supreme Court expanded free speech protections, the moral crusades against BDSM and these other groups did have a lasting effect on popular depictions of BDSM in the United States and created a cultural disapproval that persists today among some quarters of the public.

The historical record suggests that BDSM grew despite, perhaps even on occasion because of, governmental efforts to regulate or crackdown on the morals of the citizenry. BDSM clubs and groups continued to be founded and grow throughout the United States, suggesting that, at a minimum, there was an increasing and enduring level of interest in BDSM. The visibility of a diverse BDSM community in San Francisco that supported several BDSM establishments clustered together on Folsom Street was bolstered by the comparatively tolerant city climate. Even today, the Folsom Street Festival is a world renowned BDSM celebration. Still, visibility and open enjoyment of the BDSM lifestyle was not a ubiquitous feature of BDSM life in all major US cities. If it were, then the larger BDSM communities in Los Angeles, Chicago, and New York would have been far more known and San Francisco's title as the BDSM capital of the United States would surely have been credibly challenged (Rubin 1991; 1998).

Yet, popular depictions presented the world of BDSM as being part and parcel of the gay and lesbian community, despite the widespread engagement in BDSM by straight Americans. BDSM as a series of activities, ideas, and practices agnostic of sexual orientation held true, even as the popular perception of who practiced BDSM, and therefore, who was most often conceived of or targeted for being "deviant" or "perverted," clustered around the gay and lesbian population. In this way, groundwork for the surprise in how successful the book and movie franchise of *Fifty Shades of Grey* was laid more than fifty years ago. The punitive crackdown on BDSM in the 1950s bifurcated BDSM as (1) a "gay thing" or something for a group of deviants and (2) wholesome ways of spicing up the love lives of straight people—furthering the straight-gay segregation in BDSM. Had the book featured a gay male dom and a gay male sub, or two women, we doubt very seriously the sales would have come close to approaching that of the heteronormative version of the naughty couple.

In 1958, Chuck Renslow and Dom Orejudos founded the first leather bar in the United States called The Gold Coast, eponymously named for its location in Chicago. The growing counterculture in the United States around leather and motorcycles, particularly after the sensationalized depictions of the so-called Hollister Invasion in 1947 and conservative cultural orthodoxy of McCarthyism, helped make the membership in these increasingly stigmatized groups more central to individual identities and, thereby, allowed for sustained, local patronage for bars and clubs. Renslow and Orejudos also helped found global leather events such as International Mr. Leather, an annual pageant in Chicago with a host of related leather-oriented events. International Mr. Leather culminates in the annual crowning of a new International Mr. Leather chosen from a wide variety of contestants who have won local, regional, and international contests. For instance, Mr. Leather Palm Springs, chosen annually, is a contestant in International Mr. Leather every year.

The BDSM community continued to grow even after the notoriety from *Life Magazine* and viral moments in pop culture faded. Curiosity about BDSM and kink groups were overtaken in popular culture and establishment concern by the emerging hippy and free love counterculture. More extreme BDSM groups began developing at this time. Some of this can be attributed to a natural tendency to fully dive into certain aspects of BDSM while some can be seen as the community's way of creating a stronger contrast to other sexual communities and a polarizing reaction to the reemergence of conservatism following the 1968 elections. In-group guides to BDSM practices at this time such as Larry Townsend's *The Leatherman's Handbook* were readily sensationalized.

BDSM events benefitted from the social aspects of the sexual revolution in the 1960s. The United States entered into the "Swinging Seventies" with suburban swinging parties, sometimes called key parties or fishbowl parties, increasingly explored by middle-class Americans with varying politics. These parties, where couples would trade sexual partners, and their associated sexual liberation served as a symbolic demonstration of youth, vitality, and freedom such that even corporate America joined in the fun. For instance, camera and film maker Polaroid's successful "Swinger" camera, which developed photographs on the spot, found the coincidence highly marketable. These swinger parties, in addition to promoting consensual nonmonogamy, are noted for enabling a greater exploration of sexual practices including BDSM, bisexuality, and group sex. Under this background, the BDSM community hosted "Great Parties," decentralized but enduring rendezvouses that helped expand participation in BDSM beyond clubs. Unlike key parties which would be hosted residentially, Great Parties would rent out night clubs or other commercial venues for the duration of the event. Examples include the

Inferno, first hosted in 1976 by the Chicago Hellfire Club, which is still in operation today. Some of these parties would be organized around specific subgroups in BDSM or practices, allowing for enduring subgroup communities to form in their own spaces at scale for the first time.

BDSM political organizations also began to appear in the 1970s in response to America's conservative revival. The Eulenspiegel Society was formed in 1971 and based in New York City while the Society of Janus formed three years later in San Francisco. In 1978, Samois was founded as the first lesbian BDSM organization. It took a considerable amount of time for these organizations to achieve some influence within the sex rights movements and broader political currents. The outlier nature of BDSM desire meant that many in the sex rights movement were uncomfortable with what was viewed as deviant behavior. The BDSM community often found itself as sexual outlaws even as they sought to join the other sexual outlaws that pushed a more open view of sex and sexuality.

The 1980s was an era of rampant appropriation of BDSM by larger cultural currents in the United States. Pop culture icon Madonna wore leather and embraced BDSM motifs in a variety of her music videos, concerts, awards show performances, and publicity campaigns. She and her team used nominally BDSM themes provocatively, inciting conservative groups to protest her work as endangering the purity and safety of women. The notion that BDSM engaged in misogynistic practices was not new to the 1980s. To the contrary, a variety of second-wave feminists aggressively critiqued BDSM, explicitly and implicitly, on the same grounds that they objected to pornography as the objectification and subjugation of women. Lacking an empirical study of BDSM, they assumed that BDSM scenes were always structured as the men in dominating roles and women in submissive roles. This, of course, was a blurry and inaccurate caricature of BDSM. The radical feminists of the 1970s, who often believed that lesbians and lesbian culture were the vanguard of women's liberation, were some of the strongest anti-BDSM proponents. They were concerned that some growing aspects of sexual expression, while seemingly more pluralistic, were regressive attacks on the status of women. Groups like Women Against Violence in Pornography and Media and, later on, the group Women Against Pornography were instrumental in leading protests against BDSM venues and stigmatizing BDSM, particular among lesbian Americans. Just as today, the roles in BDSM scenes were not limited by gender, let alone sexual orientation. Beginning with the Conference on Sexuality at Barnard College in 1982, the Sex Wars raged within feminist circles—pitting sex-positive activists and anti-pornography/BDSM activists against each other in a series of debates, protests and counterprotests, and moments of intense vitriol.

As the BDSM community engaged in debates and faced protests from voices on the Left, they also, like society as a whole, were forced to confront the perils of the emerging AIDS epidemic. Out of concern over safe sex and limiting the spread of HIV and AIDS, most of the Great Parties and BDSM clubs shuttered their doors, casualties of fear and caution. Safe-sex guidelines at the beginning of the epidemic where highly speculative, commonly attributing actions as high risk for transmission that we now know are not actually risky at all. Some venues that remained open like the Catacombs actively participated with the Centers for Disease Control and Prevention to improve the study of the AIDS epidemic and test different community-driven public health strategies. Frightened and reactionary missives came from straight vanilla Americans, who began campaigning for the closure of remaining BDSM and LGBT clubs. Even some of the political Left argued that the perils of the epidemic overrode civil rights obligations and the commitment to the freedom of sexual expression inherent in the BDSM community.

Targeted and vilified like gay and lesbian Americans, BDSM organizations and activists began working with and within LGBT organizations. A common enemy, HIV, along with a common discriminatory culture, served to unite the BDSM and leather communities with the gay and lesbian social movements. Their institutional success is notable. Despite the stigma from some sex-positive feminists just a few years earlier, the BDSM community was able to secure representation on the planning committee for the 1987 March on Washington for Gay and Lesbian Rights which mobilized more than one thousand attendees to the rally. The march was immediately preceded by a conference in the United States Department of Commerce that is often considered the first truly national BDSM conference, in part due to its scale and sociopolitical purpose. The BDSM community also had an active role in planning and promoting the twentieth anniversary of the Stonewall Riots two years later. As Stein notes, soon after that cooperation, leather-specific events became a visible and staple feature of Pride parades and events across the country (1991).

In support of the political union of the LGBT and leather community, Tony DeBlasse designed the Leather Pride Flag in 1989 (Weiss 2006). In some ways modeling off the open network of national LGBT organizations, BDSM groups like Gay Male SM Activists and Lesbian Sex Mafia were important in helping complete BDSM's shift out of the apprenticeship codes and relatively insulated networks. These organizations put on a variety of programming for those in the life as well as to those curious about BDSM, a dual-audience dynamic that is now a staple of all large BDSM conferences today. Beginners and experts, and every skill and experience level in between the extremes find acceptance and level specific programming at virtually every BDSM conference. One consequence of the opening up of the BDSM community was that the hard linguistic codes and mores were less enforced, and the symbolic representations of the community took on greater significance as the broadening community's unifying feature (e.g., leather, flags, gear) (Stein 1991).

The 1980s and early 1990s also saw skyrocketing demand for BDSM toys, clothing, guidebooks, personal ads, and even "professional domination services." More recently, websites such as FetLife (short for "fetish life"), a social media platform dedicated to BDSM, have cropped up and expanded greatly, providing even larger and more accessible platforms for members of the community. This proliferation, however, met headwinds with groups like the Moral Majority who led a renewed push for regulating obscenity. For example, the Communications Decency Act of 1996 regulates internet pornography, but also allows for the regulation of BDSM content in particular (Weiss 2006). Antiobscenity laws and the mass media landscape resensationalized BDSM, despite the efforts of community leaders for the past decade. News outlets and political commentators had a field day mocking United Nations arms inspector Jack McGeorge when they discovered that he had earlier founded a BDSM group. The modern media landscape manufactured sensational images to stigmatize McGeorge and lampoon the United Nations.

In the #MeToo Era, the BDSM community continues to work through precarious legal distinctions as American politics has become more bifurcated and younger generations are increasingly more embracing of sexual identity and expression broadly construed and without the narrow confines of their elders' frameworks. The use of the terms "master" and "slave" have occasionally been subject of external critique and even gotten members of the community arrested under a misunderstanding by legal authorities (thinking that "slaves" meant nonconsensual and illegal sex trafficking). While *Obergefell v. Hodges* (576 U.S. 644 [2015]) was critically important for LGB Americans, it did not, for example, effect holdings such as the opinion from the New York State Supreme Court that held that people do not have a protected right to engage in consensual BDSM activity (*People v. Jovanovic* 263 A.D.2d 182, N.Y.S.2d 156 [1999]). Overtime, the American court system has slowly moved from seeing BDSM as something no reasonable person would consent to (*Commonwealth v. Appleby* 380 Mass. 296 [1979]), to existing in a liminal space between sport and sex lacking explicit protections (*State v. Collier* 372 N.W.2d 202 [1985]), to understanding and proving consent. It bears repeating that, at the moment, consent is not an affirmative defense to battery in any state or territory. Consensual sexual activity can lead, and has led, to arrests, convictions, and jail time for battery.

Data Collection

To measure the political attitudes and activities of the BDSM community, we administered BDSM-oriented versions of our two sets of questions. Recall one survey contains twenty-nine multiple-choice questions (Appendix 1.1) and the other contains eleven open-ended questions (Appendix 1.2). As with the other cases, we first collected answers to the surveys in person through a convenience sample and then collected additional responses through the virtual snowball technique discussed earlier. We also collected versions of the surveys oriented to leather and puppy play. As discussed above, once we were educated by the community, we quickly realized that leather and puppy play were subsets of BDSM and not actually separate communities. Accordingly, we have grouped all of the responses we received in these three categories under BDSM.

We attended three major BDSM conferences: Beyond Vanilla XXIV in Dallas, Texas, in 2014; DomCom in Los Angeles, California, in 2021; and Frolicon/Froliween in Atlanta, Georgia, in 2021. Each conference lasted four days and was strictly adults only. That is, no one under 18 years of age was allowed in any part of these conferences. This contrasts with our other groups who may have adult-only space, but in general are oriented toward all ages. At Beyond Vanilla, we registered for a table in the vender room where participants answered the questions in person. Because we were registered as venders, we were able to include a flyer soliciting participation in our study in the welcome bags given to each registrant at the conference. The flyer is included here as Appendix 3.1. We asked those who participated in person to share the links to the questionnaires through their social media BDSM networks and with anyone else they knew who identified as a member of the BDSM community. We also asked participants to identify closed social media groups we could contact directly to solicit survey responses. The social media groups identified by participants and contacted by us that resulted in taking survey responses are listed in Appendix 3.2. We offered participants a chance to win $50 in a drawing at the end of the conference and also kept a liberal supply of Halloween size candy at our table in the vender room.

We used four iPads to administer the surveys so that we could accommodate multiple people at one time. We had a steady stream of attendees approach our table and take the surveys. We went through well over sixty-five pounds of candy during our three days of taking surveys. We had a large sign on our table that informed people of the chance to win the drawing and we would also verbally solicit people to take the surveys. We tried to use humor to get attention like saying, "Hey little boy (or girl), do you want a piece of candy?" as the adults walked by. We were located near a paddle vender who sold paddles made out of folded sections of fire hose bolted onto a wooden handle. These fire hose paddles were about two feet long from tip to tip. The first several hours we were there, we were visibly startled by the loud cracking noise whenever any attendees would try out the fire hose paddles on someone. Every time we jumped, someone walking by our table would chuckle at us and that frequently led to those folks taking our surveys and talking with us. We initially collected over one hundred surveys at Beyond Vanilla and then collected another hundred online over the next six months through the variety of the online groups listed in Appendix 3.2. We also conducted semistructured interviews with the elites as well as any of the people who were willing to talk to us after filling out the surveys. We also engaged in participant observation and ethnographic analysis by attending some of the panels and social events and reading the literature and flyers that were made available throughout the conference. The lead organizer of the conference, Beth, proved especially helpful. In total, Beth spent more than ten hours chatting with us about virtually every aspect of the BDSM community and lifestyle that we could think to ask about or that occurred to her to bring up. She also introduced us to several other elites, people who were organizers of sessions at the conference or events in their home areas, that proved incredibly informative. Because Beth vouched for us, we entered into these conversations with more credibility and trust than we would have had we simply tried cold-calling, so to speak.

At DomCom and Frolicon/Froliween we registered as attendees and attended panels and conference social events in order to engage in participant observation and ethnographic analysis. We also conducted semistructured interviews with elites and other attendees at these two conferences. We spoke with more than 250 people across the three conferences. The conferences had many similarities and some differences which bear discussion. But for the content of the panels, the appearance of the attendees, and the gear, art, and information available in the vender room, these conferences are no different from any trade or interest area conference. Experienced academic conference attendees would find the experience familiar in many dimensions. The conferences have ongoing panels and workshops throughout the day on a host of topics of interest. The attendees wear their badges to enter into the events and there are codes of conduct posted throughout the event. There is a strong emphasis on consent to interact in the architecture of the codes of conduct. The BDSM focused conferences place sex and sexuality at the forefront of the event. There is no ambiguity or hidden undertones of sexuality like some of the other conferences for the other groups we consider here.

Rather, there are activities like "Group Masturbation Session" and "Exhibitionist/Voyeur Room" which explicitly are structured for participating in and viewing others participating in a variety of sex acts. We attended panels such as "Mind-Blowing Blow Jobs" and "An Introduction to Rope Play" which are designed to be instructional panels about specific sex acts, specific styles of BDSM play, specific products and gear used in BDSM. We attended a panel titled "Introduction to

Belts" which demonstrated restraint techniques using a common belt that you would wear to hold up your pants. The speaker demonstrated how to restrain wrists, arms, and legs using one or two belts and claimed some of the methods were inspired by, or actually used by, the Stasi, the official state security service of East Germany. One attendee, Joe, told us that over time, leather and bondage play that was actually inspired by Nazis had become described as inspired by the Stasi because it was a more palatable heritage. Joe suggested that the World War II veterans were more comfortable with Nazi gear and play than the younger generations. While we found his claims persuasive, we really have no way of verifying this, although another leather vender at Beyond Vanilla made the same claim as we were discussing leather hats with him. Many panels were about learning to navigate the communicative aspect of BDSM, learning the norms of the community for new members, and navigating your BDSM community in the workplace and with your family and friends who are not in the life. Each conference also had many panels that were more narrowly targeted, such as panels specifically for members of the LGBTQ+ community or even specific literary or role play communities like a panel for *Game of Thrones* fans and a *Harry Potter* themed playroom.

Moreover, each BDSM conference will have a "dungeon" or "playroom" where gear has been staged and any attendee can use the equipment. For instance, there will be whipping stations where one person gets struck with any number of different devices, from actual whips to canes, reeds, a cat-o-nine tails (a multistranded leather whip), or paddles. There will be ropes stations where someone gets bound and often suspended in the air by ropes. There may be wrestling mats where people engage in erotic wrestling. At Frolicon, we watched two men in their midthirties wrestle. They began their wrestling match in underwear and t-shirts and eventually they engaged in oral sex and mutual masturbation with each other after fully disrobing. There will be tickling stations where devices like feathers and restraints are used to tickle. We saw two different electric play stations where mild shocks are used in erotic fashion. At each station of the dungeon or playroom, the attendees may be fully clothed or fully nude or somewhere in between. Friends, acquaintances, and strangers alike might passively watch or, with consent, join in the sexual interactions. Each dungeon or playroom had ample seating and space for spectators. There were not dividers between the play spaces so someone could stand by a whipping station and still see, for instance, rope play in one area and wrestling in another. The scenes may lead to sex and orgasm or may end without release. Some people prefer a specific type of play, while others have broad tastes and may engage in a wide variety of activities. One important note is that safety is paramount in the dungeons. There are always very experienced volunteers who are charged with ensuring safe use of the equipment and novices are constantly encouraged to ask for help, guidance, and input. There is ample water available because the adrenaline rush, the weight and warmth of some of the gear, and the physical nature of these activities can rapidly lead to dehydration. Safety protocols around sexually transmitted diseases and body fluids are routine. Condoms and lubricants are freely and readily available. Some activities, like fecal matter play (or "scat") or blood play are prohibited in the dungeons because of the challenges of cleaning up quickly and thoroughly.

Results

The results of our research paint a picture of a predominately white, educated, and secular community with somewhat moderate political leanings. About 82 percent of those surveyed identified as white (figure 3.1). This sample is much whiter than what we observed of the convention attendees, although certainly a majority of those in attendance appeared to be white or white passing.

Like our respondents in the polyamory group, we had many more non-Hispanic whites in our response pool than appear in the general population. Also, like in the polyamory group, we observed many more people of color at the live events than are represented in the data. We believe one of the driving factors here is the additional risk of publicly being in the BDSM community is not something the community members of color might wish to embrace. In other words, white privilege allows those members of the BDSM community who identify as white to be a bit more public about it than people of color who might face higher costs for affiliation with BDSM if it intersects with other identities. The intersectional amplification of risk of disclosure meant that we were not able to convince some people of color to participate. We asked

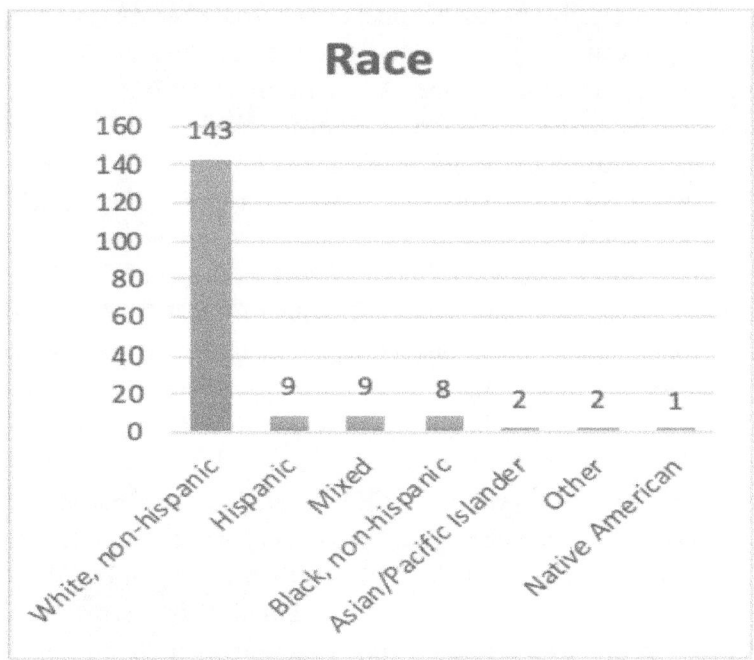

Figure 3.1. Racial Identity of the BDSM Community

one African American man to take the surveys in Dallas, and he replied, "Naw, I'm good. I've got enough headwind without going on record about any of this," as he gestured to the large room full of BDSM gear and adherents. One African American woman in Dallas approached our table and had a piece of candy then asked us what we were doing. After we explained our intent and plan for publication, she said "I'm sorry, but I'm going to have to say no. I can't risk it." We then talked with her for several minutes about her struggles as a Black female in her "white-collar job"—she joked "I don't ever wear white collars, but that's what they call it anyway!" Her bottom line was she faced overt and implicit discrimination and she believed if her employer ever figured out she was in the life she would be immediately fired. It is also worth noting that there is a large subset of BDSM made up of African American Dominatrices. For instance, at DomCon we talked at length with Queen Ana Algos, a middle-aged African American dominatrix. She identifies as pansexual and specializes in "Black" (meaning racial) and "leather" BDSM play.

Queen Ana is a full-time professional dominatrix who works primarily in Los Angeles but serves clients all over the country and on occasion internationally. According to Queen Ana, for some (especially white) men, domination by an African American woman is the height of pleasurable humiliation. Indeed, racialized play is a specific subfield of BDSM. We believe that, across the groups we surveyed, reticence among nonwhites to engage in our surveys can be mostly attributed to the intersectional risk associated with being both a racial and sexual minority. There is much more to learn about the racial dynamics of the BDSM world that goes beyond the scope of our project. We can only be certain at this point that our sample is more white than the actual BDSM population. It is also worth noting that we only took in-person surveys at the Dallas convention while we did interviews at all of them. Had we taken surveys in Atlanta and in Los Angeles in addition to Dallas, we might very well have ended up with a more representative sample as those conventions appeared to be much more racially diverse than the one in Dallas.

Given the centrality of sexuality to a BDSM identity, it is perhaps not surprising that organized religion and religious institutions are not critically important to this community. Note that "other" and "none" were by far the two most frequent response choices for religious affiliation. Just over a third, 36.9 percent, report having no religious affiliation, which is slightly higher than the overall American population. Additionally, only half of those reporting any religious affiliation report attending religious services with some frequency. At Beyond Vanilla, we met Billy, who wore several sets of Rosary Beads and several chains with crucifixes around his neck. We first asked him if he attended church very often and he chuckled and said "No, I wear these because I think they look cool but also it seems to piss off the sort of person I don't much care for." We followed up by asking him if he was going to any of the clergy kink panels, panels where Catholic religious rituals are incorporated into erotic play (discussed more below) and he laughed again and said "No way, that stuff is for people who got turned on in church and that's not my thing at all. I really just think it looks cool."

Non-traditional religions perhaps have an easier time finding converts in non-traditional communities. There are many people in the kink or BDSM community that engage in religious play. Each of the conferences we attended had panels that touched on constructing religious themed scenes, and the paraphernalia affiliated with religion, and particularly Catholicism, was highly visible. From people dressing as nuns or priests as part of paddling scenes, to sales booths offering rosaries, priests collars, and nun hats, the rituals of Catholicism seemed to be a recurring theme among some of the BDSM adherents we encountered. It was unclear if these Catholic imageries were actually driven by a Catholic-specific kink interest or if they were more simple stand-ins for religion generally. We talked with one woman who described the allure of religious kink play as the "ultimate in power play since one of you is representative of God."

We attended a panel at Frolicon/Froliween that illustrated several ritualistic piercing and hanging processes affiliated with various religions around the world. By pierce and hang rituals, we are referring to the use of metal hooks to pierce the skin in the upper torso—either back or front—and then using those hooks, attached to ropes or cables, to suspend the person in the air. The panel made references to Native American rituals and various religious rituals across India, Persia, and China. That specific panel began with the main speaker "smudging" the perimeter of the room with burning sage and "sanctifying" the space by splashing bits of water he had blessed, also completely around the perimeter of the room. As he walked the large room perimeter (it could seat perhaps 125 people), he spoke softly about sanctifying the space, releasing negative energy, expressing gratitude for "this time and this space," and other similar comments. While mainstream Christianity would likely not accept these as religious rituals, for these BDSM adherents there, it was very much a sacred and spiritual experience.

As we might expect, attendance at the facilities of organized religion is not a priority for this community. Out of our 172 respondents to our question about the frequency of attendance at religious services, 117 reported seldom or never, 18 reported yearly, 15 reported monthly, and only 22 reported weekly or more attendance.

Two-thirds of those surveyed identified as male. We found the convention spaces to be far from patriarchal with many women in leadership or panel instructor roles and we also perceived the gender makeup to be much closer to 50-50 than our surveys suggest. That is, visually, the crowds at each convention seemed to be much closer to gender parity than our survey responses suggest. There were lesbian spaces, women played roles of domination, and several of the presentations we observed made explicit the importance of values of gender and sexual equity. Because we are all male, we may not have had as many women take the surveys as if we had also had a female researcher with us. Recall we have included both the leather and puppy play communities in our survey aggregation for BDSM. This may also partially explain our oversupply of males. Puppy play, up until very recently, was primarily a gay male BDSM community. Likewise, while there are many women in the leather scene, and many straight people in the leather scene, gay men are still an outsized share of that total population. Accordingly, those two communities are more male than BDSM in general and it may be the inclusion of puppy play and leather have skewed our sample to be more male. In any event, and whatever the cause, we can safely say that the BDSM community actually has much greater gender parity than our data shows.

Our respondents were spread across age categories but skewed a bit younger than the population as a whole. Again, like all or our groups, we did not speak with anyone under 18. Of the 172 respondents to the age question, 54 chose the 18–29 group; 82 chose the 30–49 group, 35 chose the 50–64 group, and, unbelievably, only 1 person confessed to being over 65. One obvious note from our responses about age for the BDSM community is that people are hesitant to identify as older than 65. Like the polyamory group, we are certain there were people over 65 who either skipped over the age question or chose a younger grouping. Our observation of the attendees, whether in the gear hall, play rooms, panels, or social activities, was that many more older people are involved than our data suggest. Moreover, we thought that the people who took our surveys live were spread about evenly across the age brackets. In any event, as we talked with people at the events, it became clear that the people who presented as older had been involved with BDSM for much longer. In other words, people did not seem to join the BDSM community late in life. Rather, they uniformly reported becoming involved in BDSM in their twenties or thirties, or often even younger as their sexuality was emerging. We met Jeff at Beyond Vanilla and when we asked him how he entered the BDSM community, he said, "Every time my dad paddled me, I got a raging boner. Eventually, I asked one of my friends from high school who I used to jack off with, to spank me and that was it, man. I was in it for good from that point on!" Additionally, the consensus seemed to be that once you become a member of the BDSM community, you are in it for life. As one older man told us in Dallas, "Once you're kinky, you can't go back. It would be like getting rid of your hot water in your shower. You'd spend all your time from then on thinking about that warm water instead of that awful cold water. When your eyes get opened, you can't close them again."

All things considered, we think it unlikely that the BDSM world is excluding older members or that people age out of the community. The age distribution we report is probably a function of generalized societal agism rather than animosity toward older people or exclusion of older people specifically in the BDSM community. While it is beyond the parameters of this study, aging and agism in the kink communities should certainly be researched. Our belief is that the kink community is likely less agist than society at large because the premise of acceptance of people without judgment is such a foundational value to the BDSM world. Moreover, we saw many elderly people who were treated with respect and even reverence. We attribute the absence of older identification in the responses to internalized agism rather than something actively or systematically exclusionary about the BDSM community.

Members of the BDSM are overwhelmingly well educated, with over 90 percent of respondents having at least some college education. That is much higher than the overall US population and much higher than any individual age cohort. We are not sure what to make of the high levels of education except that it could be that attending college allows time and freedom for more experimentation, sexual or otherwise. Accordingly, it could simply be that the privilege of attending college for a substantial period of time as a young adult allows the inner kink to blossom. It could also be that the college educated find joining in the community to be a less risky or costly endeavor. We also note that as time goes by, some of those who are less educated may complete their undergraduate degrees or move on to graduate school. The high rate of reported education may also be simply an artifact of how we collected our data. It is possible those with less education might be more suspicious of random academics taking surveys in their safe space. It could also be that the cost of the convention attendance suppresses attendance by lower income people and given the correlation between income and education, people with a lower level of education may simply have not been in attendance. Of the 173 respondents who answered the education level question, 32 reported attending graduate school, 125 reported graduating or some college, and only 16 reported high school or less.

Our respondents were spread in almost a normal distribution across the income brackets (figure 3.2). We speculate that some in the lower income levels are the people in the youngest age bracket who are working part time because they are students. We found that 69.2 percent of our respondents were employed full-time and the plurality of members in the BDSM community are middle class. This makes sense because of the higher than average levels of college education and of the proportion of early-career adults in our sample. So the members of the community are younger but are well educated and, accordingly, have decent incomes. Again, like with the other groups, our omission of "retired" as a category combined with the older-aged people we observed suggests the "not employed" category may overstate the actual population. Also, like the polyamory respondents, the wealthier respondents seemed more unwilling to disclose their income levels. Of the 173 people who answered the question about income category, 27 chose "prefer not to answer" and 34 chose "more than $75,000." The middle bracket of $30,000–$74,000 was selected by 59 people, with 26 people choosing $20,000–$29,000, and 27 people choosing less than $20,000. Generally speaking then, the BDSM world does not appear to present anything remarkable about income. That is, the community is not particularly rich or poor and it seems to welcome all class strata. This manifests itself in the presentation of the activities as well. Almost every activity we saw demonstrated could be done with equipment or gear found in virtually every household—from clothing like belts or scarves to household items like knives, candles, spatulas, and dog leashes or collars. Other than the very specialized paraphernalia, like electrical wands that deliver mild shocks or elaborate trapeze ropes and stands, almost anyone could afford to participate.

The current relationship status of those sampled appears consistent with the age distribution in our sample (figure 3.3). That is, for instance, the 58 people who identified as single more or less align with the 54 people who picked the 18–29 age bracket match. We do have one caveat about the relationship status numbers. Because of the puppy play and leather groups, which are overwhelmingly gay men, and because our

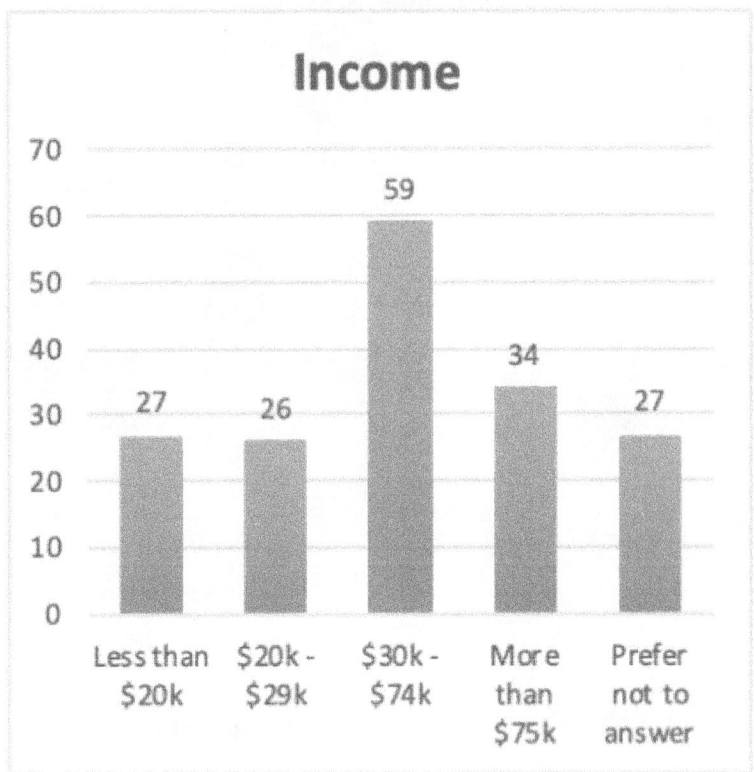

Figure 3.2. Income Brackets in BDSM

data at Beyond Vanilla was collected at the beginning of the era of marriage equality, many of those men may have been in long-term relationships but simply were not married. We do not have a way to discern how many, if any, might fall into that category. However, in general, the remarkable thing about the relationship status distribution for the BDSM community is how unremarkable it is. This suggests that, while nonkink people may view those in the BDSM lifestyle as wildly different outliers and outsiders, they are actually married and divorced at roughly the same rates as everyone else.

The BDSM community is engaged politically. For instance, more than three-quarters (77.8 percent) of those in our survey were certain that they were registered to vote (figure 3.4)

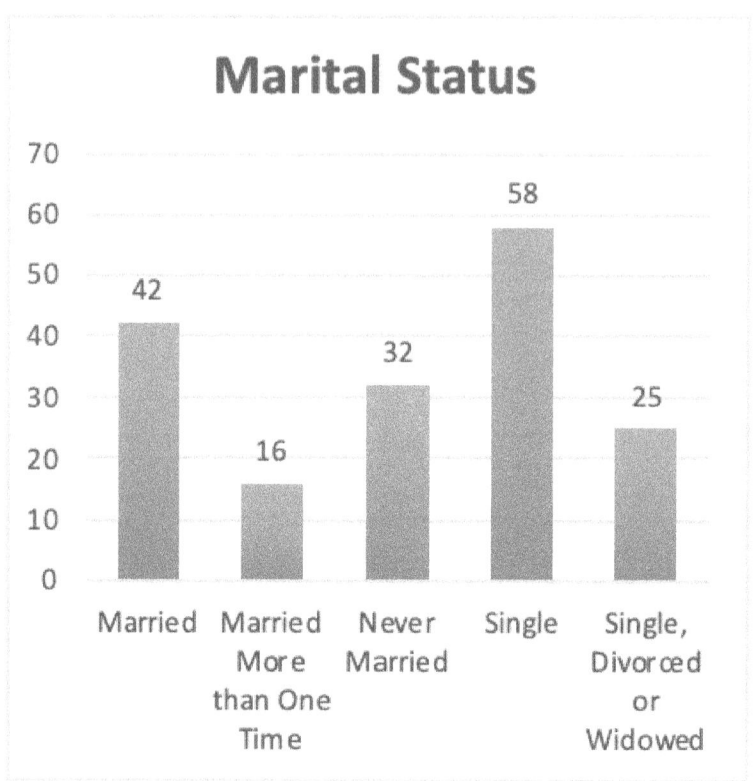

Figure 3.3. Relationship Status of Members of the BDSM Community

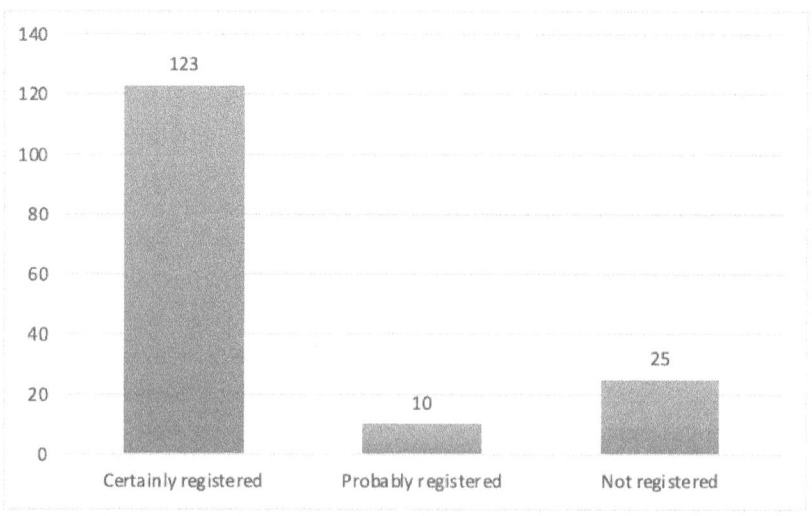

Figure 3.4. Voter Registration Among Members of the BDSM Community

The plurality of respondents were registered as Democrats, although 38.1 percent were registered independents or no party preference (figure 3.5). Not surprisingly, registration with the Republican Party comes in at a distant third. The Republican commitment to courting evangelical Christians may be coming at a cost of members of the BDSM community who are more libertarian and less interested in governmental social control and the conservative obsession with sex and sexuality.

The ideological distribution of the BDSM community skews liberal but there were about as many moderates as there were liberals, at 31 and 36.5 percent, respectively (figure 3.6).

No less than 85 percent (102 respondents out of 120) thought that the Republican party was too conservative on the issue of abortion and 90.9 percent (110 respondents out of 121) thought the Republican Party was too conservative about gay marriage. Perhaps the BDSM community has a special affectation for issues that revolve in part around bodily autonomy, like abortion and gay rights, because the right to do as they please with their bodies is central to the identity.

Across other issues, the BDSM community was often indistinguishable from the population at large, even when they overwhelmingly sided

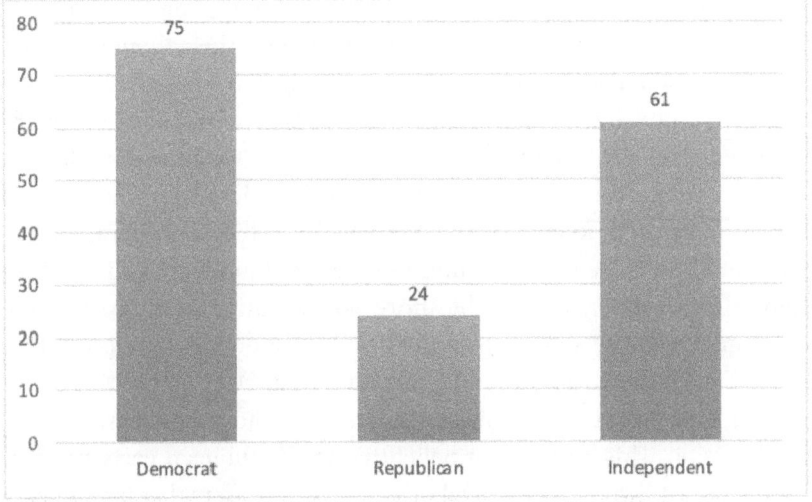

Figure 3.5. Party Identification Among Members of the BDSM Community

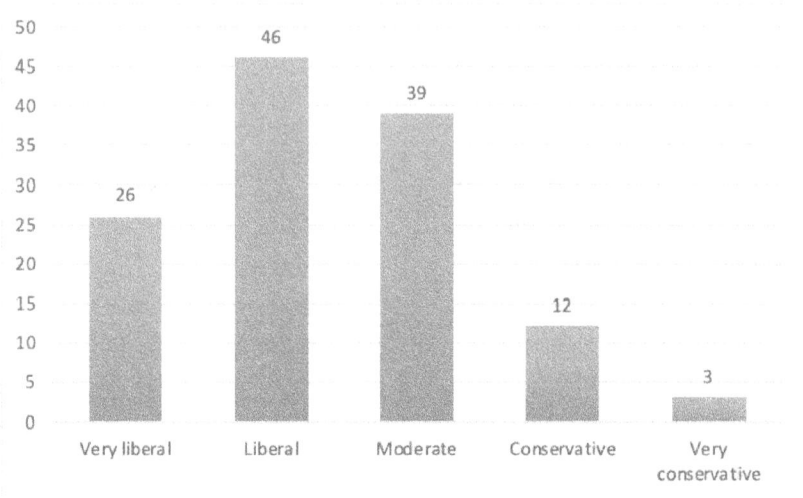

Figure 3.6. Ideological Distribution of Members of the BDSM Community

with or against one party. For example, a little over half of the members of the BDSM community thought that the Democratic Party was about right when it came to abortion, with 31.7 percent thinking that the Democratic Party was not liberal enough and 17.5 believing that the Democratic Party was too conservative (n = 120). But members of the BDSM community showed tremendous variability depending on the issue. The BDSM community was almost evenly divided on their thoughts about the Democratic Party's stance on immigration, with respondents choosing each response at about the same rate. The choice "not liberal enough" garnered 40 clicks, "about right" received 42, and "too liberal" pulled 38.

The community generally prefers political moderation, however that might be defined, to extremism. We asked whether Democratic leaders should be more liberal or more moderate (figure 3.7) and whether Republican leaders should be more conservative or more moderate (figure 3.8). By about 2 to 1, the BDSM respondents preferred that Democrats move in a more moderate direction. Over 90 percent of the respondents want the Republican leadership to move in a more moderate direction. This bolsters our belief that the Republican Party has cost itself support through the sexual oriented culture wars that have been a mainstay of their platform at least since the 1980s.

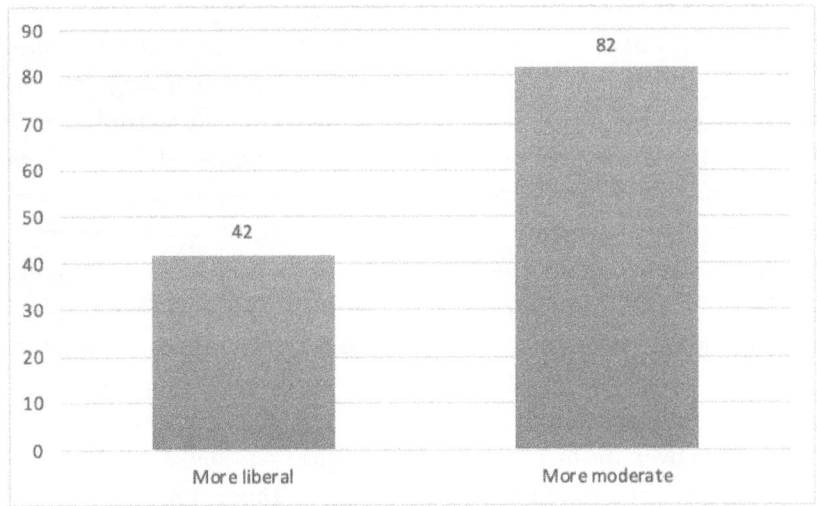

Figure 3.7. Would you like to see Democratic leaders in Washington move in a more liberal direction or a more moderate direction?

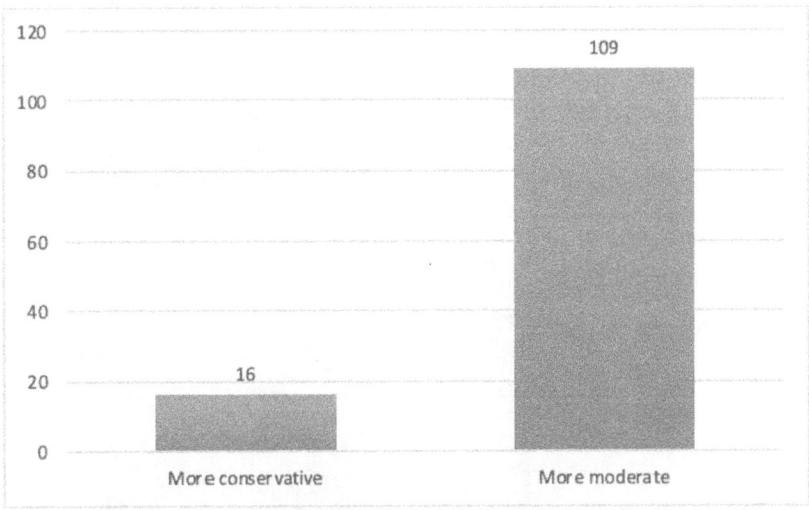

Figure 3.8. Would you like to see Republican leaders in Washington move in a more conservative direction or a more moderate direction?

The BDSM respondents were not only knowledgeable about politics, but many of them frequently discussed politics and political issues with other members of the community. More than half, 53.3 percent, talked to others in the community about politics on at least weekly basis (figure 3.9). Out of our 120 respondents, 26 hardly ever talked about politics and another 30 seldom did. So about 46 percent of our respondents were either apolitical or chose not to engage others in the BDSM community.

The responses to our open-ended questions also contained a great deal of interesting information. Without exception, every respondent identified as being a part of the BDSM, leather, or puppy play community—and, more often than not, as being part of more than one or all of these communities. The was a tremendous diversity in sexual orientation overall. Only one respondent who identified as a part of the puppy play community identified as straight. The majority of respondents who identified as a part of the overall BDSM community noted that they were bisexual and those in the leather subgroup had near equal pluralities of gay/lesbian and bisexual respondents. Interestingly, the vast majority of our respondents could not identify a unifying political issue for the community despite our findings that they consistently held liberal views on issues such as abortion and gay rights. Perhaps it is not surprising, then, that the respondents were unsure if the community

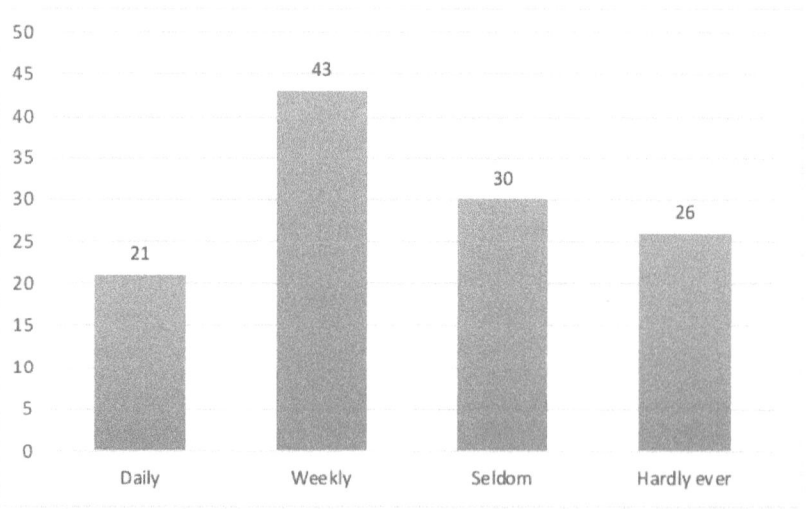

Figure 3.9. How Frequently the Members of the BDSM Community Talk about Politics

should be more active as a community on political issues. Some thought that a more politically active community might create opportunities for a dramatic reduction in the economic, social, cultural, and legal peril they face on a daily basis. Others thought that the better strategy was to avoid attracting attention or creating political enemies.

The presence of a large BDSM community that has been ignored by the mainstream political process suggests the potential for mobilization of the group. However, anyone that wants to politically mobilize the BDSM community would need to first articulate an issue that could unite the community in simple terms. We believe the easiest issue to reach a consensus on within the BDSM community is criminal justice reform. Pressing for the inclusion of consent as an affirmative defense to assault, regardless of the level of burden of proof affiliated with the defense, would almost certainly sway undecided or unengaged BDSM voters. Moreover, this issue is so germane to their identities that it could have the potential to be a cleavage issue strong enough to get crossover voters. Without exception, the issue of consent as a defense to battery was raised by the elites we interviewed and was frequently mentioned in our unstructured interviews after the surveys. BDSM conferences routinely have sessions about legal issues like the one in the opening anecdote of this chapter. We address this issue more in the conclusion where we discuss future research avenues. In the aggregate, the BDSM community differs from the non-BDSM community almost exclusively in the intimacy dimension of their lives. Otherwise, they work, earn, marry, and talk politics very much like the rest of the country. They are especially sensitive to issues where there is governmental interference with physical autonomy like abortion and gay rights. Should the BDSM community ever be unified as a voting block, they would be formidable and decisive in elections ranging from the local to the federal.

Appendix 3.1

Beyond Vanilla XXIV Solicitation Flyer

Take a Survey and Enter a Drawing for Cash!
Hello Beyond Vanilla XXIV! We are conducting research into the political attitudes, identities, and political behaviors of sexual minority groups in the United States. If you identify as a member of any (or all) of the BDSM, Leather, of Puppy Play communities, please take a

moment to take our surveys. The links to all surveys are on the back side of this sheet. Simply type each link into a web browser (on your computer, tablet, or smartphone) to begin!

Each group has two surveys—one is multiple choice and one has open ended questions where you can express yourself. You may take the surveys for any group that you think you belong to. If you identify with more than one group, take the surveys for each one!

Your answers are completely anonymous. We have no way of connecting you to your answers. Our IRB approval number at UC Irvine is 2014–1273. Feel free to pass these links along to any other members of these groups you think might be interested or to post these links on any group Facebook pages that would allow it.

What's in it for YOU: In addition to giving voice to your community, if you fill out the bottom portion of this flyer and bring it to us in the social room by 8:30 PM on Saturday, you might win $50! We will draw three names and each will win $50 in cash. We will post the name of the winners in our area in the social room at 8:30 PM on Saturday.

About the study: We are exploring the political attitudes and political behavior of several sexual minority groups in the United States. In addition to the BDSM, Leather, and Puppy Play communities, we also include the polyamory community, Furries, and nudists/naturism in our research. We are writing a book about these currently overlooked communities.

About us: Tony Smith (casmith@uci.edu) is an associate professor of political science at the University of California—Irvine and Shawn Schulenberg (schulenberg@marshall.edu) is an associate professor of political science at Marshall University.

$50 Cash Drawing

To enter into the drawing for $50, please fill in the 3 blanks:

1. What did the last question on the multiple choice survey ask for? _____

2. Name (feel free to use a unique nickname or alias): _____

3. Write down a number you can remember to confirm your identity if you win one of the cash prizes. My secret number: _____

SURVEY LINKS

Puppy Play

You are being asked to participate in a research study to explore the political attitudes and activities of the puppy play community. There are two surveys to complete. Both are voluntary and anonymous, and together they should take no longer than ten minutes to complete.

- Puppy Play Pew Public Opinion: http://tinyurl.com/PuppyPlayPO
- Puppy Play Open-Ended Questions: http://tinyurl.com/PuppyPlayOE

Leather

You are being asked to participate in a research study to explore the political attitudes and activities of the leather community. There are two surveys to complete. Both are voluntary and anonymous, and together they should take no longer than ten minutes to complete.

- Leather Pew Public Opinion: http://tinyurl.com/LeatherPO
- Leather Open-Ended Questions: http://tinyurl.com/LeatherOE

BDSM

You are being asked to participate in a research study to explore the political attitudes and activities of the BDSM community. There are two surveys to complete. Both are voluntary and anonymous, and together they should take no longer than ten minutes to complete.

- BDSM Pew Public Opinion: http://tinyurl.com/BDSMPO
- BDSM Open-Ended Questions: http://tinyurl.com/BDSMOE

Appendix 3.2

BDSM Groups

BDSM USA: https://www.facebook.com/groups/bdsm.usa.group/
BDSM Classifieds: https://www.facebook.com/groups/216108091913396/
BDSM Support and Info: https://www.facebook.com/groups/405466942904721/

ACCEPTED BY "SAM MARIE"/REQUESTED/POST BY SAM
BDSM Dating and Personals: https://www.facebook.com/groups/BDSMDating2/
BDSM Social Chat: https://www.facebook.com/groups/777362208952680/
Beyond Fifty Shades of Grey, the truth about BDSM: https://www.facebook.com/groups/259896797537291/
BDSM Learning and Growing: https://www.facebook.com/groups/BDSMlearningandgrowing/

Leather Groups

Leather Lovers: https://www.facebook.com/groups/670173656339518/
LeatherStuds: https://www.facebook.com/groups/leatherstuds/
Leather and Lace Invasion: https://www.facebook.com/groups/293738550716930/
Girls In Latex, Leather, And Pvc: https://www.facebook.com/groups/731250960220104/

4

The Naked Truth

The Politics of Nudists

Soon after we began our first visit to a nudist group, we met a divorced woman in her midfifties, scarred by mastectomies and some sort of abdominal surgery. Carol told us she joined the nudist community after her husband left her. She wanted to regain a sense of body positivity, to improve her sense of self-worth, and, in her words, "to reclaim my sexuality." Her motivation is consistent with the nudist community's positive association of social nudity with improved body image and self-esteem. It also illustrates how far many nudists and the nudist community are from the hippy, swinger, or hedonistic lifestyles that popular media associates with nudists (West 2018). The nudists in our study paint a picture of community whose politics vary similarly to the overall American ideological spectrum. Their political goals and aspirations for the community have evolved and are distinct from the nudist movements that were happening at the end of the nineteenth century and from 1945 through the 1960s. Because of this evolution of the nudism community, we will spend more time on the background and history of this group compared to our others.

Nudism is distinct among our groups because it has a long and storied history in the United States with occasionally explicit political goals associated with it. Accordingly, we spend more time on the historical record than with the other groups. Despite a (at times) prominent place in American society and culture, nudism and naturism in the United States have been the subjects of few peer-reviewed social science publications and none that we found explicitly considering the political attitudes and political activities of nudists. The first period of nudist research has since been uniformly judged as biased research without scholarly or historical merit. Most of the research on nudists during the 1950s and 1960s suffered from an array of methodological challenges and was driven by agentic sex researchers inspired by the Kinsey reports, rather than by objective social scientists. This early body of research assumed that pathology, deviance, and perversion were characteristics of nudists and nudist communities. The goal and focus of the early tranche of research was to describe and then explain the aberrant behavior that seemed to challenge the mores and dictates of polite society. Thus, this first wave of research did little more than passively and, on occasion, actively, affirm common misunderstandings about nudism in general. Specifically, the research created caricatures of the communities and their members, with unsupported claims that sexual deviance, exhibitionism, and voyeurism were the defining features of the nudist community. Sexuality and psychology scholarship in the subsequent decades has been largely successful in undermining those earlier biased studies. Social science research about nudists and naturists has generally focused on the process of becoming a nudist and member of a nudist community, the creation of nudist spaces, the linguistic strategies to differentiate themselves from the nonnude, and the psychosocial differences between nudists and nonnudists. We enter the scholarly discussion of nudism during a period of renewed scholarly interest in the topic with one of the more expansive studies of nudists in the United States and the only project that examines their political attitudes and their political participation.

Nudism entails social nudity, that is, nudism that goes beyond brief moments of being unclothed around others, like in a gym changing room or a doctor's office, and instead requires nudity among others in social settings. The community of nudists, also sometimes called naturists, are an appropriate case for us because it is an essentially contested identity (Schulenberg 2013). Going to a nude beach, skinny dipping with friends, or sitting naked in a spa with others may be sufficient for some to think of themselves as nudists, while others might disagree. Nudism seems to go beyond a specific action—social nudism—to also require a self-perception of being a nudist. That is, social nudity is a necessary but not sufficient condition for a definitional membership in the community of nudists. At Frolicon, we saw one young man repeatedly roaming through the play dungeon, venders' area, and common space who was always nude except for his shoes and fanny pack, which we found out later held the clothes he wore in the elevator to get to the areas where he could be nude. He was always alone too. We talked to him on the third day of the conference. After explaining our project, we asked if he considered himself a nudist. He hesitated at first and then confirmed that he indeed thought of himself as a nudist but that this had been, in his words, "a recent revelation" after he realized he kept seeking out activities and space where he could be publicly nude. He told us he rarely wore clothes at home and his public and social nudity was a newly discovered dimension of his identity. He was at Frolicon because he had become curious about BDSM as well. Notably, at least twice we saw him walking around the conference visibly aroused. This gives him the distinction of being the only nudist we talked with who did not demonstrate modesty about sex. Of course, unlike the nudist resorts we visited, Frolicon is an overtly sex-oriented convention, so his erection did not stand out, so to speak, among the myriad of various sexual activities occurring throughout the space.

In brief, like our other groups, nudism includes action, perception, and community (Hoffman 2015). Additionally, nudism is thought of as a deviance by many of the nonnudist public (see, e.g., Story 1987). Upon discovery, nudists might face the loss of child custody or visitation in a divorce, loss of employment, loss of housing, or any number of other types of discrimination (Martinez 1985). Accordingly, also like our other groups, nudists join the community fully aware they may face social costs for being part of the group.

Research in the 1970s found that an emphasis on supportive, familial social interactions and strong commitments to ubiquitous societal values made joining nudist communities relatively easy compared to many other forms of assimilation (e.g., Weinberg 1965, 1971). While women reported being more initially nervous than men, those involved usually experienced a short acclimation period. Weinberg found that the interviewees felt a mix of common social practices and heightened moral sentiments made the assimilation to the community more comfortable and rapid. The interviewees found that an expansive notion of family made them feel supported and that they were in a friendly and nonthreatening environment. Framing the wearing of clothes as a "ceremony," Weinberg described the nudist communities as welcoming without pretense and providing a friendly and pleasant environment. Finally, Weinberg found that his subjects regularly noted how the extranormal social interactions paired with more frequent uses of words like freedom. The respondents expressed different notions of freedom, but it was common for them to express a right to bodily autonomy. These findings were consistent with those documented a decade earlier which found, for example, that nudists held a heightened value of family (Ilfeld and Lauer 1964).

H. W. Smith built off Weinberg's findings through a comparative study of the norms and practices at French and German nude beaches. Taking for granted that France has a higher body contact culture than is the case in Germany, Smith argued that nudist spaces act as liminal spaces to interrogate assumptions underlying social etiquette (ex. 1980). Rather than being hedonistic, the people at nudist beaches were especially aware of the broader conventions that they were challenging. Nudist beaches consistently had their own social mechanisms for regulating immodesty, sexualization, and embarrassment.

Weinberg's and Smith's arguments tap into a popular theme in social science, originating most eminently in the work of the French sociologist Emile Durkheim. Durkheim saw irreconcilable meanings as a fundamental tension in the creation in a sense of self—being too much of an individual or too much of one's community leads one to alienation. At the societal level, the habit of sorting the world into sacred or profane categories leads to irreconcilable meanings. Weinberg and Smith saw that the initial unease when entering a nudist community was expecting irreconcilable values with the nonnudist world. Instead, once people recognize the shared values and understand the local terminology, assimilation can occur largely unencumbered by external norms.

Schormaker Holmes's ethnography of a nude beach in Canada explored the sexual and asexual scripts and how they challenged heteronormative beliefs, allowed for conventional boundaries to be challenged, and created limits to uphold commitments to their notions of health and modesty (2006). Nude beaches, which are almost never members-only spaces, are spaces of heightened distinction because the members of the community are not only expressing the norms of the community but also trying to clearly convey their practices to casual observers or participants. Schormaker Holmes notes that this means that the fluid space pressures individuals into adopting nonsexual scripts, rather than simply communicating that they are no more or less sexual than nonnudists. She ascribes a greater degree of intentionality than prior research.

Casler (1971) and Douglas et al. (1977) each found that nudists and naturists commonly believe a sexualized body is incompatible with the natural or pure body goals of the community. The fact that Casler and Douglas et al. looked at more sites than only one nudist beach gives their finding more comparative leverage. This is supported by Smith and King's finding that geographic isolation was an important variable in understanding how nudist communities promoted sexual health (2009). Nonetheless, the literature is unanimous that sex is no more a feature of the nudist and naturist communities than the nonnude world and perhaps is even less important as the nude body is demystified among nudists (Freed 1973).

Story found that the strict nonsexual norms in nudist communities that Schormaker Holmes also described resulted in beliefs consistent with the modesty goals constructed and promoted by nudist and naturist elites and leaders (1987). She found some evidence that nudists reported higher levels of guilt for their sexual activity compared to nonnudists although this might be a time-bounded finding since her subjects were older and reached sexual maturity before the sexual revolution had fully taken hold. Utilizing a novel comparative survey between nudists and nonnudists, she was able to conclude that there was "no direct relationship between nudity and sexually permissive behaviors" (1987). Story's work was one of the first studies to scientifically compare nudist and nonnudist attitudes, using a matched survey of nudists and nonnudists. Story also provides a wonderful history of the research on sexuality within the nudist community. She notes that most of the early sex researchers failed to rely on comparative samplings and the evident bias in the sampling was consistent with a host of methodological mistakes.

Since 2000, researchers have shown the contexts under which nudism has been exploited in entertainment (Carr-Gomm 2010) and tourism (Monterrubio 2019; Herold et al. 2021), as well as the way nudism is used in other facets of cultural life (Barcan 2004). West found that the nudist goals of normalizing the naked body, modesty, and a heightened value of familial bonds were consequential in nudists reporting higher levels of self-esteem and self-image (2018). These findings arrived just as body dysmorphia and eating disorders among men and women were occuring at record rates in the United States (Strobel 2022). Our project provides more support for this claim and suggests that the desires for body positivity and a positive self-image are motivating factors for many individuals joining the community. Nudists are motivated, at least in part, by the desire to literally be comfortable in their own skin.

A renewed academic interest in nudism in the United States can be partially attributed to Hoffman's *Naked: A Cultural History of American Nudism* (2015). Hoffman's expansive mapping of the history of nudism in the United States notes how explicitly the founders of the nudist movement sought to distance themselves from their German forebearers the Nacktkultur and their deep association with German nationalist and fascist movements. The goal of American nudism was to provide people with a respite from the stresses of the world and to be both physically and psychologically therapeutic (3). Critically, Hoffman notes how the growing popularity of nudism more recently is a product of the sexual liberation movement in the 1960s and 1970s that resulted in the American public developing a view of nudists as a sexual minority community, despite the aims of the nudist community to be viewed otherwise. Schrank compliments Hoffman's analysis by providing a similar historical trajectory while also delineating a tension where nudism is pulled between freedom, puritanism, and commercialization (2019).

Taken as a whole, the academic literature on nudists broadly demonstrates that nudists are not constructing a new value system as an alternative to the extant societal values found among the nonnude. In other words, nudists are not presenting a wholesale challenge to the social order like one might expect out of a cult. The most distinguishing values and commitments in nudism are held to some degree by hundreds of millions of Americans: connection with nature, express opposition to sexual objectification and body shaming, and reverence for family. The expression of those values exists along a continuum, just like all values. Negy and Winton found college students with greater pro-nudity attitudes were also more likely to embrace broader notions of diversity (2008). That does not mean, however, that the political affiliations of nudists skew in any particular ideological direction as a result of their identity as nudists. Our findings, which will be discussed in greater detail later in this chapter, suggest that partisanship is largely consistent with the states of residence of the nudists.

Thus far in the chapter, we have referred to and generally described individuals and organizations as nudists. That has been largely accurate insofar as most of the individuals we interviewed used the "nudist" nomenclature to generally describe themselves, their friends and families, their groups, and the larger nudist community. However, there are some key points of difference between nudists and naturists that are important to note for accuracy and for a more complete understanding of the communities. Given that both nudists and naturists are growing groups, and they hold these distinguishing elements between them with a sincere sense of importance, the difference warrants some attention. The distinction between nudists and naturists was clear early in Europe but has been an evolving cleavage in the United States.

Perhaps the biggest difference between nudists and naturists is identity. To be a nudist means, simply, to be in the nude in a social context and to perceive oneself as a member of the nudist community. A nudist associates with the activity of being nude with others. That is, social nudity is the primary behavioral marker for nudists. They may be casually nude, perhaps even just at home or nude somewhere else, but in an expressly social situation. The nudist's individual and community identities can be simply a matter of preferences or range of values that contain some ethical commitments. For naturists, nudity is an essential part of a larger lifestyle. Naturists are concerned with having as direct and respectful of a relationship with the natural world as possible. Nudity is important because clothing and other manufactured goods mediate and, thereby, inhibit a direct connection to nature. Clothing is also the clearest point of differentiation between naturists and the nonnaturist society. Common parlance in the naturist community is to refer to people outside the community as textilists, illustrating how nudity is a pillar within the naturist paradigm. Furthermore, by labeling those outside the community as textilists, they are denoting that those who wear clothes are doing something artificial whereas naturists are doing what is original and natural. This linguistic strategy avoids treating people wearing clothes as a hegemonic reference category. Nudists, by contrast, merely refer to those on the outside as nonnudists. Hegemonic cultural categories are taken for granted by nudists, meaning they are understood without labels. Nudity as a label means nudists are in a subordinated, abnormal position. Naturists make every group have a label and, thereby, make clothes wearing no longer the reference category. Naturists and nudists often share the same spaces. Most nudist resorts also have large areas for camping that have a variety of options for outdoor activities for example like hiking, horseback riding, and bouldering.

A Brief History of Nudism in America

The history of nudists and naturists in the United States is an example of a long-standing minority group vying for survival. This history draws on historical necessity and European traditions. The motivating rationale and nomenclature of nudists and naturists changed over the centuries in response to technological transformation and new sociolegal constraints. We briefly address this rich and storied history before we move to our data collection and results.

As the American experiment survived the colonial era, the history of nudism became marked at different stages by different pressures for cultural and political rebellion. When under particularly acute stigma and legal threat, the tradition of nudists and naturists evolved through and because of the formation of unlikely cooperative coalitions. They engage in some of the most pressing intellectual movements of the time such as anti-Victorianism, the Enlightenment, naturalism, transcendentalism, and, yes, hippy traditions. For hundreds of years, their motivations were nuanced, their group membership included some notable Americans, and their standing in American society vacillated. Here, we present an abbreviated sketch of the centuries-long and complex history of nudism and naturism that leads up to our present study.

There was certainly a long stretch of human history between the donning of the first loincloth and the willful, permanent shedding of articles of clothes. This gap in time creates both a sort of nostalgia for the very olden days as well as a variety of sociocultural pressures from which nudism and naturism become reasonable and predictable responses. While nudism and naturism have been practiced continuously worldwide, this introduction only attempts to sketch the most compelling forces that shaped the communities and the movements in the United States.

Colonial America

Despite a growing desire to shed themselves of the cloth of the Union Jack and many of its governmental institutions and customs, residents of colonial America, particularly the upper classes from which most of the Founding Fathers came, were not quite as interested in doing away with all the British and European customs and ideas. Furthermore, the great early American thinkers such as Thomas Jefferson, Thomas Paine, and James Madison bathed themselves in the philosophical traditions of Europe and affairs of European elites. They were interested in Rousseau's political theories as well as in his ideas about the original position of humans and how humans existed in a state of nature long before the mores and constraints of society shaped behavior. They knew the ongoing debates between the empiricists and the rationalists. Colonial American elites were often idiosyncratic in their application of many European ideas in the North American context.

Colonial American life had its formalities in etiquette, speech, and presentation. Manners, dress, and ways of courtships were European with a growing American twist. We should not forget that when the eighth president of the United States, Martin Van Buren, took office in 1837, the United States for the first time had a president that was not born while under British rule. Benjamin Franklin is the perfect example of the cultural hybridization and the embodiment of a practicing Enlightenment thinker. To call Franklin a true Renaissance man undersells his utility to the American cause. He was the chief diplomat for the United States in critical moments, domestic and abroad. Importantly for our purposes, Franklin was also a nudist.

When stuck in the sweltering heat of Philadelphia during much of the Constitutional Convention or in the French Court of King Louis XVI, Benjamin Franklin wore no clothes except the occasional nightcap to keep the top of his head warm. Franklin's noteworthy eccentricities should not overshadow the pragmatism and rationale behind his nudism. In era without the pleasantries of air conditioning, remaining bare during the humid sweltering summers was more appealing that being drenched in heavy, sweat-laden colonial fashions. But Franklin, like many great thinkers and artists of his time, felt being nude was more than just a necessity for comfort's sake because of a challenging environment. In a letter to a French colleague, Franklin wrote about his air baths as a daily ritual: "I have found it much more agreeable to my constitution to bathe in another element, I mean cold air.... With this view I rise early almost every morning, and sit in my chamber without any clothes whatever, half an hour or an hour, according to the season, either reading or writing" (Currey 2013). Franklin, raised by Puritan parents in the Old South Church of Boston, was a deeply pious man and instituted mandatory prayer during the Philadelphia Convention (Meacham 2013, 89–90). The Founding Fathers, regardless of their political dispositions or the religious traditions from which they came, routinely praised Franklin for his religiosity. Franklin's nudism was likely the common modus operandi for the time, an apolitical, largely private, and practical choice.

At this time, the austerity of the Pennsylvania Quakers and New England Puritans was certainly less than is popularly depicted today. Nevertheless, given the mores of this era, it is likely the majority of nudists, or at least those who saw their actions as more than a function of their circumstances, were in some position of privilege, not forced to labor outdoors, and inclined toward bodily experimentation as a personal exploration of science and the Enlightenment. In practice, however, many people would be far closer to contemporary notions of nudism today. With the absence of running water, people had ostensibly two options for bathing: having water drawn or making use of an outdoor body of water. Tubs for bathing did not arise in the United States until a few wealthy individuals began to order tubs of copper at the end of the eighteenth century (Mays 2004, 190). While neither nude bathing beaches or spa towns gained popularity in eighteenth-century America like they did in the countryside of England (Travis 1997), the use of public waterways for bathing was common and, particularly when away from centers of town, could be done so naked. This was true for people regardless of sex/gender, although there was greater variance in the ability of women to partake in nude bathing. Nudism here, while not labeled as such at this point in history, was a willful activity for the purposes of good health. This was routine behavior, albeit with the full expectation of modesty, especially between the sexes. When men and women took part in public bathing or swimming, women were expected to wear full-body, exceedingly heavy clothes.

President John Quincy Adams was known to visit the shores of the Potomac River and bath in the cold water of the early mornings almost daily (Kernall et al. 2018, 602–3). On one occasion, the journalist Ann

Royall sat on his clothes at the shoreline. The president would not leave the water without his clothes, and Ms. Royall would not return them to him without an interview. This further illustrates that nudism in America in the eighteenth and the majority of the nineteenth century was not tied to a political orientation or an attempt to buck societal norms. And while it was a routine of many people's hygiene or fitness, there is nothing to suggest that there was a personal or group identity constructed around it to make naked bathing in public a lifestyle choice or statement. They were naked, but they were not, perhaps, nudists in the sense of the current nomenclature.

During the Victorian Era, when a focus on hygiene grew, Americans engaged in more frequent, routinized bathing. This meant that public bathing sites became increasingly popular. Heightened use of these public bath sites coupled with increasing societal demands for modesty, meant local and state ordinances began cropping up throughout the country to regulate and, at least in some venues, suppress public nudity and criminal indecent exposure.

Nudism, Naturism, and the American Melting Pot

The cotton gin and revolutions in apparel manufacturing resulted in larger proportions of Americans owning more clothes and a wider variety of all kinds of garments. By 1900, the more prudish Americans had traded in nude bathing in public for bathing in their undergarments or in an assortment of loose, full coverage, stylized bathing suits made out of cotton, wool, or both. Cotton bathing suits were the norm simply because more water resistant and nonabsorbent fabrics had not yet been invented. However, the cotton would absorb too much water and as a result, become very heavy and would often stretch under the strain of the water saturated weight (Kidwell 2011). Some Americans, such as teachers, grew concerned at the potential for these difficult-to-sterilize suits to transmit cholera and typhoid between children as they swam in pools of stagnant water. (Note that the safe and reliable uses of any sterilant like chlorine in pools did not come about in commercial use until the 1930s.) Accordingly, it was quite common and in fact the norm for school children to swim naked in gym classes and in public pools, oceans, rivers, or lakes (Travis 1997).

The dawn of the twentieth century brought waves of immigrants to the United States. Of particular relevance here, large numbers of émigrés arrived from Central Europe during and after World War I. The availability of commercial and public spaces for the unclad, like resorts, campgrounds, and recreational and social facilities, dramatically expanded to meet the needs and preferences of the newly relocated Europeans from the Netherlands south through Germany to Switzerland (Williams 2007). The attraction to these facilities was simple and straightforward: natural, uninhibited vacation and rehabilitation. Rather than a political statement such as a revolt against the austerities of protofascism and Stalinism, an economic rebellion directed toward mass produced textiles, or promotion of sexuality or any given sexual behavior, the attraction to these places of social nudism was seen as, and marketed by the involved elites as, apolitical, noneconomic, and asexual. They varied in geography, amenities, levels of national and ethnic diversity, and socioeconomic class composition, but the commonality was that these were wholesome family recreational facilities.

Immigrants to the United States from Europe at this time were not simply the poor from major European cities, those from famine struck agrarian lands, or those climbing out of the rumbled wasteland left after World War I. Entrepreneurs wanted to move to a place where consumers had money to spend and immigrants from the upper classes wanted to keep some of the luxuries to which they had grown accustomed. So naturally, some saw opportunities to start businesses that could attract an unfamiliar and exoticism-loving consumer, just as others wanted to have nudist spaces as they did in their homelands. Nudists camps and resorts began appearing nationwide marketed to both those immigrants who were already comfortable with social nudity and to the postwar Americans who might be looking for new experiences. During the first quarter of the twentieth century children were nudists wherever they learned to swim. With the growth of nudist recreational facilities nationwide, many adults began spending extended periods of time as nudists too.

In an attempt to attract a wider consumer base, businesses and early coalitions took out advertisements in print media as well as full commercials that played in standard movie theaters ahead of the most popular films of the time between the newsreel and the feature film and alongside the other commercials. This calculated publicity push sought to convey to the nonnudists a normalcy to the behavior and lifestyles of the nudists communities as well as convey claims of health benefits to nudity in nature. The commercials aired fully naked men and women playing sports, being social, and being active outdoors. Teens and children were often seen in these ads as well. Importantly, none of the audio or the behavior of those caught on film was in any way sexualized. The advertisements instead described being nude and taking part in these functions as novel, exhilarating, and well within the values of American society. Families were always featured in these ads. Similarly, organizations banded together through the magazine *Nudist* to promote the industry and assert the wholesome family values and health benefits associated with social nudism.

A publicity campaign, particularly one that sets out to normalize something that is sensuously unlike the daily lives of most people, is as likely to gain new critics as it is to gain new supporters or recruits. In the mid-1930s, nudists faced a behemoth of an antagonist: the Catholic Church (Wheeler 2013). Many decades prior to its own scandals about the mass conspiracy to conceal the rape of young boys and girls by the clergy and protect the sexual predators in its ranks, the Catholic Church was once viewed by many Americans as a paragon for virtuous, social conservatism in the United States. This view of the Catholic Church as a beacon and arbiter of virtue even extended beyond those who identified as Catholics. Already disgruntled with the increasingly libertine tendencies of the American public during the Roaring Twenties, the leadership of the Catholic clergy and politically efficacious churchgoers saw this new acceptance of social nudism as the unbearable climax of moral decay, opulence, and the potential influence of socialist activists now thought to be infiltrating America on all fronts. Like they had done when confronting birth control activists, socialists, and suffragettes, the Catholic Church utilized their networks within many police departments nationwide to harass those who were targeted—in this case, those who ran nudist venues. The Church also circulated op-eds in major newspapers across the country, including in prominent publications like the *New York Times*, that all complained about the moral threat posed by the growth of nudism (Wheeler 2013, 11–12).

The irony is that many nudist organization were sympathetic to many Catholic social programs. One of the benefits of nudism for those who advocated it was that habitual and social nudity normalized the understanding of the complete male and female body and it would therefore neutralize the allure of most forms of obscenity and pornography in both thought and deed (Wheeler 2013, 43). Some in the nudist community believed the notion that what is unknown and also forbidden is much more alluring precisely because it is forbidden. Once people were desensitized to nudity, the body would be less sexualized and aberrant sexual behavior and perversion would diminish in substantial and meaningful ways.

At around the same time as nudism was growing into a larger and more powerful industry and, therefore, more reviled by social conservatives including the Catholic Church, a struggling group of lawyers were trying to launch their new organization dedicated to the protection of civil liberties. The American Civil Liberties Union (ACLU) had just netted a few impressive legal wins for women's health pamphleteers and erotic dancers through several free speech cases. The first two generations of ACLU leadership, ranging from their earlier forms at the start of the twentieth century into the 1930s, were often active members of the bohemian social scene in the Greenwich Village neighborhood of New York City. They were sympathetic to, if not participants in, a variety of sexual subcultures and "obscene" activities (Wheeler 2013). The early 1930s was the point in time at which the ACLU made the decisive switch to expand its mission. What began as an almost exclusive fight about free speech cases concerning government overreach in censoring allegedly obscene media, became a much broader mission to represent a panoply of infringed rights guaranteed in the Constitution. Protection of the large cluster of rights that individuals might enjoy as they seek to live their lives as they saw fit became the larger foundation upon which the ACLU sought to protect citizens from overly zealous governmental activity. This broader mission also meant a broader coalition of rights activists united in their common goal of freedom from undue governmental interference.

The ACLU leadership's sympathies were aptly piqued by both the social and media networks in Greenwich Village and the financial standing of the nudist enterprises and entrepreneurs. The leaders of the ACLU already knew the major advocates for nudism and in Greenwich Village they already had access to literature such as *Nudist*. Plus, as nudist businesses and local organizations got wind that the ACLU was interested in defending them, the ACLU for the first time had clients who were wildly successful from a financial standpoint. Women's health pamphleteers, sex workers, and exotic dancers, many of the earliest ACLU clients, did not have the financial wherewithal to pay the ACLU's bills, let alone help it expand the operation through staffing and fundraising. Nudists were the exact client, for cause and for money, that the ACLU needed at that precise moment in time.

The litany of legal restrictions that were being constructed or utilized against local nudist organizations, businesses, spaces, and printed materials—and by extension, against nudists themselves—was extensive and had to be litigated at each municipality, county, or state, and with each new restrictive law or ordinance. Some of the laws, like public indecency laws, that targeted nudists were already on the books while others were newly enacted for the purpose of harassing the nudists community. Given that obscenity and zoning ordinances were almost exclusively municipal or state affairs, most of the litigation happened at the state and local level. A private sports club that was rented out by a nudist organization in New York City had been raided by the police and the men were arrested for indecent exposure and other crimes (Wheeler 2013, 44–45). With the help of the ACLU, the men's arrests were overturned by the New York State Supreme Court (People v. Burke 243 App.Div.83 [1934]). The court found that the state laws pertaining to lewdness did not address nudity in a way consistent with the fact pattern of the case and that made arresting these men a misapplication of justice. The men were simply exercising and no lewd conduct—defined as sexual in nature—occurred. As Wheeler has noted, the decision was narrowly tailored so as to apply only to that specific case while leaving the law intact. The law had no defect, the error was simply in the misapplication of the law to the facts at bar. The decision was covered in most of the national newspapers. Days after the *Burke* decision, the Catholic Legion of Decency pushed for nudist-specific legislation, which would remove the specific requirement of lewdness, in New York and in state legislatures throughout the country to fill what they angrily decried as a loophole in virtually all of the state statutes (Wheeler 2013, 46). Some non-Catholic leaders of faith actually opposed the Legion's antinudist legislation, arguing that this treated the body as nonnatural entity and that mystifying it would only fuel truly immoral behavior (Wheeler 2013, 46–47).

Once again, the ACLU teamed up with nudist leaders, decrying these bills as invasions of the constitutionally protected right to privacy, as all nudist spaces were opt-in spaces as opposed to nudists going about their lives in ostensibly nonnudist places. From a jurisprudential standpoint, the ACLU's argument was ambitious given that the US Supreme Court did not unambiguously hold that there was a broad constitutional right to privacy writ large until 1965 with *Griswold v. Connecticut* (381 U.S. 479 [1965]). Of course, in the 1923 case, *Meyer v. State of Nebraska* (262 U.S. 390 [1923]), the court discussed at length the notion that constitutionally protected "liberty" did not have clear and unambiguous boundaries. *Meyer* dealt with the teaching of the German language to children. Two years later, in *Pierce v. Society of Sisters* (268 U.S. 510 [1925]), the court used the rationale of *Meyer* to round out the 1920s version of the right to privacy. The *Pierce v. Society of Sisters* case also dealt with educational issues and under a privacy-liberty analysis, the court decided the state did not have a monopoly on the education of children. Rather, parents, because of their constitutionally protected rights to liberty and the implication of privacy within liberty, could choose to send their children to parochial schools instead of public schools.

In a decade long battle with the federal government, a nudist leader by the name of Maurice Parmelee and the ACLU fought a seizure of a book with nudity in it (Wheeler 2013, 44). In *Parmelee v. United States* (113 F.2d [1940]), the US Court of Appeals found that social science, in its evaluation of evolving norms, should determine what is obscene and that the prevailing norms in 1940 allowed nude pictures for the purposes of science and education. *Parmelee* became the standard for customs officers and was cited with some regularity by the US Supreme Court as it began wading into more civil liberties cases. The significant legal victory in *Parmelee* affirmed to the ACLU leadership that their resources were correctly spent in expanding their efforts into this broader array of civil liberties issues.

Nudist organizations and activists formed diverse coalitions with other stigmatized groups. This allowed them to both reach more potential nudists-to-be, as well as share in resources and legal campaigns to create more legal protections for them and their coalitional partners. It is important to note that, despite the judicial accomplishments discussed earlier, nudists continued to face serious legal and quasi-legal threats. Some states did not heed the wisdom of the New York State Supreme Court, and local policing and court systems could still inflict crackdowns and enact restrictive measures. To the extent elites that were antinudists were politically powerful, nudists faced ongoing and persistent legal challenges and constant threats to their liberty.

The 1960s, Hippies, and Beyond

Nudist groups benefited greatly from the ACLU's right to privacy litigation as well as the efforts to protect gay and lesbian partners from discrimination. The benefit of the coalition-based struggle was a product of a mixture between the progressive belief in civil liberties held by the majority in the Warren Era of the US Supreme Court and the ignorance of law enforcement. Although nudism is not in and of itself a sexual identity, and nudists are not constantly sexually stimulated, nor seek sexual stimulation solely as a result of them or others being nude, some of the expanded protections for gays and lesbians as well as women's access to contraception were applied to nudists because judges and prosecutors sometimes lumped nudists into categories thought of first and foremost as sexual communities. For much of the bench, nude dancers and nudists were functionally equivalent and their rights analysis was constructed under the same architecture.

The 1960s saw large societal upheaval over issues like racial civil rights issues, the Vietnam War, the Space Race, and the cultural critiques and challenges presented by the hippies and hippy culture. Birthed out of a thirst for civil rights, opposition to the Vietnam War, and rebellion against the *Leave it to Beaver* ideals and norms of the 1950s, the nudist and naturist communities saw unprecedented growth. Part of what drew in more nudists was a disdain for what they perceived as the hypocritical sanctimoniousness of the generation before who, despite their supposed high morality, led the United States into superfluous violent entanglements around the globe. While hippies are often thought of as strong advocates for free love, or nonmonogamy, their nudity was largely a product of norm challenging rather than sex or anti-fashion. While

Goldwater conservatives branded hippies as bacchanalian and orgy seeking, and no doubt some were, the nudism in the hippy community was not exclusively or particularly a sexual act. Norms were challenged across universities by organized, and sometimes approved, naked coed runs. Nudity was part of the provocative politics of performance that was endemic in the hippy culture.

The 1960s was also the most important decade for environmental protection since the creation of the National Park Service. There was mounting concern about the effects of the insecticide DDT, acid rain, nuclear energy, and other factors on the environment and Americans ability to access reliably clean water and air. For instance, the Cuyahoga River caught on fire in 1969 and that fire is often described as a catalytic moment in the environmental movement. Although this was not the first or last time the Cuyahoga River would burn, the idea that our culture was polluting so much that river water would burn was a clear call for action. Hippy culture, the Green Movement, and naturists all shared in common the desire to create lifestyles that were harmonious with the earth. Hippies were drawn to a naturist lifestyle because it not only challenged norms but because it was responsive to their environmental concerns such as textile dyes polluting waterways. In a real sense, the combination of the hippy movement and the green or environmental movement resurrected the naturist movement. Until the 1960s, nudists, with formal clubs and spaces, really defined the nude community in the United States. Once the hippies and the environmentalists developed the idea of nudity as, on the one hand, rebellion, and on the other, as a communion with nature, growth of naturism was inevitable.

A few cities that served as flashpoints for the hippy movement also pushed to relax legal restrictions against public nudity, some of which are still largely unchanged today. San Francisco, a former military-centric city turned haven for virtually everyone not in the norm and a Mecca for gay rights, has long tolerated or even celebrated public nudity. It was not until 2012, when, under corporate pressure about the city's aesthetics, the city made all public nudity but toplessness a civil infraction with a small fine. Although, it bears mentioning that it is never enforced (Wollan 2012). Vermont, both in respect to the state government and local towns, has also been famously hospitable to nudists and naturists with facilities catering to both located all across the state. The state only forbids taking off one's own clothes in public but not the act of being nude. So, for example, you can be naked, but you cannot perform a strip show at the grocery store. Even Burlington, the biggest city in the state, which does not allow public nudity in its public parks, allows it everywhere else in the city (Baird 2018). As a result, organizations invested over the succeeding decades to create a large number of campgrounds, clubs, and other spaces catering to nudists and naturists although the state barely exceeds six hundred thousand residents.

Concurrent with the hippy movement was the creation of numerous utopian communities. They ranged in political and ideological orientations. Some were futuristic, some were highly traditional. A meaningful number of these utopian communities were progressive on a panorama of issues and were either started by hippies or those strongly aligned in belief with them. Within this batch of communities existed the common practice of familial nudity and, frequently, social nudity beyond the immediate family. While in their homes or out and about during recreation, children and parents would be nude. The rationale was a blend between the concerns for the environment and the desire to demystify the body for their children so they could develop a healthier approach to sex and sexuality as well as body image.

As we continue to see greater ideological political sorting in geographic terms across the United States, whereby there are fewer municipalities and districts where the major political parties are both regularly competitive, the ability for nudists and naturists to live their lives with dignity and without arbitrary harassment from the state and local government has been growing to unprecedented heights in some areas and concurrently facing renewed threats in other areas. Because most zoning, permitting, and indecency laws are enacted at the local and state levels, the potential for swings in the ability to exercise rights becomes more likely than some federally grounded clusters of rights and privileges. Some municipalities, such as Provincetown, Massachusetts, have intentionally never enacted laws regulating public nudity as it has carved out a reputation and a commercial industry based on the notion that it is an enclave of gay liberation and sexual freedom. In Vermont, as noted, weirdly, so long as you did not actually disrobe in public, public nudity is legal in most of the public sphere of the state. Other states, such as Maine, allow for public nudity for all of the body except the genitalia.

On the other side of the regulatory spectrum, any nonincidental form of public nudity is a misdemeanor in North Carolina and Alaska. In Arkansas, only public nudity among members of the same sex is legal.

Federal civil rights protections continue to be largely nonexistent for nudists and naturists. While some aspects of the right to privacy have been decided in state and federal appellate courts, the lack of civil rights protections for things such as housing, employment, family law, and general civil interaction is stifling and presents a constant threat to members of the nudist community. While a person might not be able to be arrested for, say, being a nudist naked in their own home, a landlord is able to cite that as a breach of contract depending on the language of the lease. Being a nudist or naturist can get you fired and there are no employment nondiscrimination laws for nudism as an identity. Parents who are part of the nudist community may face hostile family court judges when deciding custody issues. One parent who is no longer an advocate of nudism would have a powerful argument for custody of any children if the judge at hand viewed nudism as an aberrant lifestyle. We met a woman, Camile, who lost custody of her two preteen children, one boy and one girl, because her husband claimed her nudism and her involvement of the family in nudism, were sexually inappropriate. Camile said that even though her husband had physically abused her, nudism trumped those bad acts when it came to custody of the children. The judge discounted that domestic violence claim and determined it was irrelevant to the custody issue because the husband had not previously physically abused the children and, once arrested for domestic violence, he had taken a class about nonviolence and anger management as a pretrial intervention so he could avoid prosecution. Being a nudist or naturist is not a protected status under the law in the same way that any minority group is, whether based on religious, racial, or some other descriptive representation of identity. Not only may the government, whether state, local, or federal, discriminate against you, but any other person, company, entity, or organization also has the legal free rein to discriminate as they like.

While neither nudists nor naturists communities are overtly or explicitly sexual communities in group or individual activities or share monolithic sexual orientations, they continue to be seen as primarily or partially sexual, generally highly sexualized, by those outside the nudist and naturist communities. *Obergefell v. Hodges* (576 U.S. 644 [2015]), which found that gay and lesbian couples are guaranteed the same due process rights to governmentally recognized marriage and the same related benefits of marriage as heterosexual couples, and the earlier *United States v. Windsor* (570 U.S. 744 [2013]), which held the Defense of Marriage Act was a violation of equal protection and due process, may combine to offer some legal foundation for the expansion of rights for nudists. Whether this expansion of equal protection for traditional sexual minorities translates into any legal or cultural progress for nudists—or any of our other groups for that matter—remains to be seen. It is possible that nudists and naturists benefit from this expansion of rights simply because the community may seem less exotic to nonnudists after having witnessed lesbian or gay weddings. Perhaps the more interesting and salient question is whether the expansion of rights for traditional sexual minorities alters the way in which the nudists and naturists community perceives politics and the potential for expansion of legal protections through political action.

As discussed earlier, formal organizations and associations for nudists and naturists in the United States predate the Second World War. What it now called the American Association for Nude Recreation is a naturist organization that was created in 1929 by Kurt Barthel. Originally called the American League for Physical Culture, Barthel advertised their first event using German language magazines in the United States in an effort to reach recent German immigrants who were already familiar with and enjoyed nudism. The organization fractured within two short years, as other organization leaders grew tired of Barthel's propensity to micromanage. Barthel's faction, briefly named the American Sunbathing Association and then the American Association for Nude Recreation, was able to begin acquiring property for naturist spaces and leading informational outreach programs with the aid of a few affluent supporters.

Sky Farm, located in New Jersey, was the first permanent club in the United States and was founded by Barthels. It continues to operate today as a members-only club. One spin-off organization was the American Gymnosophical Society, which had Maurice Parmelee as their honorary president. The American Gymnosophical Society would hold national conventions drawing over five hundred members to locations in the Catskills Mountains in New York and the Rock Lodge

Club in New Jersey. One other organization, founded in 1980, called the Naturist Society is based in Wisconsin. They circulate an influential magazine called *Nude & Natural* and have two affiliated organizations that lead lobbying, legislative, and educational efforts for local and national policy concerns.

In furtherance of the goals to desexualize nudism, or at least make it more mainstream and subvert the popular notion that nudists and naturists are mere erotic hedonists, both the Naturist Society and the American Association for Nude Recreation credential naturist clubs to ensure that they meet the actual tenets and standards widely shared within the naturist community. Most credentialed clubs are certified by both groups because dual accreditation aides in marketing to people who are not yet members of a club but might be interested in participating. The accreditation also makes it easy for naturists who travel or relocate to find a comfortable and welcoming locale. Finally, these national organizations act as the lead in lobbying federal, state, and local governments. The elites, in this sense, control the tone, tenor, and content of the formal political dialogue or the dialogue between the community and policymakers.

Data Collection

Our team researched the nudist community through the administration of our surveys, tailored for the nudists community, and through field observations and interviews at three nudist retreats. Our three locations were Olive Dell Ranch in California, Glen Eden Sun Club in California, and Penn Sylvan (or PSHS) north of Philadelphia in Pennsylvania. Compared to our other groups, the nudists in our study were older, whiter, and represented a more balanced political ideological distribution than the furries, polyamorists, and those in the BDSM community.

We set up a table at both Olive Dell Ranch and Penn Sylvan in order to take surveys from those in the nudist community. The rules of the facilities required us to fully disrobe while in the area where we set up. We handed out small bottles of sunblock, salty snacks, water bottles and held a raffle to give away $50 at each of those two location. We administered the nudism versions of our surveys and conducted semistructured interviews with elites and anyone who would talk to us in addition to filling out the surveys. Sometimes we talked with people before they took the surveys and sometimes we talked with them once they had completed the surveys. We do not believe this variation in data collection among the subjects mattered in any meaningful or even discernible way. We did not have the Halloween size candy to hand out like at the BDSM or furry conventions because we were outdoors in the sunshine and the candy would have melted. Instead, we chose the sun-resistant premiums to hand out. Again, we do not believe this minor variation in data collection impacted the responses at all.

One interesting thing that we observed in Pennsylvania was what we called the "Winnie the Pooh" look. As the day wore on and it began to get cooler, men and women alike donned jackets or sweaters for upper body warmth but stayed nude from the waist down and even for the upper torso often wore open jackets or shirts. We talked with Jim, a man who had hung around our area for most of the day, about many different aspects of nudism as well as politics. We asked Jim about the "Winnie the Pooh" look and he said, "Well, just because we're committed to nudism doesn't mean we want to be uncomfortable!" He also let us know we were not the first to call that fashion choice the "Winnie the Pooh" look and that many nudists used some variation of that nomenclature.

At Glen Eden, although we also were required to and did disrobe, we did not take more surveys, but rather just informally talked with elites and attendees and observed the environment. Because Glen Eden is also home to a large archive of historical nudism material and literature, we spent some time perusing the contents of the archive there as well as interviewing the two elderly men who were the volunteer curators of the archive.

When we visited the nudist retreats, the communities felt like any other recreation area or club that might be populated by people who were clothed. People played tennis, pickleball, basketball, lawn games like pétanque, bocci ball, or croquet, swam, and sunbathed. Some of the participants were regular weekend attendees while others noted they were visiting that specific nudist area as a part of a vacation while also attending other nudist spaces either closer to or further from home. From the young adults to the elderly, people read books, tanned, and played sports like any vacationer might at a clothing-required resort without any noticeable presence of sexual undertones such as visual arousal or sexual activities. One of the resorts had a fully clothed live band that played cover songs by one of the pools.

Some nudists we talked with had recently rejoined the community after a prolonged hiatus. Of those in that circumstance, those we spoke with had grown up in a nudist community or home but had moved or some aspect of life circumstances had resulted in them disengaging from the community. Their desire in rejoining the community was to shed pressures from their living circumstances and to rejoin a community that places a premium on sociability and family. The experiences of the intermittent nudists were similar to those of the lifelong nudists we spoke with. For nudists who were raised in the community, they mentioned the continued positive feelings and commitment to values, suggesting that familial socialization can be extremely important in this minority community.

Our experiences engaging with nudists in person and through the survey process are consistent with the research that has studied sexual boundary making in nudist-only spaces. We found that the individuals who spoke with us did not use a high degree of orthodoxy, sharing their own experiences in their own terms. That is, there was no roster of norms that were repeated like a script for outsiders. In speaking with the managers of the facilities and later with the individuals there, we communicated the specific aims of understanding their political attitudes and political participation. Without exception, we found both the participants and the elites to be happy to engage with us. Our relaxed conversations with them about politics and the community perhaps reduced the pressure to conform and made it less likely they felt performative pressure to use common scripts that have been documented for nudists in previous research. Moreover, because we were nude, we immediately created trust bonds with others. This was the clearest signal we could be trusted that we could possibly send.

We took 142 surveys from the nudists and we had another 118 respondents for our open-ended questionnaire. Most of those 260 surveys, just over 200, were taken live and the others were taken through the virtual snowball sampling technique discussed in the previous chapters. Because many in the nudist community are retirees who travel from resort to resort in RVs, we were able to take surveys from people from a wide range of states. In fact, we collected surveys from people from twenty-seven states. The virtual snowball approach relied on nudists sharing the survey to their contacts in the national nudist community. As an aside, this network would be very similar to the one needed to mobilize the community. The racial composition in our survey had 85 percent of the respondents identifying as White, 3 percent as Hispanic, 2.3 percent as Asian American/Pacific Islander, 1.2 percent as Black, and 5.2 percent as multiracial (figure 4.1). This reflects a higher degree of whites and fewer people of color than the general American public. Given that nudist spaces are overwhelmingly located in rural locations, we believe that the racial and other demographic categories are representative of their local communities or, perhaps, the locale of the venue, but that a true national sample would be much more diverse. While nudists travel a lot, and we do have respondents from all over the country, we still have a sample that skews non-Hispanic white. To be clear, like our other groups, we observed a larger proportion of African American and Latino participants at the locales than our collected data suggests. We believe this may be in part due to the fact we are all white so we were not able to reach the additional

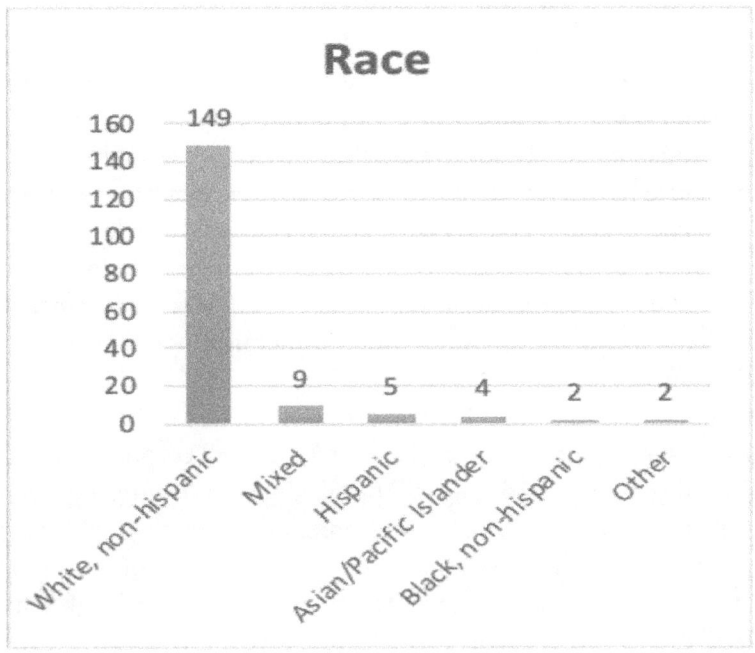

Figure 4.1. Racial Identity of Nudists

level of trust necessary to participate for at least some of the attendees. As with our other categories, we cannot dismiss the role of white privilege in skewing our results. Those who may have other marginalized identity that intersects with, and thereby enhances the risk of, identifying as a member of the nudist community may simply be less willing to participate. Further, had we gone to different locales in less rural communities, we may have had a very different mix of respondents. In any event, these are the data we have and we can draw at least some conclusions from them despite the paucity of minority representation.

The nudists we surveyed are not meaningfully dissimilar from the general socioeconomic distribution of the United States (Figure 4.2). Of our respondents, 11 percent reported incomes less than $20,000; about 5 percent reported income between $20,000 and $29,000; a third reported incomes between $30,000 and $74,000; and a quarter of those sampled reported incomes greater than $75,000. One-fifth of the respondents preferred not to provide their income. Again, we note that in our interviews we asked a few people about the issue of not responding to the income question and these people were certainly in the upper income levels. While they were disrobed, they often wore expensive jewelry including things like Rolex watches or large and flashy diamond rings. Additionally, many of the respondents traveled in large motor homes that, when new, can cost well over one hundred thousand dollars. For example, one man in Pennsylvania, Scott, who said he simply was not comfortable disclosing his income, later told us about his very large, very expensive, brand new motor home which he said cost him "close to half a million dollars." He talked about his motor home purchase in the context of us joking with him that being a nudist was thrifty since you need not spend lots of money on clothes and might never wear out the clothes you did buy.

In alignment with their income distribution, nudists were formally educated at rates only slightly higher than the overall US population. The highest degree obtained ranged from 19.3 percent having a graduate degree, 32.5 percent with a college degree, 36.7 with some college, and 11.4 percent with a high school degree or less. Like all of our groups, we did not speak with anyone under the age of 18, so the "high school or less" category is comprised of all adults. We did meet several teenagers and saw many smaller children, but they were not eligible to

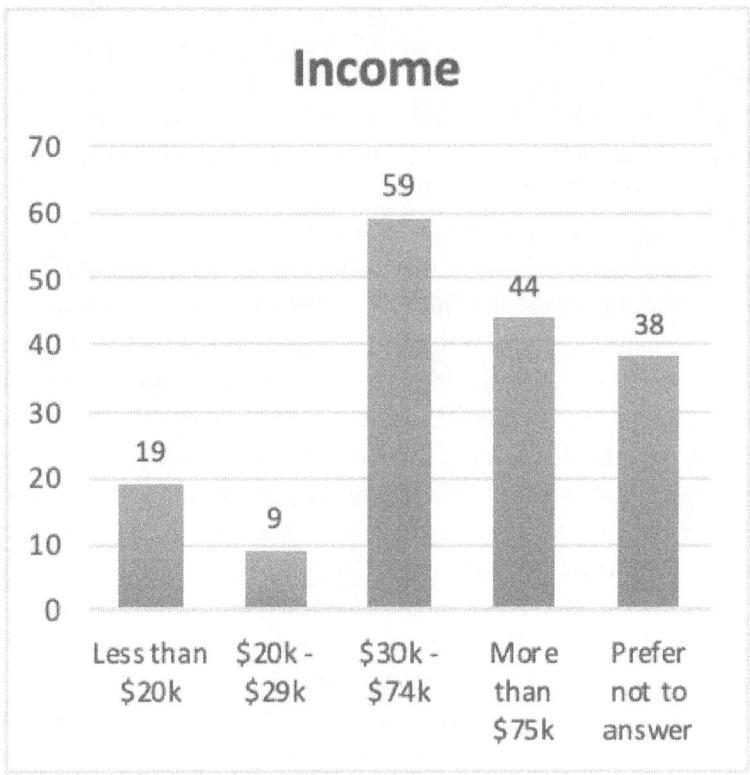

Figure 4.2. Income Distribution of Nudists

take the surveys and we did not interview them. If their parents were with them, we would answer any questions they had for us but they were outside the purview of our IRB registration. In any event, the educational attainment level spanned the range from high school to graduate school. The educational information is mostly unremarkable except to point out that, like our other groups, the community has achieved somewhat higher levels of formal education than the general public. We talked at length with an older couple, Amy and Gary—they were probably in their late sixties, perhaps early seventies—who were retired academics. She had been a vice provost at her Midwestern research university, and he had been a department chair and associate dean. Amy told us she found the academic life particularly accommodating of their nudist lifestyle. They spent the summers and winter breaks traveling around from nudist campground to nudist campground in their large motor home. Gary chimed in and explained how they had a large mesh tent room they would set up for their shared research office while they traveled. He said "I'm pretty sure over 75 percent of my publications were drafted when I was naked and in the research tent!"

The nudists may have higher levels of formal education for a host of reasons. Again, it may be that college experiences allow a person to experiment with various lifestyle and identity choices without serious consequences. It may be that some normative pluralism in college shapes their future choices and creates an openness to new experiences that those who did not have the experience of higher education do not develop. It could also be the case that our sample has some confounding variable that pushed the higher education responses upward. For instance, perhaps it is more likely that people without a college degree may work on the weekends and since our in-person data collection happened between Fridays and Sundays, we simply did not get those nudists without formal education at a representative rate. This is an avenue of inquiry that might be appropriate for further research.

The age distribution of nudists in our sample approached a normal distribution and closely mirrors the overall American population. About 18 percent of our respondents identified as aged 65 or older. Roughly 44 percent reported being aged 50–64. About 21 percent reported being aged 30–49 and about 15 percent were aged 18–29. Again, we should note that we did not take any surveys from minors although there were younger children and teenagers at each of the facilities. Indeed, all three had elaborate playgrounds and each had regularly scheduled special programming for both younger and older children. Approximately 72 percent of our respondents identified as male. Perhaps because the research team is all male, we had fewer women step up to take the surveys in person. We cannot be certain of why our survey respondents skewed male, but we can state that as we mingled among the people at the facilities, the distribution looked much more evenly divided between male and female. As an interesting aside, we spoke with Angie, a woman in Philadelphia who identified as a lesbian and she said that one of the things she liked best about the nudist lifestyle was that "everybody leaves all the gender appearance bullshit at the gate."

The marital status of our respondents was as follows: 40.7 percent were married for the first time; 7.2 percent were married after being in a previous marriage (remarried after divorce or death of spouse); 7.8 percent reported being never married (but in a long-term relationship); 24.6 percent single (never married or in a long-term relationship); and 19.8 percent reported being single (divorced or widowed) (figure 4.3). The marital status of the nudists breaks down in essentially an unremarkable way. That is, the nudists do not appear to marry any more or less frequently than the nonnudist population and the divorce rate seems somewhat lower than the general population where divorce ends around 50 percent of new marriages. This arguably gives at least some evidence to the idea that nudism, or perhaps merely belonging to a community that is central to your identity and that of your spouse, positively impacts the longevity of marital unions.

As we could expect, because organized religion in the United States frequently targets any behavior that can be, correctly or not, identified as

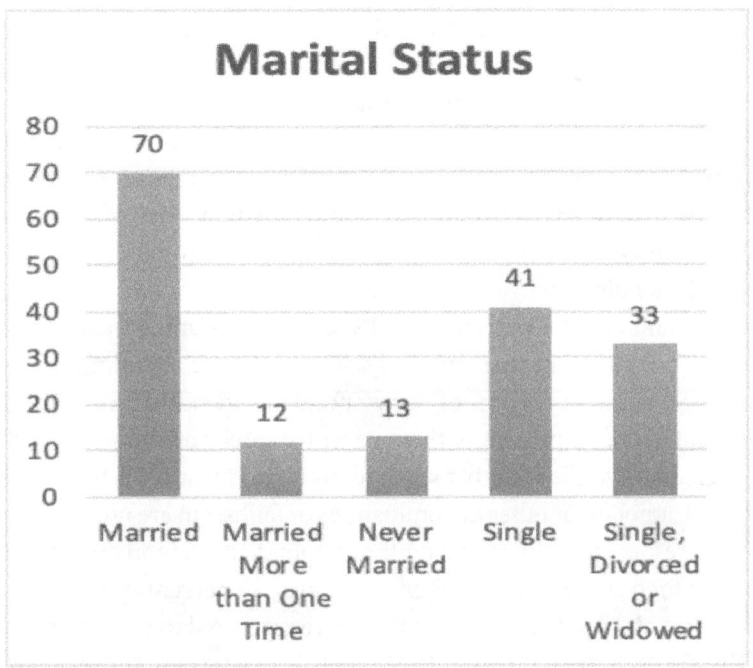

Figure 4.3. Marital Status of Nudists

aberrant sexual behavior, those in the nudist community may be somewhat less religious than the general population. Also, as discussed above, there is a long history in the United States of organized religion specifically targeting nudists. The religious identity of the nudists surveyed is reasonably similar to the overall population. Approximately 16 percent of nudists we surveyed identified as Catholic, 11 percent as Evangelical Christian, 26 percent as Protestant, 1 percent Jewish, 13 percent as other, and 32 percent as not religiously affiliated. This represents a somewhat larger number of "nonreligious" individuals than the population at large. Note that we also have no way of clearly interpreting the "other" choice. At least one of our respondents, Michael at Olive Dell Ranch, said, "This is my religion, outdoors in nature as nature made me." In other words, some of our "other" responses could be from classic naturists like Michael.

Morever, one of the interesting components of this approach of reliance on self-identifying religious affiliation, and perhaps an error on our part, is that there is no way to distinguish between a deeply held state of religiosity and a cultural affiliation. That is, for some of these respondents, they may have been raised Catholic, for example, but are no longer active or devout in any meaningful way. Of course, some light can be shed on the distinction between a cultural background and a sincere belief when we examine attendance at religious services.

We found that although the nudist respondents claimed religious participation at higher levels than our other groups, a significant number still chose the seldom or never option regarding the frequency of their attendance. Of those who expressed a religious affiliation, only about 24 percent reported attending a religious service at least weekly, about 6 percent attend monthly, and about 8 percent attend yearly. A substantial majority of 61 percent (n = 98 out of 161) reported seldom or never attending religious service. So while 32 percent of our respondents identified with "no religious affiliation," 61 percent of them never (or rarely) attend services. This lends credence to the idea that some respondents identify as, for instance, cultural Catholics, or other denominations or faiths, but are not practicing.

With respect to politics, the nudists respondents demonstrated a consistently high sense of political efficacy. Over 89 percent of nudists surveyed were absolutely certain that they were registered to vote (figure 4.4).

The partisan breakdown of the nudists broke toward conservative at a much higher rate than our other groups but came closer to being a

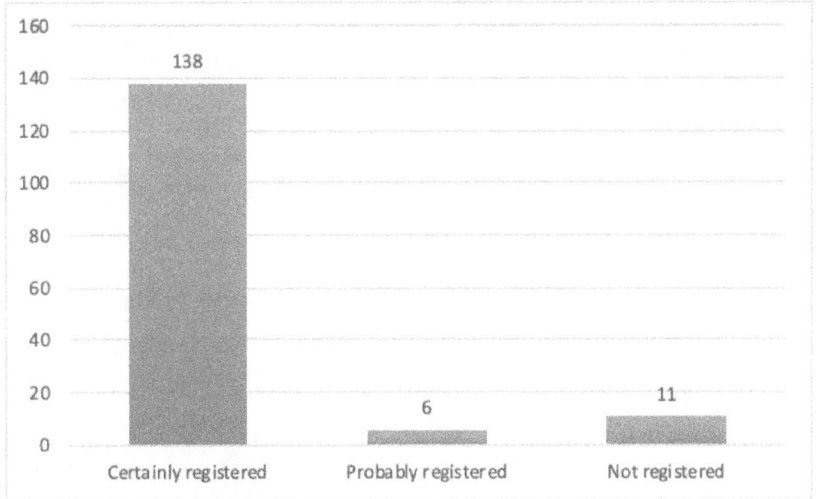

Figure 4.4. Voter Registration of Nudists

reflection of the general population, with nearly equal numbers of Republicans, Democrats, and independents (figure 4.5). We ask nudists who responded that they were independents which party they leaned toward. They were slightly more likely to lean Democratic. When we count the slight majority of leaners who are more likely to vote with Democrats, it balances the slightly higher number who identified as registered Republican nudists, so party affiliates and leaners combined parrot the general public in their distribution.

Our time at the Pennsylvania facility coincided with the final stages of the Hillary Clinton versus Donald Trump presidential election in 2016. Many of the people mingling around our table were discussing the race and playfully giving grief to those who were of a different political persuasion. One person, Russell, spent most of the day hanging out around our table. He seemed to know almost everyone that came up to talk to us. He was constantly joking around with the other nudists and he was not particularly enthralled with either candidate. During one very friendly conversation with two other nudists, a woman was expressing support for Clinton and a man was expressing support for Trump and Russell observed "Clinton thinks she knows everything about everything but didn't know her husband was whoring around and Trump doesn't know

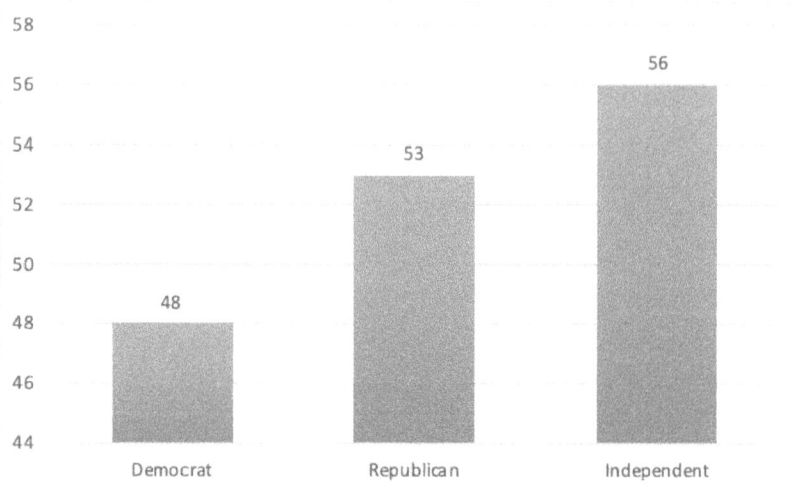

Figure 4.5. Nudist Political Party Registration

anything about anything and doesn't realize that's a problem!"—all three of them belly laughed at his observation. One interesting take away from our time in Pennsylvania at the height of the presidential campaign was that the community ties were stronger than the political ones. That is, while many, perhaps even most, of the people we interacted with that day talked about the election, no one got angry at anyone or acted as if the opinions of the others were ridiculous or outrageous. They may have rolled their eyes and scoffed in private, but in the group or social setting, they were able to talk politics without anger, outrage, or disrespect.

Overall, our nudists respondents self-identified as centrist even when also leaning conservative or liberal. Those who chose either very liberal or very conservative were outliers (figure 4.6). Of course, this is a crude measurement. It is certainly possible that those who identified as merely "liberal" or "conservative" would be thought of as "very liberal" or "very conservative" by the other group. But at least from a self-definitional standpoint, the members of the community do not perceive themselves as extremists.

On the political issues, the nudists respondents consistently found Republicans to be too conservative on social issues like gay marriage and abortion and found Democrats to be about equal numbers "about right" or "too liberal" on the same social issues. In particular, 70 out of 126 respondents said that Republican leaders in Washington were too conservative on the issue of abortion. Only 30 out of 126 thought Republican leaders in Washington were "about right" about abortion and even fewer, 26, thought Republicans leaders should be more conservative on the issue of abortion. Similarly, regarding same-sex marriage, 78 out of 127 respondents thought the Republican leaders in Washington are too conservative. As with the issue of abortion, many fewer, 25, thought Republican leaders were about right on same-sex marriage and fewer, 24, thought Republican leaders should be more conservative on the issue. It is a bit of a puzzle to figure out what "more conservative on gay marriage" might mean at a time when there was virtually uniform opposition to marriage equality from almost every elected Republican in the House and Senate. In any event, regardless of whether those responses were really just a declaration of strong antigay sentiment, when taken overall, our data suggests a community of mostly centrists. The data also strongly suggests that Republican nudists believe their party is out of step on issues that are about personal autonomy. As an aside, nudists were consistently more conservative on tax and immigration issues than our other groups which gives support

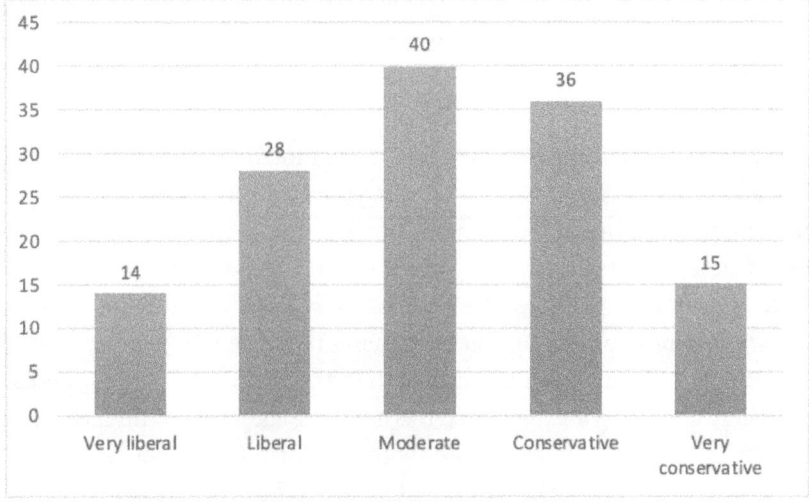

Figure 4.6. Ideological Distribution of Nudists

to the idea they are generally more reflective of the general population than the other groups.

Generally speaking, a majority of the community seems to prefer the center to the peripheries, but each end of the spectrum does have adherents. For instance, while 78 out of 132 respondents want Republican leaders in Washington to move in a more moderate direction, a substantial number, 54 out of 132, want them to move in a more conservative direction (figure 4.7).

Similarly, 99 out of 130 respondents wanted Democratic leaders to move in a more moderate position while only 31 wanted them to move in a more liberal direction (figure 4.8). While the specific issues of abortion and same-sex marriage were outliers, overall, the nudist tend towards centrism and eschew extremism.

The centrist inclination does not act as a damper on political conversations. Indeed, politics and political issues are frequent topics of conversation among about two-thirds of the nudist community (figure 4.9). We asked Russell, who had been engaged in day-long playful banter with others at the camp in Philadelphia, about whether political conversations ever made anyone angry or uncomfortable. He laughed, as was his usual preface to sharing his opinion, and said "Once you're hanging around flapping in the wind, it's easy to not take yourself or others too seriously. And after you've had conversations about being a nudist with people who don't get it, you realize you can't easily change people's minds about stuff they care about. So, you know, laugh have fun, be friends through out!"

Although those in the nudist community watch the news, collectively, they found news organizations to be more liberal than conservative at a more than 2 to 1 ratio. This suggests a stronger belief in liberal bias among news agencies than our other groups and is suggestive that, as a whole, nudists are, again, more like the general public than the other groups we studied. We have actively considered whether this question is now outdated. Because many more people get their news from social media and other outlets than the mainstream news media, whether broadcast or cable news, it is a bit of a challenge to discern what these results actually mean and how they inform our understanding of the community. Our other groups slant a bit younger than the nudists,

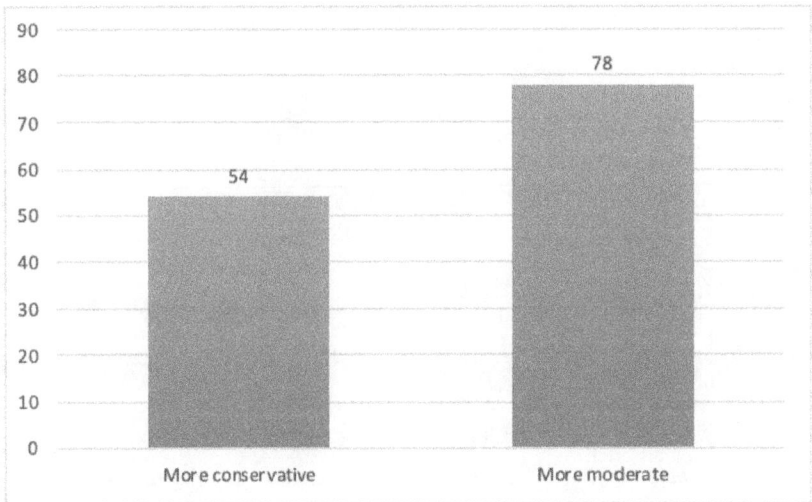

Figure 4.7. Would you like to see Republican leaders in Washington move in a more conservative direction or a more moderate direction?

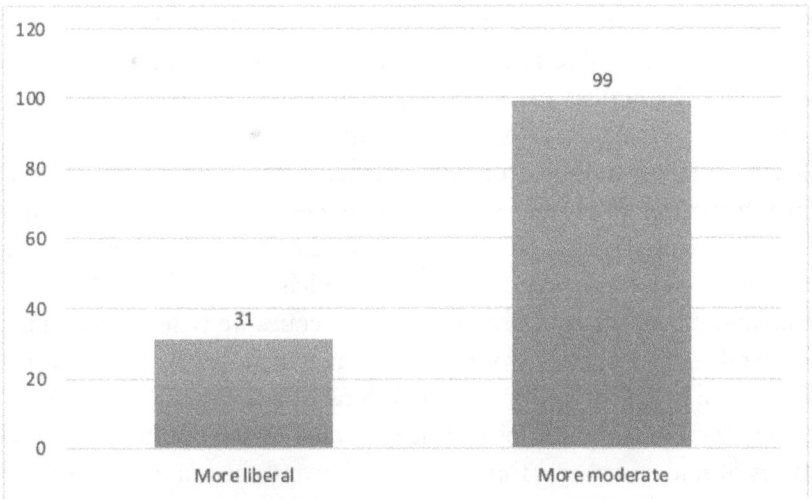

Figure 4.8. Would you like to see Democratic leaders in Washington move in a more liberal direction or a more moderate direction?

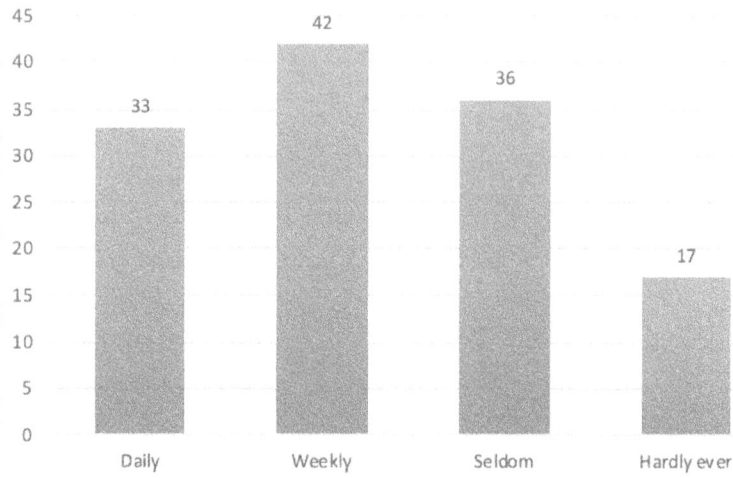

Figure 4.9. How Often Nudists Discuss Politics

so it could be that the nudist responses about news coverage are an artifact of the age distribution of our sample of the community.

In the open-ended portion of our survey, some unique patterns emerged. The nudists surveyed overwhelmingly self-reported as being straight. This is distinct from the other groups in our study, which each had significant numbers of self-reported bisexual, gay, and lesbian members. This might be explained by the existence of many gay and lesbian oriented nudist facilities. Because the community has a longer and more storied history, perhaps nudism has had market differentiation and mostly straight people go to the venues we visited while most gay and lesbian nudists would go to venues that target their marketing to the LGBTQ+ communities. Several of our elite interviews suggested there was significant sorting by sexual preference in the various types of nudist venues. This issue goes beyond the parameters of our research here but may merit additional consideration in future research endeavors.

With few exceptions, the people in our study noted that they felt being a part of the community and having a sense of community were very important to them as parts of their identity. Several noted that they have had at least a somewhat active presence on nudist chatrooms and websites, suggesting that some find meaning in the community beyond simply being nude around others in the social settings of the venues. We note that several people mentioned they are nude when they enter these nudist chat rooms and one man at Olive Dell Ranch, Glenn, spoke about it at length. Glenn had dyed his pubic hair pink and had several genital piercings. Glenn talked about his global network of nudist friends and how they stayed in touch through their frequent virtual meet ups. When we asked about how important the community was to them, they consistently offered responses denoting that nudists were "like a family." Some noted that, despite the closeness, they were less likely to discuss politics with fellow nudists than they do in nonnudist settings—but recall that a majority of our respondents said they frequently discussed politics in the community. It could be that some of our respondents have opinions that they believe would be unpopular among other nudists and they therefore self-censor. These open-ended responses may have come from people at the margins—the extremists who identified as very liberal or very conservative rather than the centrist who represent a majority in the community. Given the prospect of some self-censorship as well as the friendly political banter we witnessed, it is perhaps unsurprising, then, that the nudists in our study almost uniformly said that their politics were not influenced by other members of the community.

The responses to the open-ended questions strongly suggest that laws limiting nudism and a general value of freedom are the only unifying and ubiquitously shared political issues among the community. That said, the nudists we studied actively thought that the nudist community should more routinely be more politically active as a group. The consistent impediments to additional political action by the community was the inaccurate perception of the broader American public who believe that nudism is primarily about deviant sexual behavior and that politicians do not know or care about nudists. In sum, members of the community believe that the wider public thinks that they are perverts and that politicians are either hostile or cowards.

From an organizational perspective, we anticipate that nudists would have a comparatively easy time mobilizing politically if a salient issue were to arise. The credentialing organizations that we previously discussed are well positioned to alert and communicate with local nudist leaders and centers, and to help initially frame the issues and why they matter to nudists. Having over two hundred thousand dues-paying members is sizable in two important ways. First, it has the potential to be a large donor base given that their membership already demonstrates a willingness to put their money toward their community. In an era when even local campaign fundraising has gone national thanks to the success of social media fundraising, tens of thousands of potential donors could be impactful at the local and regional level in opposing candidates pushing harmful new laws and ordinances. Second, the two hundred thousand dues-paying members represents only this tip of the iceberg, as many times more nudists are actively involved in the community but only hold local memberships or pay per visit. Also recall that many of these memberships are family-level memberships which means any given membership represents at least one person but possibly many more. In light of the rate of marriage, each membership represents at least two people is more accurate. By some estimates, 15 percent of the US population, or about 67 million people, regularly engages in some form of social nudity (States News Service 1989). If there was a mobilizing, consensus issue, this is a large and potentially decisive constituency even if the estimate is larger than the actual number of nudists. Given the large number of venues expressly for nudists located in literally every state, as well as the other sorts of facilities like day spas, which entail social public nudity, but are simply marketed as health or recreation locales, the true number could be many times higher than the estimates.

Dues-paying membership is a unique feature for nudists among the groups we studied. While LGBTQ organizations like Lambda Legal, Gay and Lesbian Alliance Against Discrimination (GLAAD), and the Trevor Project sometimes do have annual donors or members that financially support the missions of those organizations, those members joined precisely because of their advocacy work. The number of members of nudist organizations exceeds most local unions or even many statewide union groups throughout the country. As a result of *Citizens United v. FEC* (558 U.S. 310 [2010]), independent expenditures from unions and other groups with shared interests have been influential in political campaigns at the federal, state and local levels. The sway of regular deployments of tens of thousands of dollars to challenge city council members who oppose pay raises, or whatever unions perceive as adverse to their interests, has grown despite the dwindling union member roles nationwide. As the 2020 and 2022 election cycle very clearly demonstrated, Americans are willing to donate to candidates and causes outside their district if they feel like their values or their broader community's rights are at stake. The nudist community is an essentially untapped constituency that could be mobilized rapidly for the right cause.

But the monetary impact of the nudist community pales in comparison to what we see as their potential significance as a voting bloc. As mentioned earlier, the community was diverse in partisanship and ideological leanings. This means that there is a tight identity-based community that does not vote routinely for one party over the other. This lack of committed party affiliation is a rarity among religiously affiliated groups, within racial or ethnic groups, and among many other types of subconstituents (Bishin 2009). Given the high level of voter registration and the broad political engagement among the nudist community, coalescing these voters could lead to a stable and reliable voting block that could deliver votes and resources to the right coalition.

Mobilizing the nudist community on behalf of one party or a candidate does not necessarily require most candidates to even speak about nudism or nudists specifically. Indeed, we believe that leveraging key values of the nudist community in broader debates can win over nudist voters and avoid alienating antinudist voters as a direct result of a nudist alignment or perhaps realignment. For nudists, any party that has a platform plank or campaign pillars grounded in environmental conservation, outdoor recreation, resources for families, and a strong support for the freedoms of expression and association could easily pitch these values directly to the nudist community. If a candidate were to appeal to nudists in this way, a straight forward strategy for communicating with the nudists community would be to utilize the national accrediting organizations that serve as gatekeepers. These organizations are run by credible elites who could signal to their members that a given candidate or party is truly aligned with the nudist commitments to the environment, family, and free expression and association.

The naturism movement has been driven by the desire to regain an unmediated relationship with nature. This is not inconsistent with our finding that the party affiliation is not much different from the larger polity that nudists live in or from the general public. At least at the outset, the history and development of the conservation and environmental movement had no direct or exclusive affiliation of affinity with one political party over the other. Republicans have several historical examples of their leadership on the environmental front including Theodore Roosevelt who created the National Park Service and Richard Nixon who passed both the Clean Air Act and Clean Water Act. The Democrats adopted the environmental mantle through the efforts of presidents and other political leaders. Jimmy Carter led the call for and investment in major renewable energy and engaged in a fair amount of symbolic action like the installation of solar power panels at the White House. The Udall family, with members in both houses of Congress, pushed for legislative expansion of environmental protections. Both Bill Clinton and Barack Obama designated hundreds of thousands of acres of lands as national monuments for the purposes of recreation and conservation. For many conservatives, environmental conservation is as self-evident as proper policy as the fact that conservative and conservation come from the same root. Liberals, at times, opposed environmental regulations out of concern for union jobs. Today, the salience of climate change and broad environmental issues tends to be more pronounced among Democratic voters, but there is considerable variance if you look to environmental issues at the state and local levels. States like Alaska, Montana, New Mexico, and Colorado have large natural resource and extraction commodity sectors, but also large tourism economies that are dependent on the pristine environment. Nevada has maintained decades of bipartisan opposition to storing the nation's spent uranium rods from power plants at Yucca Mountain. In essence, concern for the environment crosses the political boundaries among most voters and many political elites.

Tapping into the importance of outdoor recreation has been an effective way of framing environmental concerns in a way that receives bipartisan voter support. Hunters, hikers, and tourism workers have often formed formidable coalitions at the state and local level in opposition to well-financed logging and energy interests. We believe a focus on the naturism dimension of the nudist community would resonate across the political spectrum of nudists because of the long history of framing their community along a common value in outdoor recreation and rehabilitation. This focus on the environment as an integral part of the nudist world dates back to the prolific advertising campaigns in the 1930s and 1940s and of course is rooted historically in the very early nudist communities. In general though, political actors have avoided even acknowledging that there is such a thing as a nudist block of voters. We think this is a missed opportunity for political mobilization.

The previous research on nudists repeatedly found that nudists place an immense importance on the role of the family in their lives. Most of the research suggests that nudists are more focused on the family than the overall or general American population. Virtually every candidate for almost any level of office makes related, trite, unremarkable, and vapid claims in their campaigns about how their family, or your family, is the driving motivation for their decision to run for office. Claims that the person commits to fight for "our" or "your" family are as frequently found in political campaigns as they are in the radio and television advertisements of personal injury lawyers. For social conservatives, it means that the government should play a role in maintaining the heteronormative patriarchal family unit led by a husband and wife by opposing the acceptance of unwed, gay, lesbian, or polyamorous households. Liberal framing has been more focused on work, making it easier for parents to provide for their families so they do not have to work second and third jobs. That has underpinned, for example, the growing push by Democrats to require longer periods of maternity and family leave. Either party could easily expand their approach to defining what "pro-family" policies are in a way that would resonate with the nudist community. Whether Republicans could overtly do this without alienating their white evangelical base remains to be seen.

Despite the seemingly dichotomous ways that family values are used by Democrats and Republicans, nudists of all political affiliations can still be appealed to. Municipal governments regularly sponsor family events, state parks across the country sponsor free-admission family weekends at varying points during the year, and things like the child tax deduction and Earned Income Tax Credit have maintained broad public appeal. Some states have modified their approach to child protective services in response to the growing opioid crisis, moving away from putting most to all children in the foster care system. Instead, some have created avenues for treatment that support families as a parent, or parents, works their way through drug treatment programs and into sobriety. The policy avoids a parent being placed in the difficult position of choosing between recovery and custody. To be clear, neither our research nor the preceding large body of scholarship suggest that nudists hold some heightened commitment to a nuclear family, but rather for the members of the nudist community, the bonds that might make families special are central to their identity. It would follow then, that it would be highly implausible that the nudist community would mobilize around any anti-LGBT legislation, especially about restrictions on adoption or other familial rights or rights that focus on individual autonomy.

There is a particular kind of social libertarianism that runs through the nudist community in the United States, and that orientation is prominent in over a century's worth of activism. Maurice Parmlee's legal activism and work resulted in the Supreme Court narrowing what the government may properly consider obscene. Nudists worked with a diverse coalition to challenge what they saw as censorship and government overreach. In the decades since, large participation from European immigrants and then counterculture movements demonstrated a consistent approach to a commitment to inclusion and embracing diversity. Negy and Winton's more recent work shows a broader connection between pro-nudity and pro-diversity attitudes that suggests parties or candidates that seem to be discriminatory or exclusionary would likely be labeled as bigoted and would have a hard time mobilizing nudist support (2008).

Supporting certain kinds of speech and association also might resonate more immediately than other types of issues for the nudist community. Nudist resorts and campgrounds tend to be located in rural or lightly suburban areas, but some cities have noticeable pro-nudity populations like San Francisco, Chicago, and Austin. While our survey respondents were less racially diverse than the nudist or general population as a whole, we did have respondents from a large number of states and their claimed religiosity was not meaningfully different from the at large population. When we consider the geographic, ideological, and age spread of the nudist population in our sample, we can make at least some modest assumptions that it is fairly representative of the nudist population as a whole. This then suggests that, even if nationally political elites may be afraid to associate with nudists, an appeal to the shared values of a specific nudist community under threat, for instance because of zoning regulations, might be more effective at specific election mobilization and more effective for building a sustained mobilization effort. And, because nudity is not an out-group discursive act for most nudists, meaning that nudists are not being nude in order to communicate something to nonnudists, campaigning on protecting political speech would be unlikely to mobilize those who are hostile to nudists any more than the average American. In other words, while the mobilization of some voters brings with it the mobilization of voters who are opposed to the first group—pro-life activism also mobilizes, pro-choice voters; racial justice initiatives may mobilize racists; pro-LGBTQ+ activism may mobilize homophobes and so on—nudist do not as yet have an organized and persistent antinudist activist opposition.

On the other hand, appeals to protecting the freedom of expression and association in the private sphere would be much more likely to appeal to nudists. For example, judges in the tradition of Antonin Scalia and Clarence Thomas reject that the Constitution affords citizens a right to privacy. Their dissents in *Lawrence v. Texas* reveal their explicit denials of that right (2003), and, of course, in 2022, Thomas joined Samuel Alito and other like-minded conservatives in overturning *Roe v. Wade*. So, while nudists may hold varied opinions on abortion, gay rights, sodomy, or birth control, there is a tremendous opportunity to recast the debates in terms of privacy and realign nudists. For example, Justice John Paul Stevens and Justice David Souter were Republicans at the time of their appointments through their retirements but were wrongly perceived as having become liberal because the rise of constitutional originalism. The Christian Right drowned out the right to privacy in elite conservative circles. If a politician or party could effectively brand their opponent(s) as being morally prescriptive and undermining nudists' right to privacy, then there would be a ripe opportunity to realign nudists under one party.

Digital censorship could also be another avenue for mobilizing the nudist community. Social media and companies like Facebook, Twitter, TikTok, and Google filter content algorithmically and through human reviewers. At present, the algorithms have not meaningfully accounted for context, erroneously taking down images like pictographs about breast cancer as though it were pornography. This poses a risk for the nudist community, potentially stifling its capacity to advertise on the predominant media platforms and its ability to share photos and memories with members of the community. Nudist groups tend to utilize private group features of social media platforms, thereby minimizing the likelihood that their images would be flagged by another human. But it is nonetheless important to see how Facebook's proactive image filters might affect nudist groups in the future. Digital freedom may become a critical issue for the nudist community.

In addition to the nudist community using social media platforms to maintain social ties, there is the commercial advertising that hinders nudist organizations from recruiting new members. Search engine algorithms, again like those used by Google, Bing, TikTok, and Yahoo, can filter out websites that have been assessed as containing mature content from appearing in a search. If a prospective member is looking to find nudist spaces or communities that exist near them, they might never find out because of search engine protections. Once again, a heteronormative patriarchal normative environment, in this case encoded in sterilized searches, results in the nudist community having a harder time staying connected and growing. The commercial risk to the community could be a useful angle to pique the interests of the community gatekeepers, the credentialing organizations, and business owners. Given the present bipartisan skepticism about social media companies' ability to self-regulate, this could be a promising avenue for aligning the community and non-nudists in the process. The shared skepticism and confusion around social media companies has been a rare unifying topic in Congress, and a budding politician could optimize the utility of that issue without the need to focus exclusively on the partisan approaches of whether social media companies unfairly target conservatives' perspectives or whether they fail to stop the spread of conspiracy theories and hate.

5

Lions and Tigers and Bears, Oh My!

The Politics of Furries

In this chapter we turn to Furries—the members of the community known as the furry fandom. This community and its members have been understudied in virtually every discipline. There are two exceptions to this lacuna of research. First, there is a substantial body of scholarly work about the aesthetics of the furry fandom, and second, there is some scholarship about the psychology of its members (see, e.g., Coyote 2020; Dunn 2021; Ngai 2012; Patten 2017; Reyson et al. 2020; Strike 2017). While the work on the aesthetics is largely laudatory, the work housed in psychology tends to assume or look for pathologies and deviance among the members of community. Here, however, we engage in the first foray into any consideration of the group from the standpoint of their political beliefs and political behavior. We conceptualize the furry fandom and its members both collectively as a community and individually as a constructed identity. Furries have a chosen personal identities that, for many of them, are inextricably linked with sexual identity (Hsu and Bailey 2019). Like our other groups, this chosen community presents an essentially contested identity structure that bears further consideration.

The furry community, or furry fandom, is a subculture that developed out of the larger cosplay, or costume play, community. The connecting interest and unifying premise behind the furry fandom is an appreciation and embrace of anthropomorphic animal characters, art, and costumes. Moreover, for many members of the fandom, elaborate and usually custom-made costumes called "fursuits" are worn, and members adopt detailed, meaningful identities called "fursonas." (Dunn 2021). Not all furries actually wear fursuits (the elaborate costumes) or have fursonas (the assumed identities) and some furries have fursonas but do not have costumes. A fursona may be expressed through art, online chatrooms, or in many other ways beyond wearing a fursuit. Some furries have some representative parts of a costume but not the full fursuit. For instance, we met Kip the Fox who always wears a set of fox ears on his head and often wears a tail on the back of his pants, but has never worn paws, a nose mask, or a full fursuit because they are too restrictive for him.

As a practical matter, furries actively engage with the community in full fursuits primarily during in-person gatherings because of the weight, cost, and maintenance of the fursuits. There is a robust online and virtual community which includes interactions in chat rooms, viewing and showcasing art, promoting fan fiction and other literary endeavors, and even participating in support and advice groups. All furries identify as fans of and participants in the activities of those who create the art, don the suits, and assume the identities. According to the International Anthropomorphic Research Project, one of the first groups that committed to study furries and furry culture in a systematic way, a "furry is a person who identifies with the Furry Fandom culture" including "individuals who have a distinct interest in anthropomorphic animals such as cartoon characters. Many, but not all, furries strongly identify with, or view themselves as, one (or more) species of animal other than human" (Gerbasi et al. 2008, 198). Seabrook agrees, emphasizing that "the single defining characteristic of this sub-culture is its interest in anthropomorphic animals; there is no widely accepted or unifying tendency in the Fandom" (Seabrook 2010, 13). In other words, a furry identity is an essentially contested identity.

We see two very different but important variations in the approaches of members of the furry fandom to understanding the mores, rituals, and fursonas of furries. For most members of the community, the critical defining characteristic of a furry is anthropomorphism. That is, ascribing human traits, including behaviors, motivations, emotions, and physical characteristics, to animals is a foundational and nonnegotiable premise. Anthropomorphism in furry culture plays out through a variety practices, including but not limited to artwork and the creation and use of a fursuit. When a furry wears their fursuit, which means dressing up in an mascot-type animal costume, they still embody the psychosocial traits of a human being but add in some characteristics which differentiate the fursona from a human. For instance, we talked to a young woman, Rebecca, who had an elaborate chipmunk type fursona and fursuit she named Blossom. Whenever she was in her full fursuit, she kept a small plastic squeaker in her mouth and only verbalized through clicks and squeaks. The squeaker is the small piece you might remove from a dog's squeaky toy. She would also mostly keep her arms bent at the elbow so her paws/hands were always located just below her chin as if she was about to bite into an acorn or some other chipmunk preferred snack. Still, Rebecca, even when in character as Blossom, still presented as a human. That is, she behaved like a typical human by walking upright on her "hind" legs, she wore clothes, spoke her own language but perfectly understood English, and interacted with others in cultural settings normally reserved for human beings. In other words, furries assume their fursonas but are still very present as humans.

Similar to anthropomorphism, there is a smaller but significant sector of the furry fandom that approaches being a furry from a therianthropy point of view. That is, therianthropy ascribes animal traits to a human (Maase 2015, 1). We spoke to a man and a woman at Califur who told us that they both "had dragon blood" and were "spiritually dragons." The therianthropy community is a subset and distinct minority within the furry community. As the dragon couple talked to us, a full fursuited rabbit named Buddy was standing nearby. Buddy made squeaky noises and pantomimed belly laughter at them. They responded by both holding up their hands and "roaring" at Buddy the Rabbit. This was all done in a good natured way and they perhaps were acquainted. Buddy hugged them both before hopping away.

In many cases, furries wear portions of animal costumes like ears or tails and may act like an animal for instance by purring like a cat, growling at a stranger like a wolf, or sniffing unfamiliar things like many animals would. There are many different types of furries, with each animal genre comprising a distinct subset of the community with specific animal-representative characteristics (Jeansonne 2012, 73). For example, the wolves hang around together in a pack while more solitary animals like crocodiles may be part of a smaller crew or roam through the conventions alone. Because of the broad diversity across the fandom, with members drawing from the mores, expressions, and stylistic presentations of both humans and nonhumans, the social space shared by the community of furries is wildly dynamic and diverse.

One critical differentiation of the furry fandom from other types of cosplay and other fan-based groups—like devotees of Star Trek or Star Wars—is that furries have no canonical guidelines or specific characters that must be adhered to (Dunn 2021). This means furries are free to develop their identities and characters as they see fit with no concern of running afoul of the "rules" of the identity. At Califur, we spoke at length with a giant pink wolf we will call Spike. We spoke to him both as Spike and as the human inside Spike. He led several panels including ones about the aesthetics of the furry fandom and about the historical trajectory of the furry fandom. Spike impressed upon us the critical importance that a lack of canonical constraints has for the furry fandom. The members of the community can literally be anything they want. They do not need to conform to any costume vision thought up by another or a roster of preestablished characteristics for their constructed identity. They are free of the constraints of their character as they are their own authors and they are complete masters of their own identities.

In the United States, the exact number of furries has not been determined and estimates of the number of self-identifying members of the furry fandom range from hundreds of thousands on the very conservative end to several million to perhaps as many as ten million depending on who you ask and how you calculate the size of the community. The political attitudes and the political behavior of those who identify as members of the furry community have to date been completely neglected in the explicit study of the furry community regardless of the discipline in which the research is grounded. We strive here to better understand this large community and to make an initial foray into determining who makes up this community and how these people engage in politics.

Importantly, we are interested in determining how primary the furry identity is for the members of this group. That is, is being a member of the furry community a more reliable indicator of political attitudes than other demographic characteristics like age, income, and race? Is the furry community a peer network wherein political talk is mediated? Our objective is to examine the intersection of identity politics and political attitudes and political behavior in the context of this chosen identity and chosen community. How does choosing to be a part of the furry community influence how individuals behave politically. Like the other non-traditional sexual minority groups in our study, we answered these questions by administering the same in-person and remote surveys and open-ended questionnaires that were used for the other groups but tailored for the furry fandom. We only took surveys from or interviewed those people who self-identified as members of the furry community. We interviewed elites and participants in the live events and we engaged in participant observation and ethnographic analysis.

In-person surveys and elite interviews took place at events including AnthroCon in Pittsburgh, Pennsylvania, Califur in Pasadena, California, and FurCon: Further Confusion in San Jose, California. We also conducted in-person elite interviews and engaged in participant observation at Sakura-Con in Seattle, Washington (an anime convention with a strong furry presence), and at Frolicon in Atlanta, Georgia (a combined BDSM and anime convention with a strong furry presence). Each furry convention attracted several thousand members of the furry community. With our collected data, we show that, while furries are clearly invisible to politicians and policymakers, they are politically engaged, participate civically, and are a cohesive social group. In short, they are a substantial voting bloc that may have the ability to sway local, regional, and national elections. We should also note that we saw a strong furry presence at the BDSM conferences we attended, which included some people in costume and a scattering of panels directed toward furry-specific interests. There was also a significant amount of furry art at the other conferences as well. Furry art runs the gamut from fun for all to explicitly sexual in nature. At the more overtly sexual BDSM conferences, the furry art was more sexually explicit and the furry gear included, on occasion, sexual toys. For example, at Beyond Vanilla and Frolicon, venders sold erotic vibrators and artificial phalluses designed to look like what one might expect the genitals of an anthropomorphized animal found throughout the furry fandom.

As a caveat, as is the case with each of our groups, we do not claim this is a representative sample of all the members of the furry community in the United States. Rather, because we employed the novel use of a virtual snowball sample, the sample might be younger, perhaps more educated, and more technologically sophisticated than the furry community in the United States as a whole. Furthermore, because we were limited to engaging with members of the furry community that approached us at the conventions and those who followed the links shared by those who came up to us, some demographics may be oversampled while others might be under sampled. Specifically, our sample could be young than the overall population because the conferences attract a younger audience and thus, presumably, our participants and their friends might also be younger than the furry population in general. Before we detail the results, we first discuss the extant literature and where this scholarship fits into that landscape. We also provide a brief history of the furry fandom.

Current scholarship provides us little insight into the demographics of the furry community and no insight into the political activity or preferences of this group. Although some members of the community would disagree, being a furry is not an innate characteristic as classically defined. One becomes a member of this community by deciding to join it. For a variety of reasons, sexual communities that individuals effectively opt into might be missed by the scholarly analysis of more familiar and frequently studied groups defined along traditional demographic variables (Bobo and Gilliam, 1990; Uslaner and Brown, 2005; Barreto and Pedraza, 2009). The furry identity is formed on the basis of choice and, likewise, the community is one of choice as furries come together to be a part of a group that shares an identity and a collection of shared interests. Furries are a prime example of chosen sexual communities. We recognize, and discuss below, that not all furries embrace or agree with the notion that the furry fandom is a sexual community. Still, the role of erotica and erotic play in the culture strongly suggests that for at least some—and given the data, perhaps even a large majority—their sexual identity is intertwined with their furry identity in substantial ways (Hsu and Bailey 2019).

There are many popular misconceptions about who is a furry, what it means to be a furry, and what it is that furries do as part of their identity and community. Before further clarifying what we have learned about furries, it is important to consider a general identity question: does engagement in a community rise to the level of a core identity or is it simply an action that one does? That is, is action identity? Does having a fursona and wearing a fursuit make you a furry or are you a furry who has constructed a fursona and fursuit to present your identity? At least some research suggests a significant portion of the furry community believes that engagement represents identity, and mere activities are not enough. In other words, for many members of the community, being a furry is who they are, not simply something they do.

In a survey completed by the International Anthropomorphic Research Project, roughly 38 percent of their furry respondents believe being a furry "is not a choice," and thus an innate characteristic, compared to 32 percent who believe "it is a choice"; 30 percent selected "I don't know" (Plante et al. 2016, 45). Cleary, if this survey is correct, a plurality of furries believe it is part of their core identity. While many furries believe they were born a furry, identity "is constructed through a complex interplay of cognitive, affective, and social interaction processes, occurring within particular cultural and local contexts" (Vignoles et al. 2006). Like many other identities, "although furries argue that being a furry is not something they do, it is something they are . . . sociologically we can say that becoming a furry is a social construction" (Jeansonne 2012, 74).

We point this out not to argue that these respondents are wrong; on the contrary, we take them at their word that they are furries. The fact that such a large portion of the community sees being a furry as inextricably linked to their fundamental sense of self, despite the dynamic, changing boundaries of the community, illustrates the passion and commitment furries have to their communities and to their identities as furries. Moreover, how they came to self-identify as a furry is not critical for our purposes. It would be misguided to suggest that simply because an identity is socially constructed it is any less profound, valuable, or meaningful than those rooted in more conventional categories like race or gender. For our purposes, the point is that the socially constructed nature of the furry identity allows us to classify them as what Schulenberg calls "essentially contested subjects": social groups with a fixed identity label, but no universal, objective definition of who is and is not a member of the group or groups with "contestable boundaries" (Schulenberg 2013, 45).

The idea of an essentially contested subject is significant here because it means that there is no universal definition of who is and who is not a furry. We may see competing definitions used by different people with different levels of engagement and different levels of identity salience. Some may be more inclusive in their assessment of who is a member of the community while others may be more exclusive. The nebulous boundaries of the community are important especially when we consider the role of sex within the furry community. As we will discuss later, some see sex and sexuality as intrinsic and important features of the community while others believe it has little or even nothing to do with being a furry. Some in the furry community uses the group-specific term "yiff" or "yiffing," named after the sound a fox makes when it has sex, to refer to sexual interaction, particularly penetrative sexual contact, but yiffing can also generally refer to pornographic art, stories, or any erotic endeavor (Maase 2015, 122).

Being a furry, like any other group-based identity, often delivers a lot of value to the individual through the psychosocial experiences associated with the identity. Furries interact with one another in an individual and group capacity both online and in physical spaces. Furries have a very large online presence, meeting together on popular furry-oriented websites such as furaffinity.net, where they chat, develop strong relationships, and share furry-oriented artwork (Maase 2015). However, furries also interact in public spaces, both within local social groups and large regional and national conferences, such as Anthrocon, the world's largest furry convention, held in Pittsburgh, Pennsylvania, every year. In both online and in-person environments, most furries adopt a "fursona," which is their online and offline animal persona that they use repeatedly over time, both as an act of play and an act of identification (Brown 2015). It is through this fursona that furries frequently, but not always, interact with another. A furry may have more than one fursona at a time, drawn on depending on context or mood, and many change their fursonas over time.

A Brief History of Furries

The adoration of animals and the contemplation of the role of animals in human society have existed longer than written history. The symbolic use of animals in religion, culture, art, war, and society in general is evidenced from prehistoric times forward across every era. From cave paintings by early humans, to the ever-present animal iconography in the early empires like the Romans, Greeks, Aztecs, Incans, and Egyptians, to the diverse smaller Indigenous populations in North and South

America and sub-Saharan Africa, the use of animals to portray strength, dominance, and wisdom, among many other traits has been a constant. Royal families from the czars in Russia to the kings and queens in the United Kingdom and across Europe and Asia frequently incorporated animals into their crests and other symbolic family paraphernalia to represent their aspirational traits. Likewise, anthropomorphism, the attribution to animals of human emotions, traits, and characteristics, has also been a central dimension of the human perception of animals. Moreover, anamorphism, where a human or human-like being transforms into an animal, is also ever present in the stories of human culture and society. Common anamorphism stories include people turning into werewolves, vampires turning into bats, a host of ancient gods and goddesses turning into swans, snakes, horses, or birds, or any number of different animals. The furry fandom, or "furries," embrace sensibilities from all of these animal-centric tropes and in many ways is the culmination of the confluence of these ideas (Morgan 2008).

The specific moment of origin of the furry fandom as currently defined is murky at best and controversial among many members of community. Early cartoons from the likes of Disney and Warner Brothers depicted anthropomorphic characters like Mickey Mouse, Robin Hood portrayed as a fox, and Bugs Bunny (Donaldson 2018). Cartoonists like Robert Crum made a cultural impact with characters like the titular character of the film *Fritz the Cat*. Throughout our interviews, people often mentioned these types of cultural icons as the trigger for their awakening as a furry and sometimes as their sexual awakening as well. A person we interviewed at Anthrocon in Philadelphia described watching the animated Disney movie *Robin Hood* at the cusp of puberty, and that became his sexual fixation. He imagined himself as the Robin Hood character—a smart, sexy, quick witted fox and the hero of the movie. The movie had such an impact on his life and development that, even as a twenty-four-year-old, the fursuit he wore at Anthrocon was a tribute to the Robin Hood character. As a side point, we saw many fursuits that seemed inspired by the Robin Hood cartoon and the similar, if perhaps less well-known, 2009 Disney film *Fantastic Mr. Fox* based on the book by Roald Dahl of the same name.

As cartoons became a television fixture, more people were exposed to more artistic representations of humanistic animals as they grew up.

Anime, a particular style of animation developed originally in Japan, built a large following in the United States after the animated anime series *Speed Racer* broadly introduced the graphic style to American audiences beginning in 1967 (IMDb 2022). What has been termed the "proto-furry" era of the late 1970s and early 1980s was notable for the beginning of a convergence between some elements of science fiction fans and fans of anime (Silverman 2020). What is believed to be the first anime fan club in the United States was founded in 1977 by Fred Patten, who went on to become a prominent historian and chronicler of the furry fandom (Annett 2014, 120). By the 1980s, a contingent of furries were fixtures at the many science fiction conventions across Southern California (Patten 2012). In 1989, Mark Merlino and Rod O'Riley—the organizers of those early furry gatherings—organized ConFurence 0, the first convention solely devoted to furries, at a Holiday Inn in Costa Mesa, California (Patten 2017, 57). ConFurence had less than forty attendees the first year. They dubbed it "ConFurence 0" because it was a proof of concept effort rather than a full blown convention, but quickly grew to become prominent as the model for furry conventions. Some common thematic aspects of Furry conventions include furry-specific art exhibits, sales by costume designers and creators, a parade of attendees in fursuits, and dance contests for the participants, among others.

The advent of the internet meant that Furries, like so many other small or marginalized groups, were able to much more easily connect with their like-minded compatriots. As with our other groups of interest, there is not a clear and obvious line between membership in the furry fandom and sexuality. For some, the fandom identity is unrelated to sexuality in any meaningful sense and for others, sexuality centrally informs the parameters of the identity and is a critical, perhaps even driving, dimension of their membership in the community (Brooks et al. 2022).

Stigmatization in Popular Media and Academia

Popular mischaracterizations and prejudices have maligned the furry community almost since its inception. The general public often has skewed opinions about what furries are and do, and, overall, the community suffers from widespread misunderstanding, stigmatization, and discrimination. Perhaps not surprisingly, given US puritanism about sex, more than any other factor, "sex is the most commonly associated negative attribute of the fandom" (Maase 2015, 118). The general public approbation "is based in the stereotype that furries are sexually deviant or have a mental disorder . . . (often) the idea is that furries are into bestiality and their activities are based on sexual behavior" with animals (33). In other words, the nonfurry world misinterprets and mispresents the sexuality of furries and frequently focuses on the misconceived notion of sexual activities within the community as the entirety of the fandom. Of course, this tendency in the dominant heterosexual and heteronormative culture to pervert the reality of any subculture and then distill the entirety of that subculture into that one perversion is not limited to furries.

Members of the LGBTQ community as well as the other groups we study here are all too familiar with this process. Indeed, this also routinely happens to religious and racial minorities. Some politicians, in their never-ending quest to find groups to demonize and therefore scare and mobilize some voters, like when they overtly attacked furries during the 2022 midterm elections (Bishin et al. 2021; Kingkade et al. 2022). Specifically, at least twenty republicans running for offices, ranging from a sitting member in United States Congress (Laura Boebert, R-CO) to the ultimately unsuccessful Republican nominee for governor of Minnesota (Scott Jensen) and a host of candidates seeking many lower offices, falsely claimed that schools were placing litter boxes in restrooms to accommodate children who identified as furries (Kingkade et al. 2022; Strobel 2022a). This was designed to shock gullible voters who are unfamiliar with the furry fandom. Typically, those pushing this false story used "cats" instead of "furries" to describe the situation but would eventually refer to the furry fandom either directly or indirectly. Conservative media influencers like Tucker Carlson and Joe Rogan repeated the lie and furries found themselves in an invented controversy not of their making, where the whole community was demonized apparently in an attempt to belittle the educational system and educators, LGBTQ people, and even the furries themselves.

Despite the stereotypes, the extant research shows that the view of the role of sexuality within the community, while very prominent for many furries, is far from homogenous across the community. Orientation and sexuality are not universally seen as key attributes of the community. Perhaps because of the fear of disapproval from the general society for all the wrong reasons, many in the furry community believe "sexual explicitness in visual representation is a divisive issue in the Furry subculture and one that provokes attacks on the sub-culture both from external critics and from those within the sub-culture who perceive themselves as moral police" (Seabrook 2010, 134). This concern with the general societal perception of furries as sexual deviants can have profound personal and group implications because "this stigma also goes as far as stopping furries from being open as furries," and thereby inhibits individuals from openly acknowledging who they are and thus creates a furry closet, so to speak (Maase 2015, 119).

More often than not, the popular press and the entertainment industry present furries and the furry fandom as "sexual deviants . . . or as suffering from psychological disorders" (Healy and Beverland 2013, 227). Beyond the general negative framing, at least four specific press and entertainment events gained notoriety among the furry fandom. Negative and unfair portrayals were popularized in a 2001 article in *Vanity Fair* (Gurley 2001); a 2014 episode of the *Dr. Phil* television program; a 2003 episode of *CSI: Crime Scene Investigation* (Lewis 2003); and a 2014 episode of MSNBC's news commentary program *Morning Joe*. In each case, the interviewees/subjects were chosen or portrayed for their "for shock value" and not because they were a fair presentation of furries (Nast 2006, 319–20). This is of course reminiscent of the early television portrayals of African Americans and members of the LGBT community, as well as any number of racial, religious, and ethnic minorities.

Vanity Fair interviewed several furries about their sex lives, their psychological struggles, and their generally desperate and unhappy lives. The interviewer also pushed them to claim all furries were just like these select few. Dr. Phil interviewed a single furry who, for the show, ate out of a dog bowl and barked. Dr. Phil overtly ridiculed Boomer the furry with a sarcastic "Go figure" after Boomer claimed he had never been on a date. The episode, rather than being an exploration into the culture or psychology of the furry fandom, was little more than an exploitative caricature of the community, with Dr. Phil leading his live and television audience in mocking Boomer specifically and furries generally. The *CSI* episode was titled "Fur and Loathing." It portrayed a furry in full fursuit taken into the police station for questioning about a murder. The suspect is always present in his fursuit and both the character and the community are ridiculed throughout the episode. Another character was presented as little more than a stripper who wears furry bunny gear. The episode of *Morning Joe* featured a panel of commentators that discussed furries in general. Cohost Mika Brzezinski laughed so long and so persistently at the opening of the segment, that she had to leave the set to get back in control of her laughter. The point of the episode was to laugh at the expense of the community and its members, not to inform the viewers about the community in any meaningful way.

The scholarly world has also treated the furry fandom poorly. For instance, in an article titled "The Complexity of Deviant Lifestyles" in the journal *Deviant Behavior*, furries are one of the cases analyzed for their "episodic dress deviance," where they are described, in a wildly inaccurate way, as

> people who enjoy dressing like animals. They are apart from other groups who wear animal costumes as a route to socializing with others and who share common interests such as anthropomorphic art and costumes. The furries see their costumes (fursuits) as part of a lifestyle. A furry is a person with an important emotional/spiritual connection with an animal or animals, be they real, fictional, or symbolic. They see themselves as someone other than human and who desire to become more like the furry species they identify with. Indeed, a small percentage of furries do not consider themselves to be human at all. Another small subgroup within the furry fandom attach a sexuality to their activity, dressing like an animal while having sex. Furries having group sex are referred to as fur-balls. (Bryant and Forsyth 2012, 531)

This scholarly description is flawed in many dimensions. First, branding furry behavior as deviant—which has specific negative clinical implications, but is also a generally negative social category—frames the group under an assumption of perversion. Second, the article categorizes furry identity as a "lifestyle" which replicates the negative framing commonly used to justify discrimination toward the LGBT community. No one publishes papers about heterosexual "lifestyles." The nomenclature presents a foundation of and language for disapproval. Finally, the article makes broad generalizations about furries as a group, including the scintillating reference to group sex as "fur-balls." None of our respondents used that term, no one we interviewed said they had even heard the term, and we were unable to find it in any other academic articles or any furry fandom websites. Notably, the authors do not actually interview any furries for the article. Additionally, is it unclear whether they actually researched any other scholarly articles on the subject as there are no citations to any peer-reviewed research on furries.

The International Anthropomorphic Research Project began to study the furry fandom in 2007 using scientific methodologies common in psychology to assess the accuracy of some of the popular and academic perceptions of the furry fandom. The principles of the project are closely affiliated with Anthrocon, the self-proclaimed world's largest furry convention which, as mentioned, is held annually in Pittsburgh, Pennsylvania. The multiple studies and papers produced by the project have revealed a lot about the demographics, desires, and practices of those in the furry fandom, even though some of the early work and some aspects of their approach are controversial.

Their initial publication focused on the demographics of the furry community (Gerbasi et al. 2008). Unfortunately, they also purport to test for personality disorders among furries and ultimately suggest that further research is needed to determine whether psychologists should add "species identity disorder," modeled after the discredited and transphobic "gender identity disorder," to the Diagnostic and Statistical Manual of Mental Disorders. There is no science or data-based evidence in the literature or in our observations that suggest that a furry identity should be considered pathological or as a disorder in any way. The demographics of the study's control group, community college students, are simply not a representative sample of society in general and cannot credibly be the metric for measuring disorders in other groups. Additionally, the study did not use a consistent symptomology for its diagnostic assessments; for an in-depth critique, see Probyn-Rapsey (2011). Simply because an identity or behavior is not common cannot be the basis for declaring it a psychiatric disorder. The response by Gerbasi et al. (2011) to Probyn-Rapsey's critiques suggested that their work contained positive contributions to understanding the furry fandom even if these criticisms were valid.

The popular and scholarly mischaracterization of the Furry Fandom has, on occasion, led to disagreements within the community over how the fandom should be represented in public and whether the extreme and the eccentric examples that the media seeks out can be counterbalanced by more mainstream members (Maase 2015, 23). Thus, the furry fandom is actively involved in self-image battles known in other marginalized groups as the "politics of respectability," the presentation of self that is most likely to avoid negative sanctions from those outside of the group (Jones 2021). As an example, each convention we attended had a specific panel for first time attendees, always open to all attendees, about how to speak to the press. In each of these presentations, the speaker specifically mentioned some or all of the cultural slights (that were infamous in the community) from the *Vanity Fair* article, *Dr. Phil* show episode, *CSI* episode, or *Morning Joe* episode.

Internal Battles: Respectability Politics

Many marginalized communities regularly face internal battles of "respectability" as they struggle with putting their best face forward to win acceptance or at least avoid being targeted by more dominant groups (Higginbotham 1993; Vaid 1995; Jones 2021). This can result in internal policing that takes the shape of removing or downplaying any elements of the community that might increase the odds of external disapproval (Goffman 1963; Katz 1976; Gould 2009).

The negative media, scholarly missteps, and the perception of strangeness by the general public lead many in the furry community to be wary of discussing the furry fandom with the nonfurry world. At Anthrocon, for example, any members of the media who attend the convention are required to be escorted by a member of the event staff. Some exceptions to this rule are granted if the journalist has been vetted and determined to be fair, which is defined as less likely to exploit eccentric examples or focus on the salacious (Brown 2015, 3–4). Anthrocon's long-running chairman, Samuel Conway, leads a session every year at the convention called "Furries and the Media." This recurring presentation is geared toward new attendees to the conference and is simply about how to interact with the press. Conway coaches attendees on best practices for engaging with the media to avoid unintentionally fueling negative stereotypes to outsiders (5).

We attended that panel and the underlying thematic suggestion was that the press hoped to embarrass and ridicule the community at large and any furry who spoke to them in particular. Accordingly, there were strong suggestions about how to manage questions from reporters including how to downplay the role of sex, not reveal anything especially unusual about yourself or the community, and keep the answers short and boring. The panel on managing the media that we attended was packed full with perhaps as many as two hundred people present and engaged. Many of the attendees of Brown's talk nodded their heads enthusiastically as he described the motivation of journalists as looking for the weird and sensational and being primarily focused on the furries' sex lives. We interpreted Brown's instruction to those present as an effort to engage in respectability politics and downplay or completely dismiss the role of sex within the furry fandom. One way some furries have responded to the focus on sexuality from those outside the furry community is definitional and boundary setting within the community. For instance, "many non-yiff furries don't consider yiff furries part of the furrydom at all, and they sometimes resent the attention yiff receives from the general public, fearing that yiff gives the impression that all furry activity is erotic" (Reid 2006, 122–23).

Some furries who believe that sex plays a significant role in the community, but prefer the sexual aspect be de-emphasized because of the associated negative publicity, might employ a different strategy and remove or limit the sexual references from some types of furry spaces. Online, we see routine efforts by nonerotic artists to exclude the erotic furry artwork from creative spaces with the argument that the association between the erotic and nonerotic might diminish their credibility as serious artists (Seabrook 2010, 124). Moreover, controversy has also engulfed many furry conventions over the visibility of sex-related products and representations in convention spaces, with continuously changing protocols regarding what can and cannot be sold or displayed in the vendor and dealer rooms (126). Each conference we attended had adult-only space, which seemed to thoroughly hide the sexually explicit gear and art from the underage attendees in particular but also from those who prefer not to see the erotica.

Some organized groups within the furry fandom have actively tried to sanitize the community with efforts to remove the sexual aspects from both online spaces and offline spaces. Some of the activities of these groups have been described as follows:

> Within the Fandom, the issue of explicitly sexual Furry art came to prominence in September, 1998 when "Squee Rat" (Charla Trotman) and several associates. . . . formed the "Burned Furs," an association of Furries who felt that the explicit art and actions of Furries at ConFurences undermined and degraded membership in the Fandom. The Burned Fur "Manifesto" launched "The Great Internet Flame War," an episode in Furry history that went on for several years and finally ended with the demise of the Burned Furs website on December 7–8, 2000, although the relentless pursuit of Furry Internet "pornography" continues. . . . Various "backlash" groups have formed since the Burned Furs, among them Antifur, now inactive, Something Awful, an active and intrusive Internet presence, and Portal of Evil, as well as Crush Yiff Destroy, and Third Rail Furs, characterized by Furry essayist, Simo, as "another crop of self-righteous dumbasses with delusions of cleaning up Furrydom." (Seabrook 2010, 127)

These efforts are at the extreme frontier of the politics of respectability and go beyond just ensuring the sexual aspects of the furry fandom are contained and those who are uninterested are insulated from the erotic. Like most communities, there is a wide range of opinions among the members of the Furry Fandom regarding the role of sex and sexuality in the community. So while some might prefer there be no association between the furry fandom and sex and sexuality, there are also many members of the community who see the link between furry identity and sexuality as inextricable with varying degrees of intensity. Importantly, the nonfurry world absolutely links sexuality and the furry identity, so the debates about sex and sexuality within the furry fandom are not dispositive of the topic. As long as the general population perceives the furry fandom as a community that at least in part revolves around sexual identity, the dynamics of sexuality politics will still come into play.

Sexuality and Furries

Two large surveys have specifically asked members of the Furry Fandom whether sex and/or sexuality are central to their furry identity. The results of these surveys support the notion that sexuality is central to the furry identity for many within the community. In a 2008 study, 16.9 percent reported that sex played an extremely large or large part of the furry life, with 31.6 percent reporting a medium role, and 51 percent reporting small or extremely small role (Osaki 2008, 28). Essentially half of the furry population reported sex and sexuality as a critical dimension of their furry identity. Another survey found a higher level of interest with 33 percent of respondents revealing they had a "significant sexual interest" in being a furry and 46 percent responding that they had a minor interest (Evans 2008, 16–17). The different response ranges in these surveys may be due to wording of the questions. Osaki asked how large of a role sex plays while Evans ask if it plays any part. Despite the variations in wording or methodology, both surveys suggest that sexuality is intertwined with furry identity for a significant number of furries. These numbers should be thought of as a floor rather than a ceiling because it is possible that some furries would have been shy about disclosing their conception of sexuality or at least not comfortable responding to a stranger about what might be thought of as aberrant behavior. That is, we should assume that some people are unwilling to disclose details or opinions about sexuality especially when those people or the sexuality at issue is associated with some sort of taboo or stigma.

Other surveys about other aspects of sexuality within the furry fandom confirm the prominent role sex and sexuality play in the community. Erotic and sexually graphic art, while disfavored by some in the community, are routinely created and viewed by a large number of the members of the community. For ease of use and to align with the extant studies, we use the word "pornography," but we recognize these types of art may or may not fall within the legal parameters of actual pornography. Rather, we use the word in the colloquial and casual sense in the same way that members of the furry world mean it and the same way the cited studies mean it rather than in a definitional or legally specific way. We recognize that there is a debate about whether the sexually explicit furry art is pornographic or not, but we leave that to others to settle.

According to surveys from the International Anthropomorphic Research Project, 96.3 percent of male furries and 78.3 percent of female furries view or have viewed furry pornography (Plante et al. 2013, 15–6). That survey did not have any option between having viewed it regularly or not so we cannot determine how habitual the consumption might be. When asked about their view of furry-oriented versus non-furry-oriented pornography, roughly 4 percent of the respondents reported having a negative view of furry-oriented pornography while 34 percent said they had a negative view of non-furry-oriented pornography (18). Moreover, roughly 51 percent of the respondents answered that they prefer, to varying degrees, pornographic over nonpornographic furry artwork (20).

While we discussed the furry pornography with many of our subjects after they had finished the surveys as well as with some of the elites, we did hit a slight barrier to fully candid exchanges. While the males we spoke to were much more comfortable talking about their affinity for the sexually explicit furry art at the conferences, the women were much less interested in discussing it. We believe the fact that we are all male made the conversations about the erotic and sexually explicit art and, as was often the case when discussing it with males, the concurrent conversation about masturbation, led some of the women to be less comfortable talking about it. Nonetheless, we did have several conversations. For instance, one woman, Kat (short for Katherine) told us she found drawing the erotica of the furry fandom to be a form of foreplay and she and her boyfriend have "the best sex right after I've spent an hour or two drawing." Kat was in her early forties and sold art at furry conferences and online. She kept her other job, as a veterinary assistant, for the benefits and because she enjoyed it, but said she actually made a larger income off selling her art.

We also talked to a man in his thirties, Javier, who told us that the furry fandom art really helped him understand his own sexuality. He used his fingers to put air quotes around the word "cartoon" when he told as that, at first, in his early twenties, he was ashamed that he was masturbating to "cartoons." But once he realized there was a larger community of furries where he could feel he belonged and could avoid judgment, he knew there was nothing to be embarrassed or ashamed about.

Beyond issues of sexually explicit online art, online roleplaying also has a significant sexual dimension for some members of the furry community. Male furry respondents reported that about 34 percent of their online furry roleplaying was sexual in nature, while female furries reported about 21 percent of their online furry roleplaying was sexual (Plante et al. 2013, 22–23). We asked one couple about their online roleplaying, and they made the interesting point that it was not any different than anyone else's online sex play except that it also involved furry aesthetics. Although about 23 percent of the furry community reports that sexual attraction has nothing or very little to do with their furry interests, about 37 percent of the respondents stated that sexual attraction to furry content is an important and significant motivator of their participation (Plante et al. 2016, 43). The responses to questions about the role of furry-oriented pornography varied significantly by gender with only 27 percent of males respondents but 64 percent of female respondents choosing "not at all" when asked whether furry pornography played a role in their entrance into furry fandom (Plante et al. 2013: 19).

Like many communities, "while furry fandom is sexually open, this doesn't mean that everyone in it is sexual" (Howl 2015, 52). Or, as put elsewhere, "we can say that furry is not wholly sexual in attraction. It is a strong element of furry, but it is not the entirety of furry" (Evans 2008, 17). Because the existing research shows that sex and sexuality are important components of furry identity for many members of the community, the furry fandom is an appropriate case to include as we assess the political attitudes and identities of these marginalized non-traditional sexual minority groups.

Data Collection

Both online communities and furry conventions are critical forums for the furry community. The furry fandom might exist without either or both of these components, but it would be much smaller in every regard if either did not exist. We attended three exclusively furry conventions and two conventions that expressly included furries as an aspect of their overall and broader themes. Recall that the exclusively furry conventions were Anthrocon in Pittsburgh, Pennsylvania; Califur in Pasadena, California; and FurCon/Further Confusion in San Jose, California. The two conventions that were not exclusively furry but still had a significant formal furry presence were Sakura-Con in Seattle, Washington, which also included anime and other kinds of cosplay, and Frolicon/Froliween in Atlanta, Georgia, which was primarily a BDSM and fantasy convention. The Sakura-Con and Frolicon/Froliween conventions had several venders geared toward furries, many panels about the furry fandom, receptions or events specifically for furries, and a significant group of attendees who appeared to be part of the furry fandom based on their fursuits or other furryifferrnalia. We note too, that the BDSM conventions we attended, in addition to Frolicon/Froliween, often had either an informal furry presence or a formal or more minor furry presence. That is, there were frequently some attendees who are furries and a few germane panels, events, or venders, but this was sparse.

We collected survey responses at Anthrocon and Califur. We interviewed elites and attendees with semistructured interviews at all the conferences. We engaged in participant observation as well as ethnographic analysis at each conference. We used the virtual snowball technique described earlier to obtain survey responses from people who identified as furries that were members of closed online social network groups. We took our leads for the virtual snowball technique from the elite interviews as well casual conversations we had with any conference attendee who identified as a furry. We also allowed anyone who self-identified as a furry at any of the other data collection sites to take the furry surveys. That is, if a furry walked up to us at, for instance, a BDSM conference, we let them take whichever survey they preferred.

The Conferences

Before we discuss the results of our surveys and elite and attendee interviews, we want to generally describe the conferences and some of our efforts at those conferences. The furry conferences in many ways would be familiar to anyone who has attended any academic or trade conference. There are panels throughout the days that cover a wide variety of aspects of the furry fandom. Some may cover artistic or aesthetic aspects—like building or designing a fursuit, developing graphic skills, or discussing color and design theory. Other panels focus on topics about communication—like how to navigate your disclosure to family and friends that you are part of the furry fandom, how to find like-minded furries, or how to keep your squad from squabbling when you all go to conferences. Other panels may focus on very practical issues like hydration, health, and first aid issues for those in the fursuits, care and maintenance for your fursuit and other furry gear, or very typical orientations for first time attendees or novices of any sort. As discussed previously, at Anthrocon, we roamed the conference venues and our hotel lobby to acquire survey responses, while at Califur and FurCon, we had a table set up in the venders' room. We had Halloween size candy to hand out and drew a name for a $50 prize at each event. For the conferences that were not mainly about the furry fandom, we would conduct informal semistructured interviews with anyone we saw that seemed to be a furry and we attended some of the furry-oriented panels.

The furry-focused conferences are overtly and intentionally family friendly and all have straightforward codes of conduct which prohibit public lewdness and any inappropriate behavior towards or around minors. There are a host of etiquette rules regarding photography—you should ask before you take a photograph of anyone in a fursuit and you should never photograph someone in a fursuit if they have taken the head off or are otherwise only partially suited. Every conference had an area exclusively for putting on or removing fursuits. The person wearing the fursuit usually had a helper with them who could assist in putting the suit on or taking it off. Only those with fursuits and their helpers were allowed into these areas. These fursuit prep areas also had seating and hydration stations for those in the fursuits. The weight and heat retention of the costumes mean the wearer must be especially conscious of hydration. These areas also had steam wands, brushes, lint rollers, clothing repair tape, masking tape, and many other items that might help get the fursuits into top presentation shape.

Exceptions to the "ask permission before taking a photograph" rule exist for the furry parade—where all those with fursuits line up and march through the venue and outside along the preselected parade route—as well as during a panel presentation. The furry parade is a highlight of the conferences where all those in fursuits literally march through the event and often the surrounding area in full regalia. This invariably attracts local television, radio, and newspaper coverage and is truly a remarkable spectacle. While each suit is impressive in its own right, a line of several hundred at the smaller conferences or as many as several thousand people in unique fursuits, playfully marching along the corridors of the conference and surrounding area, rivals the large-scale national parades like Macy's Thanksgiving Day Parade in joy and excitement. All the other (nonfursuited) attendees as well as lots of other spectators that are not conference attendees, line the parade route and applaud nonstop for the passing furry menagerie.

The different species types have different aesthetic sensibilities (although, bear in mind that since there is no literary canon that dictates authenticity, each member of the community can construct their fursona, or fursonas, as they see fit). Some fursuits include movable jaws connected to the chin of the wearer, and these can include a device or prop that allows the wearer to make nonhuman squeaks or squawks or noises that replicate a language. Some furries are mute. Some wear elaborate costumes, others wear only the basics. We talked with one furry in Philadelphia at Anthrocon, a twenty-three-year-old white male, who asked us about the larger project. He was very excited about our brief description of the plan for the research and explained, "I'm also a nudist! My family are nudists! See my fursona only wears a hat, shoes and a weapon and I'm always nude under the fursuit so I can always be true to myself!" He pulled on the thinnish material of his fursuit to demonstrate via his clear genital outline that he was not wearing any underwear. His fursuit presented as a primarily reddish brown fox with a white belly and neck. He had a green cloth vest that was open in the front. He carried a bow and arrow and had a small hat with a feather. The inspiration for his costume was the 1973 Disney animated film *Robin Hood* which, recall, many people mentioned as one of their earliest examples that piqued their interest in anthropomorphic anime or the furry community.

In addition to the panels, there are also receptions of different types, social events like dances, contests, meet and greets, and a vender room. Some conferences also have a guest plenary speaker—like the San Diego Chicken (the fursuited mascot of the San Diego Padres baseball team), a prominent artist, or social media entertainers and influencers. In short, furry conferences are very similar to every other fandom conference, but also every other academic or trade conference.

Results

We collected a total of 360 surveys that have provided novel insights into the furry community. Because we had to rely on data collection at the conferences and through the virtual snowball sample, we cannot claim that the survey is a fair and complete representation of the furry community as a whole. That said, the furry fandom in general may look different from a representative sample of the overall, nonfurry, US population. First, given the relatively short history of anime fandom and its subsequent subgenres, we would expect that the population would be younger than the national average. Additionally, although we cannot be sure, given the prominence of the conferences and the online community in the way in which members engage their community, this actually may be a fairly representative sample of the general furry population. Similarly, we would expect the racial and ethnic diversity of the furry community to be closer to their younger age cohort than the less diverse overall US population. We make these conclusions with some level of confidence based upon our elite and participant interviews and on our informal observation of those in attendance at the conferences and those engaged in the online community.

One immediate observation from our data is that either we have dramatically under sampled African American or there are many fewer African Americans in the furry community than in society at large (figure 5.1). We only had 6 respondents out of 221 respondents who answered the race question with "identify as Black, non-Hispanic." We believe it is a sampling defect rather than an absence of African Americans in the community. Not only did we see specific programming for African Americans at the conferences, but we also observed a much higher ratio of African Americans at the conferences than our responses would indicate if accurate. Like the other groups, we expect that intersectional concerns and the fact that we are all white, meant we had a lower ratio of African American respondents than is present in the population. Out of the 221 respondents, 152 identified as white, 26 as Hispanic, 14 as Asian/Pacific Islander, and 14 as "mixed." The "other" category was chosen 7 times. The racial designations, like all of the demographic questions, parroted the Pew Research Center survey that we used as our form. We are uncertain if any pathologies are introduced into the responses by the way the race designations are listed. For instance, some respondents may have been offended or even just annoyed by the "Black, non-Hispanic" designation instead of "African American." In any event, although our racial clusters may not be representative of the community as a whole,

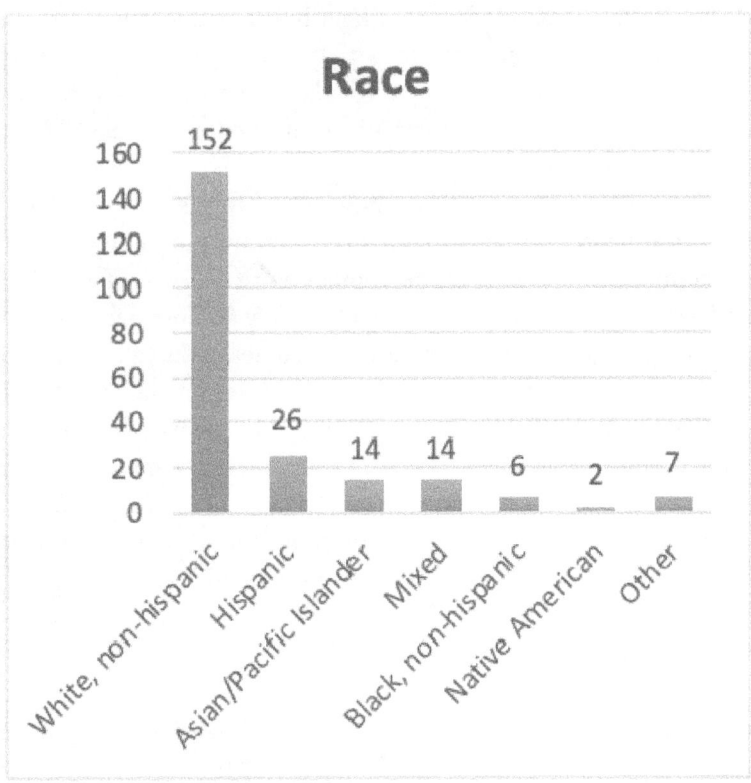

Figure 5.1. Race of Furries

we still can discern a great deal about the political attitudes and actions of the furry fandom.

As you might expect given the newness of the community and its reliance on social media for growth, furries are on the young side. Our survey participants skewed very young with 68 percent, or 150 out of 220 respondents, identifying as between aged 18–29. Like our other groups, we did not allow anyone who was under 18 to take the surveys. We had many more people under 18 want to enter the drawing or interact with us in this group than in any of the other groups, but, simply put, it was likely because there were many more children and young teens at these conferences. We had 49 respondents say they were aged 30–49, and 19 respondents say they were aged 50–64. Note that only 2 people out of the 220 claimed to be over 65. Like our other groups, we are certain some of our respondents chose younger brackets than their actual age and, in particular, we are certain perhaps as many as 25 to 30 people were really over 65. Still, although we take the data as it is, this may be another avenue for future research on agism even in very accepting but marginalized groups.

Despite our skepticism about how accurate the self-selected age brackets are, we do think in general this community is younger than our other communities as well as the population in general. In addition to the relatively short period of time that the furry fandom has existed, the continuity and growth of the community comes, in large part, through the ability of its members to engage over the internet and social media. Using memes, short-motion images (GIFs), chat rooms, and self-created digital graphics tend to be skills that younger Americans, socialized in the digital age, have in abundance.

Furries are highly educated or in the process of being highly educated. A very high, 86 percent, of those surveyed identified having at least some college education. That is, out of 221 respondents, 103 of them chose "some college," 70 of them chose "college graduate" and 17 of them reported attending graduate school. Because so many of our respondents are in the normal age bracket for those who are attending college, it is possible that a significant number of the 47 percent of respondents with "some college" will later convert to college graduate status or attain an even higher level of education.

We also attribute the relatively high "high school or less" group to the age cohort. Many of those respondents were about to graduate or had just recently graduated from high school. Like our other cases, we did not take surveys from or interview anyone under 18 years of age, although we did have several teenagers who were not yet 18 talk to us about the project at each site. We answered their questions but did not ask them anything. Younger children on occasion asked if they could have some of the candy from our table to which we always replied positively but that they would first need to ask whoever they were with.

A large number of respondents, 56 out of 219, declined to answer the question about income. Likely as a result of the young age of our respondents, 71 reported income of less than $20,000 and 21 reported income in the range of $20,000 to $29,000. While 55 people reported income in the range of $30,000 to $74,000, only 16 reported more than $75,000 (figure 5.2).

Also perhaps, at least in part, as a result of the age distribution, our respondents tended to be single. About 88 percent, or 193 out of 221, responded that they were single or never married (figure 5.3). With the benefit of hindsight, we should perhaps have not simply used the Pew Research Center survey categories. In retrospect, we were not especially well served by the Pew Research Center survey question design for this question and this community. The overlap of "never married" and "single" and the category for serial marriage were not especially useful for understanding a younger community like furries. We had more than

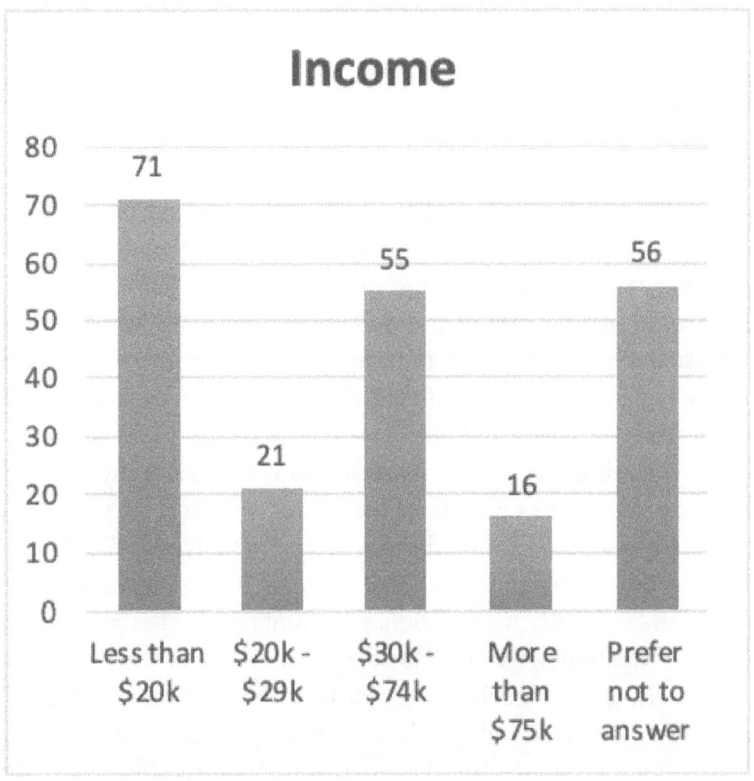

Figure 5.2. Income of Furries

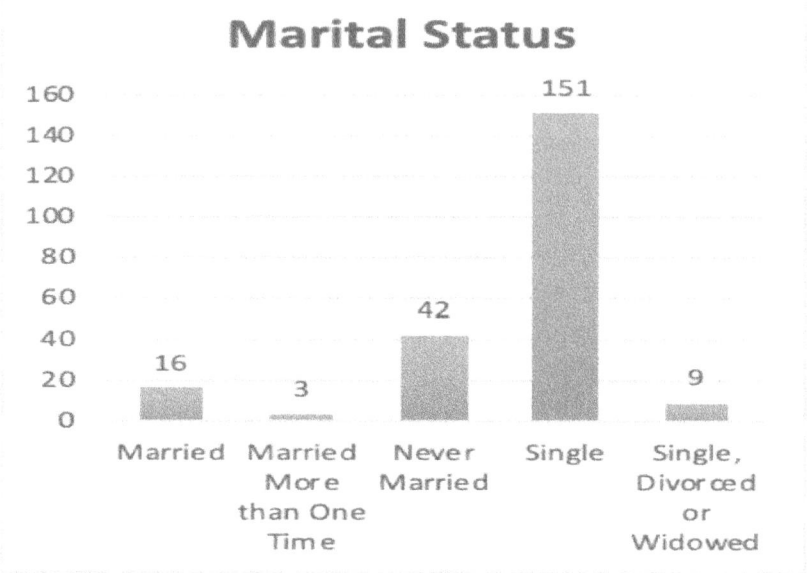

Figure 5.3. Marital Status of Furries

one respondent ask us the difference between single and never married. We were not able to come up with a reasonable explanation. We were told by an academic at a political science conference that the designation was meant in part to capture gays and lesbians with the "never married" designation to differentiate them from heterosexuals who were not married. We were not able to confirm this, but it makes as much sense as anything else we could think of.

Overwhelmingly, our furry respondents were certain they were registered to vote (figure 5.4). Out of the 212 respondents, 151 were certain they were registered, 14 thought they were probably registered, and 47 of them said they were not registered. Some of the younger respondents who had only recently turned 18 may account for a larger proportion of those who said they were not registered.

Politically, an overwhelming majority of our respondents identified as either Democrats or independent with independent beating Republican by about a 5 to 1 ratio and Democrats beating Republicans at about a 3.5 to 1 ratio (figure 5.5). Specifically, out of the 209 respondents, 113 identified as an independent, 74 identified as a Democrat, and only 22 identified as a Republican. That the largest segment of respondents claimed to be "independent" rather than a member of either of the two major parties bears some consideration. There are several possibilities that might explain why party identification is spread this way in the furry community. First, as we have discussed, this group is on the

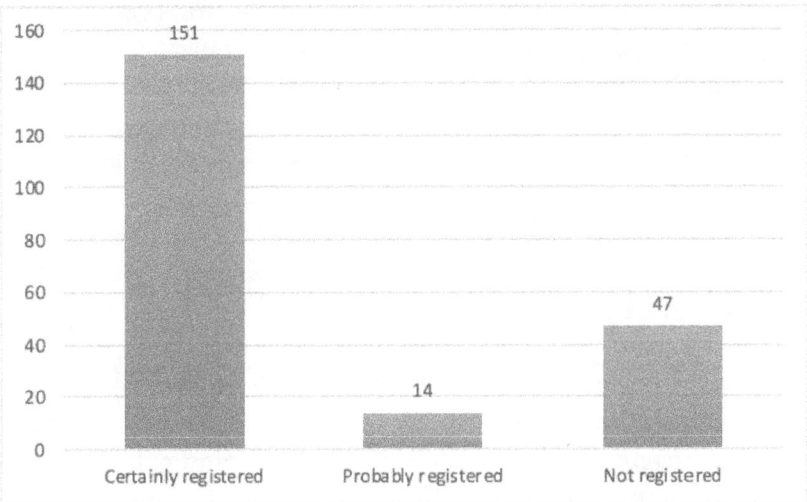

Figure 5.4. Furry Voter Registration

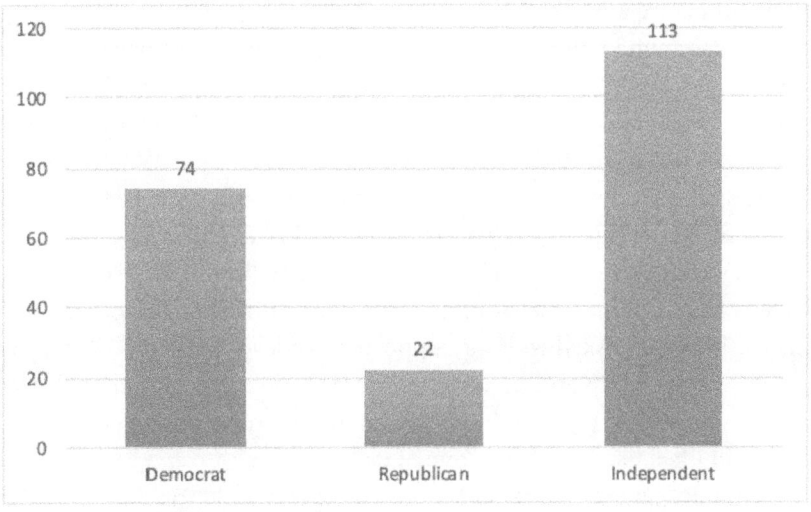

Figure 5.5. Political Party Affiliation

whole younger than the other groups we consider. Young people may have less affection for the two major parties as their political ideology and belief structure is forming. A twenty-year-old independent might very well affiliate with one of the two major parties as they begin to be concerned about a host of issues that coincide with being older. For instance, mortgage interest rates are not of a major concern to most twenty-year-olds. The half of our sample who are progressive and liberal, but are also apparently wary of the establishment parties, may simply be discouraged by polarization and the hostility between the parties. The furry community seeks to be one of harmony and peaceful interactions. Accordingly, it is possible those who find comfort and comity in the furry world find the political world too distasteful. Another possibility was suggested to us by a furry named Skipper. Skipper's fursona was a canine, although he did not engage in "puppy play" like is covered in the BDSM chapter. After he had taken the surveys, we asked Skipper about his political affiliation and he said he identified as an independent. When we pressed him as to why he was an independent instead of affiliated with a party, he said, while smiling and slightly shrugging, "Well, I mean, Skipper spends most of his free time online with other furries doing Skipper stuff. Peter the human doesn't really pay that much attention to what is happening on any given day, although he always votes. Peter pays attention to politics like a week and half before any election but Skipper doesn't care!"

We also met a woman called Skittles who, because of her multicolored rainbow hair, was given the nickname by coworkers at the beauty salon where she worked. We did not find out if Skittles had a fursona or fursuit, but she did identify as part of the furry world. When she finished up the surveys, she said, "Hey is Bernie [Sanders] a Democrat, a Republican, or an independent. He's the one I like." This was during the primary when Sanders was challenging Hillary Clinton, so we explained he was in the Democratic primary but called himself a Democratic Socialist. When we asked why she supported Sanders, she said, "The way is hair is all fuzzed up and he wears the same little outfit, he sort of looks like a muppet—if he would just put an animal nose on, he could be a furry. So I feel like he's sort of one of us."

While in general we expect more younger people to align with the Democratic Party than with the Republican Party, this is still a stark imbalance for Republican affiliation. The very high rate of independents is also remarkable. Given the large number of people who identified as independent, one might imagine the community might be up for grabs between the parties.

However, beyond party identification, the majority of respondents, 164 out of 185 respondents, placed themselves in a range of moderate to liberal and very liberal on a Likert scale (figure 5.6). Only 17 of the respondents identified as conservative with only 4 claiming the very conservative mantle. That ideological distribution roughly aligns with the general US population given the age cohort and educational attainment of our respondents. That is, young people between age 18 and 29 with at least some level of college education tend to identify as moderate to left-leaning in their political orientation. The old and less educated are more likely to be conservative but also much less likely to be furries.

Beyond the general descriptive notions of party affiliation and self-described ideology, we also were able to gain insight into the attitudes of the community about some specific political issues. The respondents found the Republican party to be too conservative in each substantive area that we asked about, including government spending (64 percent), abortion (81 percent), gay marriage (83 percent), and immigration

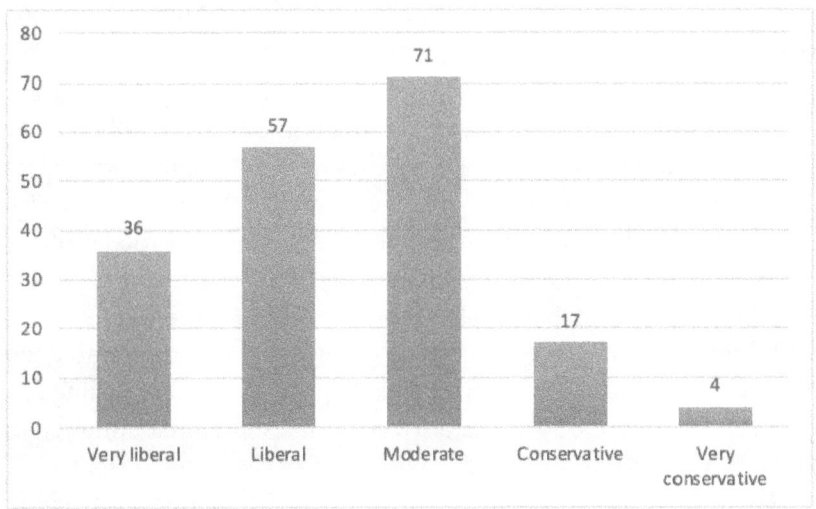

Figure 5.6. Political Ideology of Furries

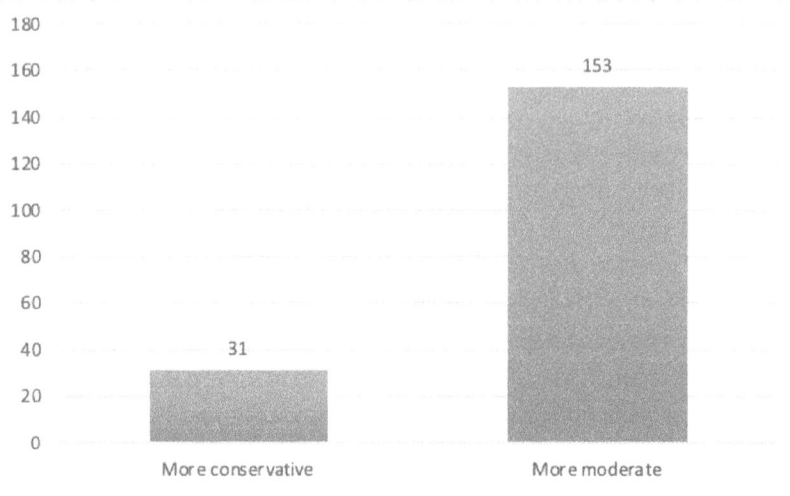

Figure 5.7. Furries: Would you like to see Republican leaders in Washington move in a more conservative direction or a more moderate direction?

(69 percent). Furries had similar feelings about Republicans in Congress, with 83 percent saying they wish leaders would become more moderate (figure 5.7).

Conversely, when asked the same questions on the same topics in regard to the Democratic Party, the plurality, if not majority, of respondents found the Democratic Party to be "about right" with the narrow exception of government spending (figure 5.8). Out of 178 respondents, 39 thought the Democrats were not liberal enough, 112 thought the Democrats were about right, and 30 thought they were too liberal. For gay marriage, 45 thought the Democrats were not liberal enough, 112 thought they were about right, and only 23 thought they were too liberal. In general, the furries did not think the Democrats were too far off on most of the issues, but they were somewhat split on whether the leaders should strive to be more liberal or more moderate (figure 5.8).

While the modal response from furries was that Democrats were too liberal with regard to government spending, no question regarding any political issue resulted in a majority, or even a substantial minority, of our respondents indicating the Republican Party was "about right."

About half of our respondents reported that they frequently speak with their friends and families about politics (figure 5.9). Out of our 185

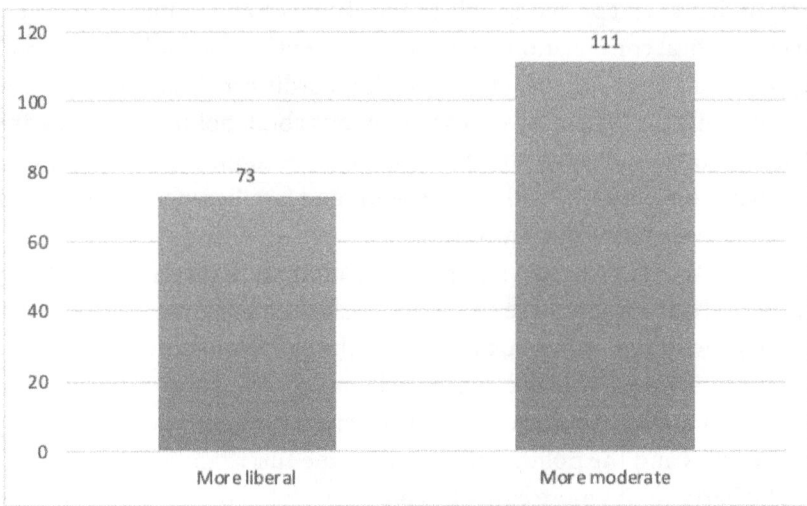

Figure 5.8. Furries: Would you like to see Democratic leaders in Washington move in a more liberal direction or a more moderate direction?

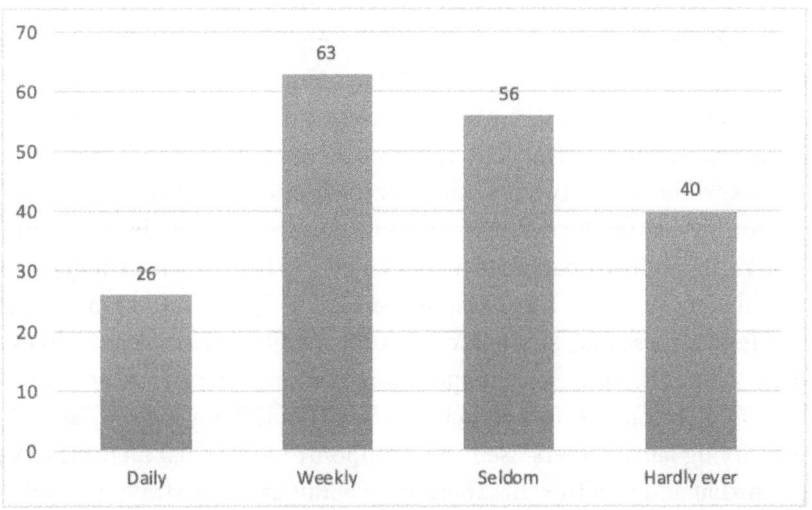

Figure 5.9. How often do you discuss political issues with your friends and family? Daily, weekly, seldom, hardly ever?

respondents, 63 reported weekly political conversations and 26 reported daily political conversations. Yet, 56 respondents chose the "seldom" category, and a large number, 40, chose the "hardly ever" category.

So, while the furries have strong opinions about politics, and they are left-leaning overall, only about half of them are comfortable engaging in political conversations with their friends and families while half choose to limit those political conversations.

Given that the members of the furry fandom that spoke with us or answered our surveys were conversational about politics and essentially familiar with the policy positions of both the Democratic and Republican parties, a party could conceivably mobilize this constituency with modest amounts of outreach. Of course, given the policy positions of the two parties and the policy preferences of the furry fandom, the Democratic Party would more easily be able to appeal to the community than the Republican Party without the Republicans reevaluating some of their policy positions. Like our other groups, the issues that involve personal autonomy, like abortion and gay rights, seem to be insurmountable barriers for the Republican Party to appeal to furries unless it dramatically changes its roster of and posture on these platform issues. Of course, at the moment, some Republican candidates have embraced attacking and mocking the furry community as an electoral strategy, so it seems unlikely that Republicans would be too concerned about accommodating furries while the party is currently actively alienating the community. We found that the furries who responded to the open-ended questions had an incredibly nuanced way of describing their own sexuality and sexual identity. While some responded succinctly that they identified as gay, lesbian, bisexual, straight, or asexual, many others took time to explain where they were on the spectrum of sexual interest and sexual attention. For example, one respondent listed "bi leaning straight" as their identifying label. Others used less commonly used sexual identities like pansexual and demisexual. There were about as many straight respondents as there were gay or lesbian respondents, at 26 and 23 percent respectively. About 38 percent of our respondents identified as bisexual, pansexual, or with other terms that are under the umbrella of bisexuality. We also found that about 9 percent of the respondents identified as asexual or demisexual. The asexual designations set the furries apart a bit from our other groups as no other group had more than one respondent who self-identified as asexual. Likewise, only the furries had demisexual respondents. We attribute this added nuance about sexual identity in the furry community to the relative youth of the community. These terms that go beyond gay or straight may be less familiar with older people so, accordingly, a younger cohort might have the vocabulary for the more nuanced categorization. Additionally, younger people are less judgmental about sex and sexuality than the older generations (see, e.g., Smith 2011). A community with an older profile might combine more shame and embarrassment with greater ignorance about the evolving definitions of sexual identity.

When we asked our respondents about what first drew them to the furry community, we found similar explanations as the other groups. Many respondents noted that the internet and close friends tended to be their first points of exposure to the furry community. Others mentioned a television show, movie, anime series, or toy. Interestingly, we found that 14 percent of our furry respondents mentioned that the driving factor that led them to discover the furry community was interest in or their own creation of art. The art aspect of the furry fandom sets it apart from the other communities we study. While there is a tremendous art community in BDSM, it was never mentioned as the driving or motivating factor behind someone's involvement in the community. Rather, for the BDSM community, the art aspect seemed ancillary. Art is a central part of the community and individual expression for a significant portion of furries.

Our respondents are committed to creating a nurturing community and the values that might accompany a broadly understood "come as you are or as want to be" safe space, as one fursuit designer explained to us at Anthrocon. One respondent noted that, "The community aspect is constitutive of the fandom." Another said, "The whole point is a place to belong, no matter your quirks." Almost all of the respondents said that being a part of the furry community had little to no effect on their political attitudes. Some noted that they perceived some common attitudes among the furry fandom. In particular, and perhaps not surprising, those we interacted with and took surveys from believe the furry fandom is widely supportive of gay, lesbian, bisexual, and trans rights. Many people also mentioned animal rights to us or referenced animal rights as a unifying issue in response to the open-ended questions about what political issues might motivate the furry community.

The responses to the open-ended questions indicate that, at least among those who took our surveys, there is a belief among the members of the furry community that, collectively, there is broad support, and even perceived unanimity within the community, with respect to LGBTQ rights, animal rights, and the need to combat media misrepresentations of the furry community. As one furry responded, "I do however, feel the fight for the right of gay marriage definitely effected the community. The community is full of people who are outcasts and I never have seen an instance of gay shaming in the community. I've seen plenty of it still online in the nonfurry community. But when it comes to being different to normal society, it's really welcoming."

While many seemed unaware of any political activity taking place within the community, or organized by the community, many replied that political fundraising around animal and LGBT rights was something they had seen and/or engaged in through their local furry community, with national furry groups, or with other individuals from the community who acted informally. One respondent noted that fundraising for a variety of different charities is common both online and at the conferences. In particular, some charities sponsor activities at the conferences and, in turn, the convention will sponsor that specific charity. For example, at Anthrocon, a therapy dog organization had their team of therapy dogs available for play and relaxation near the main entry to the convention center. Each convention had at least one no-kill animal shelter raising money and sometimes offering up pets for adoption. In our experience, the charities sponsored by the conventions or conferences are most often local animal rescue or shelter groups. Furries overwhelmingly responded that they think most politicians have either no idea who furries are or, if they did, that furries are sexual deviants. Representative comments include "they think we're all perverts" or "they want to think we're kinky because they're so vanilla." Generally, the furry fandom does not believe the general public is sympathetic to or supportive of them and certainly there is a common belief that the general public does not understand them.

There was a stark divide among respondents when we asked if the furry community should be more politically active, less politically active, or stay at its current level of political involvement. The plurality of respondents did not answer the question as asked and instead answered that participation was up to an individual. This is idea of individual level decisions being preferred is consistent with the general ethos of individuality in the furry fandom. The notions that you are alone are responsible for the nuances and characteristics of your fursona, and that no one can tell you that you are wrong, are critical to the constitution of the furry fandom.

Many identified a fear that political activity might cause division and discord within the community and those respondents preferred the community to be as apolitical as possible. Across many of the questions, we saw a significant number of respondents suggesting that it was the division that politics can cause, and not politics itself, that should be avoided in a community that prides itself on inclusivity and collegiality. One respondent who exemplified this perspective wrote that, "Unless the cause is unified; I feel that 'furry' isn't really a political party; Any more than 'gamers' or 'writers' are." This suggests to us that there may be limited avenues for mobilizing the furry community beyond rallying around broad consensus issues like LGBT rights and animal rights.

Implications

Furries are cognizant of the political landscape and have clear ideas about how candidates and parties might help or hinder their community. As a group, they have distinct preferences about the policies that should be implemented by the government and they share a desire to be free to pursue their best lives. The marginalization of the furry fandom has been driven by elite disregard and it can be overcome through education and mobilization (Bishin et al. 2021). Although minority groups are often faced with an inability to easily effect policy change, on occasion, politicians will defy their constituents to expand rights for minorities (Smith 2007; Bishin and Smith 2013). Moreover, once sexual minorities obtain rights, whether through litigation, legislation, or executive action, the public will move toward acceptance and support of that progress (Bishin et al. 2015). Accordingly, to the extent the furry fandom can converge on broadly agreed upon policies, like LGBT rights and animal rights, they should not fear mobilization.

6

All Bi Myself

Bisexuals in Non-Traditional Sexual Communities

In 2015, President Barack Obama became the first president to mention bisexuals in his state of the union speech. While President Bill Clinton mentioned "gays" in his 2000 state of the union speech, no president had ever before specifically acknowledged the existence of bisexuals, lesbians, or transgender people in this important forum. Just like presidents, political scientists have largely ignored the *B* in LGBT and have used "gay" as a short cut to describe anyone who is not heterosexual. The invisibility of bisexuals has been an issue for the larger LGBTQ community as well as for the academic and political world. While changing the politics and culture may be beyond our reach, we can make an initial foray toward extending the academic literature about bisexuals.

The *B* in LGBT is frequently neglected in the investigation of sexual minorities in American political processes (Smith 2011). In the bimodal model of sexuality assumed by much of the political science literature, and the academic literature in other disciplines as well, bisexuals are categorized and incorporated within the larger LGBT community simply as "not straight." The goals, challenges, and rights claims of the bi community are assumed to be identical to, and therefore subsumed within, the goals taken by the academic literature to be shared by all sexual minorities and in particular the gay and lesbian communities.

The literature reflects the reality of political discourse for bisexuals in the United States. They are mostly invisible both within LGBT communities and within our larger political system as a whole—some notable exceptions are the recent national attention given to openly bisexual Oregon Governor Kate Brown and Arizona Senator Krysten Sinema, who was the first openly bisexual member of Congress. Lesbians and gay men have historically served as the primary faces and forces of the LGBT movement, although in more recent times, many transgender activists have also emerged as recognizable figures with their own policy priorities, including fighting transphobia within LGBT communities. Bisexual "issues," while overlapping in some areas with other sexual minorities, are distinct as they face unique forms of discrimination including biphobia and monosexism, to name two examples, from both members of the LGT community as well as heterosexuals. In the end, the agendas of the major national LGBT groups have mostly not incorporated the rights-based claims of the bisexual community and, moreover, the broader public does not distinguish bisexuals as a marginalized group with specific concerns. Given this lack of visibility and power within the LGBT community, some bisexuals have instead found themselves better incorporated into polyamory and BDSM political communities, which provide them with a venue for political action and interaction as well as perhaps a more empathetic community.

Like other members of the LGBT community, bisexual Americans represent a distinct type of minority group because their members come from every demographic across the categories of age, income, religion, gender, ethnicity, socioeconomic status, and so on. The only universally shared traits or experiences are based on the animus from some sectors of society and a lesser roster of rights than heterosexuals. Bisexuals are born into a diaspora and, like most gay, lesbian, and trans people, do not find their community until they are adults. One significant difference for bisexual Americans is that at some points they may appear to many as indistinguishable from heterosexual Americans because they may form durable sexual or romantic relationships with members of the opposite sex. It is this ability to glide from the targeted group or lesser rights group, LGBT, to the dominant and full rights group, heterosexual, that perhaps accounts for the invisibility of the *B* in LGBT political science. At Olive Dell Ranch, we spoke with one man in his fifties, Michael, who explained "I dated girls and guys all through high school although in different ways. I dated girls just like everyone goes on dates and when I say I dated guys I mean we would hang out and then fool around after when we slept over at each other's houses. I thought everybody was like me until I went to college and realized there were plenty of guys that had never been with another guy."

We had not anticipated how many members of the polyamory, BDSM, nudist, and furry communities identified as bisexual. That surprise has punctuated some of the most important aspects of the communities we studied and their politics. In this chapter, we provide an overview of scholarship in bisexuality studies and how bisexuals have and have not fit into American gay and lesbian history. The second portion of the chapter presents the data from our open-ended surveys about the sexual orientation of our respondents and its relationship with the community and political aspects of our four cases. We argue that there are specific elements to these communities that provide a uniquely inclusive space for bisexuals. In this chapter, we use bisexual in two senses. In describing the history of bisexuality in the United States and in scholarship, bisexuality refers to the intimate attraction to more than one sexual or gender presentation. In our data sets, the survey respondents provided a variety of identities that fit within the historical umbrella notion of bisexuality. We present the respondents in their own terms and explain the differences between some of these lesser-known identities, and then aggregate them for the purposes of comparing these communities against larger demographic studies.

Bisexuals before Bisexuality

History has been replete with examples of social customs where individuals would engage in both same-sex and opposite-sex intercourse. The arrangements were, depending on the context, based on sexual attraction and/or a functional mechanism. In parts of Ancient Greece, the practice of pederasty served as an early form of sexual education. Alexander the Great has been noted for his attraction to men and women. Most of human history has lacked the language to describe what is now known as bisexuality. The Abrahamic holy books, for example, refer to sexual acts like "laying with another man," demonstrating that the language around sexual identity is a relatively new development. When the Irish playwright Oscar Wilde attempted to sue the Marquess of Queensbury and was subsequently tried and found guilty of sodomy (1893–1895), there was a debate about whether the decadence of the age led married men and women into same-sex affairs or if these individuals were only married and perhaps even only had children in those marriages for the sake of social expectations and to satisfy the demands of societal norms.

The beginning of the twentieth century marked an important and critical juncture in the societal discourse about sex and sexuality. The term "bisexuality" is first attributed to American neurologist Charles Gilbert Chaddock in his 1892 translation of *Psychopathia Sexualis* by the German psychiatrist Richard von Krafft-Ebing, the same source as the first use of the term "homosexual" (Angelides 2001). Moralists deemed those who engaged in intercourse with both men and women to be nihilists often led astray by decadence and secularity. Early psychologists and psychoanalysts, including Sigmund Freud, characterized same-sex attraction and the attraction to both men and women to be a pathology or slippage of psychological stability. Yet, the new terms "bisexual" and "homosexual" were initially seen only as designating the kind of sexual act suggested by the modifier attached to "sex." For example, social elites and the barristers during the trial of Oscar Wilde referred to the men with whom he had sex with as his homosexual partners, meaning partners in homosexual sex, and did not characterize Wilde as a homosexual or bisexual. It would not be until later when bisexuality would be a recognized as a legitimized identity rather than merely a description of a range of acts. So initially these terms that modified "sex" began as mere descriptions of types of sex acts or desires, but they were not descriptions of people or communities.

Prior to the advent of the gay rights movement, there are few examples of famous, openly bisexual Americans. There is historical debate about several famous Americans. For instance, there is some debate whether Walt Whitman was gay or bisexual. There have long been questions about the sexual orientations of the anthropologists Margaret Mead and Ruth Benedict, who shared a close relationship with one another throughout their lives. During this early period, perhaps the most famous openly bisexual American was the Pulitzer Prize–winning writer Edna St. Vincent Millay (Milford 2001). Despite the fact that the public memory might not recall many bisexual Americans from the early twentieth century, bisexuals were absolutely targeted by the state-sanctioned morality police shortly after World War I (Chauncey 1994). Homosexual sex and homoeroticism were seen by conservative reactionaries as a plague brought on by the decadence of the Roaring Twenties and the moral failings of recent European immigrants. The association between homosexual sex, decadence, and moral decay has been a recurring framework that was used in the public uproar around Oscar Wilde but dates back through at least the fourteenth century (Khaldun 2005, 288). Conservative reactionaries specifically targeted bisexuals with propaganda and campaigns. Bisexuals, they reasoned, were in fact innocent, straight Americans being corrupted by the bacchanalia of nihilist, godless immigrants. Often invoking Christian scripture, these moral crusaders would liken bisexuals to Adam facing sinful temptation from a serpent in the Garden of Eden.

Bisexuals, presumed or otherwise, were among the five thousand federal employees fired by the Truman and Eisenhower administrations during the Lavender Scare, the fear created by Joseph McCarthy that sexual minorities and other "moral subversives" were vulnerable to blackmail by Soviet counterintelligence, if they were not already communist sympathizers (Johnson 2004). Although McCarthy, a middle-aged lifelong bachelor, later rumored to be gay, left targeting gays to other operatives in his purge brigade, the movement stirred up the fear that closeted bisexual, gay, and lesbian government employees would betray the United States in order to keep their sexual activities hidden so as to avoid legal repercussions and intense social stigma. The irony should not be lost that a movement driven by extreme, right-wing, Christian nationalist, anti-immigrant, and anti-communist sentiments dramatically increased the stigma against homosexuality and homoeroticism and served as the political base that moved Joseph McCarthy from a fringe ideologue into a national political power broker. Had they not exacerbated the stigma and repression of sexual minorities, then the threat of the Soviet Union using a government employee's sexuality as leverage would have been *de minimis*. In other words, demonizing the private consensual sexual relations between adults actually could have created a reason for blackmail where acceptance of the private sex lives of Americans would have eliminated the threat.

In addition to their shared persecution with gays and lesbians, American bisexuals have been active members in the gay rights movement over its many decades and areas of focus. Yet, despite sharing in the hardships and triumphs of the gay and lesbian Americans, bisexuals have often occupied a contested position within the LGBT community and in scholarship. There are a variety of persistent stereotypes of bisexuals that have stigmatized them even within sexual minority communities. These include the belief that bisexuals are gays and lesbians who simply have not fully "left the closet," are in some sort of phase, or failed to fully understand their sexual identity. Others argue that being bisexual is not an essential political identity in the way that being gay or lesbian is because bisexuals in monogamous heterosexual relationships are able to live as bisexuals with full legal rights and without persecution while gays and lesbians must face legal and societal indignities if they are to enter into same-sex relationships (see Angelides 2001; and Sedgwick 1990). There are also enduring yet unfounded myths that bisexual women are the cause of HIV in lesbian communities (Eisner 2013).

The earliest academic work on bisexuality was in psychology and psychoanalysis before and during World War II. Led by an interesting combination of Freudians and zoologists, they largely understood bisexuality in reference to homosexuality and hermaphrodism in the animal kingdom. Much of this theorizing was nonscientific by today's standards in that there were no clinical trials, surveys, samples, or genetic profiles to substantiate their claims. They found that bisexual attraction was a process of learning mating rituals prior to peak virility or when the role as a desired procreator had passed. The ideas that bisexuality is transitory and subordinate to one-sex attraction would have a lasting influence in future sexuality research and uniquely undermined bisexuals' claims that their orientation could be enduring and grounds for an identity claim.

While bisexuality was a tertiary focus, the Kinsey Reports, published in 1948 and 1953, spurred a groundswell of research of sexualities that included bisexualities in studies even when research questions were often more focused on the differences between homo- and heterosexual people including their behaviors, attitudes, and development (Kinsey et al., *Human Male*, 1998; Kinsey et al., *Human Female*, 1998). The Kinsey Reports contained data from thousands of interviews of men and women about their sexual behavior, orientation, and desires. The reports were controversial for their coverage of sex and sexuality and through their use of nonrandom sampling methods. Despite the Kinsey Reports' methodological shortcomings, they were made popular for the Kinsey scale and for positing that sexual orientation exists along a spectrum ranging from fully heterosexual to fully homosexual. The spectrum approach to sexuality would also prove important for the attempts by academics, clinicians, and activists to challenge the natural-unnatural binary that had been ascribed to heterosexuality and homosexuality (see Van Wyk and Geist 1984). The Kinsey scale allowed researchers on bisexuality and bisexual activists to pivot the focus on sexual orientation as determined by who a person presently has sexual relationships with to include historical and prospective considerations of sexual attraction and behavior. In other words, this created the nomenclature to discuss bisexuality as an enduring trait rather than a specific and transitory series of choices.

Much of the first research specifically on bisexuals began off the momentum of Second-Wave Feminism in the late 1970's and early 1980's. While not used directly by many researchers on bisexuality at the time, the popular reception of Foucault's *The History of Sexuality Vol. I*, published in 1976, and his argument about the social construction of sexuality gave researchers in bisexual studies a wider and more hospitable audience. Bode's *View from Another Closet: Exploring Bisexuality in Women* comprised a series of extended interviews of bisexual women from which she found that heightened egalitarian and nonpatriarchal ideals in lesbian relationships were present for bisexual women regardless of the gender of their partner (1976). Bode also detailed how bisexual women have felt caught between and stigmatized by both straight and lesbian populations. Blumstein and Schwartz found that at least some people who might be labeled as bisexual did not choose that identity out of fear of stigma and a social expectation to label one's sexual orientation based on their most current relationship ([1977] 2000). MacDonald published a series of important theoretical papers critiquing the prevailing approaches to research and teaching about sexuality, which assumed that people are either straight or gay (1982, 1983). One of the more important and lasting critiques by MacDonald was the methodological errors in counting anyone with same-sex attraction as homosexual out of convenience (1981, 1983). MacDonald's seminal article in the *Journal of Homosexuality* used the limited existing research on bisexuality to challenge other ideas like bisexuality being purely and uniformly transitory (1981). This work is remarkable in that, while it relied on a thin amount of data, much of it has stood up to rigorous testing over time as bisexuality studies has grown into a field of multidisciplinary research. Klein made some of the first sustained forays of research specifically about bisexuality. His 1978 book, *The Bisexual Option*, and Klein Scale, which mirrored the Kinsey scale but measured desires over behaviors, were important for solidifying bisexuality as a topic of study and not purely a byproduct of studying heterosexual or homosexual sex acts.

In the late 1980s, several sex researchers used research on bisexuality to challenge some of the more recalcitrant ideas about sexual orientation that had lasted since the Freudians or that developed out of the Kinsey Reports. McConaghy reviewed the then recent findings on the effect of varying hormone level on gestational development and studies building off the Kinsey Reports to argue that many studies have systematically underreported the number of people within a straight-gay continuum because studies have overemphasized sexual activity over desires and fantasies and have persistently let coding convenience obscure and override the issue of variation in sexuality (1987). Ellis et al. treated sexual orientation as a continuous variable rather than a Likert variable in the Kinsey Reports, which enabled them to find that there was a far more even distribution than previously understood in the extant research of the time (1987). Coleman designed a nine-prong model that moves away from sexual categorization being determined by the genitalia of sexual partners to include gender identity, social permissibility, sex-role identity, fantasies and ideations, and current relationship status (1987). Coleman's model, while not seminal, does bear some similarities to the current portfolio of identities that our survey respondents used that will be explicated later in this chapter.

The movement in bisexuality studies to de-emphasize sexual activity as the sole criteria was stalled by the "performative turn" that swept up sexuality studies along with many fields in cultural studies (Angelides 2001). The performative turn further complicated bisexuality's place in sexuality studies, fueled by the impact of performative turn in cultural, gender, and sexuality studies. The performative turn was ushered in by West and Zimmerman's "doing gender" conceptualization in 1987 along with Butler's *Gender Trouble* in 1990. Drawing on the work of ethnomethodologists and semioticians, the performative turn challenged an array of essential definitions of gender, particularly those on biological grounds. They argued that our social identities are things that we fashion by drawing from a varying of social norms and symbols, and how both the ways we express these identities and how they are recognized by others matter. Butler's *Gender Trouble* also had an important effect in propelling the performative turn, having a greater influence outside of the social sciences than West and Zimmerman. Butler found that the presentation of one's gender and gender expectations have noticeable class, racial, and sexual variations such that to be a "good" man or women can mean noticeably different things (1990). Feminist and queer theorists expounded on that argument to claim that bisexuals were in a state of limbo because, while there are heterosexual and homosexual sexual arrangements, they do not believe that there are bisexual sex acts. Sedgwick is one of the more notable theorists making this argument.

While not a return to the behaviorism of past decades, the performative turn complicated the academic study of bisexuality. Because bisexuality had long been hidden under the banner of homosexuality, there were fewer, if any, clear bisexual symbols. Performative bisexuality was difficult to conceptualize in a bimodal world. Schilt and Westbrook note how that, while not rejecting the performative framework, people's performances are deeply informed by heteronormativity, a world where being and doing heterosexual is the norm, expected, and socially approved orientation (2009). Darwin identified how traversing male and female stereotypes makes it difficult for transgender individuals to perform their gender in a society that has generally seen gender and sexuality as a starkly contrasted binary (2017). As a result, bisexuality was read as sometimes performing straight and sometimes performing gay or lesbian but never as performing as bisexual.

Sedgwick's work encapsulates how the performative turn was a helpful step forward for understanding homosexuality but not bisexuality. Despite correctly critiquing the notion that sexuality exists in a straight-gay binary, Sedgwick argued that bisexuals, in sum, do not count as sexual minorities as gays and lesbians do because, she argues, bisexuality is not an essentially political identity (1990). To identify and be identified as gay or lesbian entails a political cost (and even more so at the time Sedgwick was writing). A gay or lesbian American could be fired, lose custody, and face a variety of other legal and social consequences for being out. Sedgwick claimed that a bisexual in a heterosexual relationship or marriage could avoid those legal and extralegal risks without limits on their sexual behavior. In other words, because bisexuals have an easier time passing as heterosexuals, they are not true sexual minorities. We strongly disagree with this analysis and think it is deeply flawed on nearly every level.

Bisexuals are often stereotyped as hypersexed and predatory, and that negative portrayal has been used to push the trope that bisexuals, regardless of the relationships they may currently hold, are a danger to children and other innocents. If bisexuals need to be closeted in order to avoid stigma, then it is at best a frivolous distinction between closeted bisexuals, gays, and lesbians. Because homophobes consider bisexuals to just be "gay," bisexuals suffer all of the same discrimination gays and lesbians do in straight world, compounded by some serious levels of lack of acceptance in gay world. Sedgwick's highly influential work demonstrates the segmented progress afforded to sexual minorities, even by those most likely to be their allies. In essence, Sedgwick might have said feminine lesbians or straight presenting gay men cannot be discriminated against because they can hide in plain sight. This is an untenable argument. It is also worth noting that many foundational theorists of sexuality and queer studies, such as Foucault and Butler, reject the presence of a sex binary while also utterly failing to evaluate the liminal position of bisexuality (Callis 2009).

Although the performative turn posed challenges to the more nuanced approaches to the study of human sexuality, its popularity in several disciplines helped balloon interest in sex and gender studies. The growing public health research on LGBT Americans in response to the HIV/AIDs epidemic also brought more disciplines into a more routine engagement with sexuality in general and bisexuality in particular.

Just as Klein founded the American Institute of Bisexuality in 1990, there was a convergence of writers and academic who sought to understand the unique nature of bisexuality and the lives of bisexuals as a community unto itself. The institute continues to manage the peer-reviewed *Journal of Bisexuality Studies* and maintains several affiliations with academic research associations. Hutchins and Ka'ahumanu edited the anthology *Bi Any Other Name: Bisexual People Speak Out* in 1991. The volume is a compilation of nonfiction, fiction, poetry, and art that communicates aspects of bisexuality and being a bisexual from the vantage of bisexual writers and artists. It was a publishing success and is credited with launching or expanding the careers of many of the contributors, further developing bisexuality literature.

Colker provides in important comparative legal study of how Americans who hold bisexual, multiracial, and nonstandard categories can face intersectional discrimination and how legal binaries generally reinforce discrimination within the American public. Most importantly, discrimination serves to gird the in-group hierarchies and power structures even within marginalized group (Colker 1996). Colker's work is a useful example of intersectional feminist literature, drawing on Collins's notion of a matrix of domination, or how the multiple marginalized identities can create compounded and unique forms of discrimination (1990). Intersectional approaches to feminism and queer studies have been fruitful intellectual homes for bisexuality studies given their shared foundational aim to challenge hegemonic stereotypes of the LGBT community as really only meaning gay white men with high socioeconomic status. Of course, throughout our discussion we have noted the intersectional challenges of membership in these out-groups and race, and a bisexual identity in combination with these other identities simply adds an additional layer of complexity as well as an additional avenue for discrimination or approbation.

Hertzog found that bisexual voters, which at the time of his study, were estimated to be about the same size as the Latino American vote, were not politically mobilized, and did not overwhelmingly support one political party (1996). He found that the 1992 presidential election had some effect of unifying lesbian, gay, and bisexual partisan support and was especially notable for the larger LGB community with turnout at 72 percent. Hertzog attributes the political mobilization and effective turnout efforts to the Reagan and Bush administrations woeful handling of the HIV/AIDS epidemic. This was a driving force not only behind the LGB turnout success, but also as the origins of consolidation behind the Democratic Party. Of course, the Republican Party also began to publicly demonize gays and lesbians in the Reagan era and then used fearmongering about gays and lesbians to drive turnout for decades (Smith 2007).

Activism about bisexuality and activism by bisexual activists are different but overlapping topics. As mentioned earlier, American bisexuals have been targets of stigma and persecution similar to that of gays and lesbians. Leaders of bisexual activism have been at the frontlines in the efforts to fight discrimination and enact pivotal LGBT civil rights protections. Rather than retread the entire history of the LGBT rights movements, we will highlight the unique efforts and actions within and outside of the LGBT community directly targeted toward the promotion of the well-being of American bisexuals.

In the 1970s, author and activist Stephen Donaldson, during a period of frustration caused by the feeling of bisexual exclusion within the gay rights movement, put on an impromptu workshop during the 1972 Friends General Conference, an annual meeting of quakers in North America. The conference, which had more than one hundred attendees, culminated in the release of the Ithaca Statement which is commonly acknowledged as the first pronouncement of a bisexual rights movement (Donaldson 2005). Brenda Howard, a militant activist who organized efforts to oppose the Vietnam War and promoted the causes of both the feminist and the LGBT movements over the span of three decades, is credited with leading several advances in LGBT rights as well as the normalization of efforts on behalf of the bisexuals in the LGBT community. Howard is commonly referred to as the "Mother of Pride," who, along with Donaldson and gay rights activist L. Craig Schoonmaker, is credited with the initial concept of Pride.

Bisexuality organizations began appearing locally and nationally in the United States in the late 1980s and 1990s. This period saw many sex rights organizations appearing on the political scene in response to the Reagan neglect and malevolence toward the victims of the HIV/AIDS epidemic. These groups provided important social and health services for the LGBT community. Gay and lesbian organizations had existed since the Mattachine Society in the 1950s, with local and national groups growing rapidly after the Stonewall Riot in 1969. Bisexual activists and groups have strategically worked in concert with and even sometimes in opposition to other LGBT and marginalized groups. Take, for example, the Bisexual Political Action Committee (BiPAC). BiPAC was founded in New York City in 1989 by radicals seeking to combat the erasure of bisexuals from the LGBT community. At the near height of the HIV/AIDS pandemic, they disrupted the meetings and events of LGBT organizations that had been overlooking or even rejecting that plight of bisexual New Yorkers during the crisis. BiPAC worked in coalition with community organizations serving specific LGBT ethnic groups to help cast a broader light on the mass pain and isolation that the pandemic caused. Since then, groups like the Coalition for Unity and Inclusion adopted reformist approaches to move toward greater bisexual inclusion in LGBT organizations and activism. These strategies of assimilation into the LGBT movement included adopting more conventional campaigning strategies and assuaging LGBT organization elites. Other groups have drawn members from existing bisexual and broader LGBT organizations to focus on specific issues. One example of this is Bialogue, which was created in the mid-2000s in response to a controversial and deeply flawed study suggesting that as many of three-fourths of bisexuals were, in fact, gays or lesbians in denial (see Carey 2005). The Bisexual Network of the USA, Inc. (Bi/Net USA) was another group that formed in 1990 shortly after the first Bisexual National Conference. Bi/Net USA worked with many of the previously mentioned groups and activists and is perhaps best known for the efforts of former organization president Wendy Curry and activist Tom Limoncelli to harness the power of nascent social media platforms for strengthening a national bisexual community and for facilitating bisexual activism. Gary North, one of the founders of Bi/Net USA, also published a popular and important newsletter beginning in 1988 called *Bisexuality: News, Views, and Networking*.

The bisexual community also has important regional and national conferences and conventions in addition to working groups within most major LGBT organizations. Bisexual Empowerment Conference: A Uniting, Supportive Experience (BECAUSE) is a large annual bisexuality conference held in Minneapolis, Minnesota, which marked its thirtieth anniversary in 2023. Administered by the Bisexual Organizing Project since 1999, they have expanded their reach by partnering with Fritz Klein's American Institute of Bisexuality to put on the Bisexuality Research Conference USA (BiReCon USA). It was inspired by a long-standing bisexuality research conference in the United Kingdom. Klein and other activists also organize the International Conference on Bisexuality.

Bisexuality+ Day is an internationally observed annual event on September 23 aimed at promoting the visibility of bisexuals and the bisexual community, the history of bisexuality, and the unique challenges faced by bisexuals. The day was initially created in large part due to the efforts of Wendy Curry along with other Bi/Net USA affiliates Gigi Raven Wilbur and Michael Page. The "+" has been added over the years to recognize the array of identities that can be seen falling under or adjacent to the umbrella of bisexuality like pansexual, polysexual, queer, omnisexual, and other identities that we detail later in the chapter. We noted in the furry chapter a wide range of these types of identity designations, but we saw wide spread use of these terms in all the communities (save the nudists). Bisexuality+ Day, whose official title varies slightly between countries and sometimes changes slightly from year to year, was first officially recognized in 1999. This came after nearly a decade of national and international conferences put on by several bisexuality awareness groups and, later, by coalition building with larger LGBT organizations like the Gay and Lesbian Alliance Against Discrimination (GLAAD).

Bisexuality+ Day slowly began to be recognized by official governmental actors through a combination of efforts and interests of local groups and politicians as well as a general proliferation of awareness days, weeks, and months aimed at highlighting marginalized groups, their grievances and interests. Berkeley, California, is usually referred to as the first municipality to formally recognize Bisexuality+ Day, doing so in 2012 (Associated Press). Importantly, the White House hosted its first bisexual-specific event the following year, a meeting with a few dozen bisexuality advocates and members of the Obama Administration, which raised the profile of bisexuality as a discreet topic of concern. Also in 2013, the British Parliament, through its Minister for Women and Equalities, recognized Bisexuality+ Day. It is worth noting that the British Parliament was in a coalition government led by the Conservative Party, whereby decrees, proclamations, and policies required a consensus from politicians of various ideological approaches. In 2014, groups like BiNet USA drew from this momentum to create a Bisexuality Awareness Week which was meant to have six days of events and programming, and then culminate with Bisexuality+ Day. In 2021, Democratic Pennsylvania Governor Thomas Wolf made the first proclamation in recognition of Bisexuality+ Day by a governor on behalf of a state government. In the proclamation, Wolf noted, "I am proud to recognize your determination to face and overcome adversity, your commitment to breaking down barriers, and celebrating individuality. I am confident that this example of conviction, compassion, and camaraderie will inspire many for years to come" (Martin 2021).

The bisexuality flag consists of three horizontal bars, one pink, one lavender, and one blue. It was created by Michael Page and unveiled on December 5, 1998. Page believed that the rainbow flag symbol of gay and lesbian pride did not resonate with most bisexuals simply because it did not expressly acknowledge them. The pink has been a common color used in gay and lesbian activism since the pink triangle was affixed onto suspected gays and lesbians by the Nazis during the horrors of the Holocaust. The blue is meant to contrast with the pink. As a playful acknowledgment of gendered color, the blue denotes opposite-sex attraction. The addition of the lavender represents a blurring of the heterosexual-homosexual binary. Lavender is also an important color in the history of LGBT rights. Examples of the symbolic role of the color lavender in the LGBT struggle for rights include the Lavender Scare discussed earlier in this chapter and the Lavender Menace which is a reference to radical feminists who protested the Second Congress to Unite Women in 1970 over the program's explicit exclusion of lesbians and of issues that lesbians were facing.

In hopes of demonstrating that bisexuality is an enduring sexual orientation, both during one's life and historically, groups like the American Institute of Bisexuality actively catalog famous bisexuals. The American Institute of Bisexuality identifies famous individuals who are believed to have been attracted to both women and men using things like personal correspondence, photographs, or diaries among other types of evidence. This approach by sexual minorities advocacy groups and activists of outing other sexual minorities and ascribing sexual orientations to the dead is a controversial method of achieving representation. The premise behind this approach is that by showing some sexual minorities succeed only by hiding some fundamental aspects of themselves, the disclosure can demonstrate the harm caused by discrimination. The goal of this strategy is to assert the idea that all people should be able to have the same opportunities available to heterosexuals. One complexity to this strategy of outing is that some of those who may have publicly had relationships with both men and women may never have identified as bisexual, which raises the question whether you can be bisexual without self-identification as such.

They could have identified as heterosexual, gay, lesbian, queer, or any orientation available at the time. It is precisely because of the stigma of identifying as gay or bisexual that public health research often uses the phrase "men who have sex with men" or "MSM" to account for the gap between behavior and identity. Resolving the dubious question whether one is truly bisexual or not is beyond the purview of our research. However, this question demonstrates that bisexuality is in fact an essentially contested identity just like our other groups.

The essayists and novelist Gore Vidal may perhaps be the earliest well-known American bisexual; he also spent time and effort to combat America's conservative attitudes toward sex, homophobia, and biphobia. His 1948 novel, *The City and the Pillar*, caused an uproar over its matter-of-fact portrayal of same-sex attraction. Sex was a central, but certainly not exclusive, facet of Vidal's cultural criticism. In this way, he harnessed the controversy over his bisexuality and provocative writing on bisexuality and sex. Vidal, a consummate provocateur, was also relatively protected from any potential public backlash; he was born into an elite, upper-class family with ties to two American political dynasties such that financial security was never a real concern for him. He fearlessly told Esquire in 1969:

> We are all bisexual to begin with. That is a fact of our condition. And we are all responsive to sexual stimuli from our own as well as from the opposite sex. Certain societies at certain times, usually in the interest of maintaining the baby supply, have discouraged homosexuality. Other societies, particularly militaristic ones, have exalted it. But regardless of tribal taboos, homosexuality is a constant fact of the human condition, and it is not a sickness, not a sin, not a crime ... despite the best efforts of our puritan tribe to make it all three. Homosexuality is as natural as heterosexuality. Notice I use the word "natural," not normal. (140)

Vidal would remain one of the few major American figures to be so open about being a bisexual. Two reasons may help account for this exclusivity in the famous bisexuals club. First, the immense social stigma faced by sexual minorities throughout the twentieth century and continuing at least among white evangelicals and conservatives hangs as a threat over anyone who might choose to disclose their bisexual identity

(Bishin et al. 2021). Second, the use of the queer identity nomenclature by sexual minorities and in the arts became increasingly commonplace in the 1980s, perhaps at the expense of bisexual nomenclature. Many Americans with both same- and opposite-sex attractions began identifying as queer out of a particular desire to not be defined by their sexual orientation. Being queer was often in direct response to the gay panics of the 1980s that sought to bar gays and lesbians from teaching in public schools and the homophobia generated by social conservatives during the HIV/AIDS crisis. In contrast with Vidal's often explicit demarcations of gay and bisexual characters, movements like New Queer Cinema utilized homoerotic themes and imagery but without explicitly categorizing the nature of the sexual attraction.

The British artist David Bowie told a reporter for *Playboy* magazine in a 1976 profile that he identified as bisexual, at an early stage of his career (Crowe). Bowie retracted the statement a few years later during an interview with *Rolling Stone* magazine (Loder 1983). Almost twenty years later, Bowie reflected on the how that unfolded, telling the magazine *Blender* that:

> I had no problem with people knowing I was bisexual. But I had no inclination to hold any banners or be a representative of any group of people. I knew what I wanted to be, which was a songwriter and a performer, and I felt that [bisexuality] became my headline over here for so long. America is a very puritanical place, and I think it stood in the way of so much I wanted to do. (Collis 2002)

Bowie, an icon of glam rock whose use of cosmetics and gender-nonspecific costuming was iconic for challenging gender norms, found that sexual norms in the United States were far more rigid than in the United Kingdom and were something that would be difficult if not impossible to challenge, even for someone with his celebrity and public image.

George W. Bush's reelection to a second term in the White House is, for many, the most defining event of the 2004 general election in the United States, but this election carries a different significance to those concerned about the LGBT community or rights contestation generally. On that same day in 2004, eleven states approved state constitutional amendments explicitly banning same-sex marriage, all by ample margins indicating widespread resistance to same-sex families. Smith demonstrates widespread homophobia which results in the "electoral capture" by the Democratic Party of gay and lesbian Americans (Smith 2007). Electoral capture may happen in a two-party system when a specific demographic group very closely aligns with one political party but not the other (Smith 2007; Frymer 1999). In essence, one party has no interest in gaining votes from the demographic groups captured by the other so the party that has captured the group does not have to expend political capital to deliver policy because the group will never vote for the party that ignores or attacks the group.

The electoral capture of the LGBT community in the 2004 general election resulted in sparse direct appeals from Democrats for votes from the LGBT community because Republicans were actively attacking the LGBT community. Karl Rove, the primary strategist for the George W. Bush campaign and no fewer than thirty state and national races that year, proudly admitted that the Republican Party made a concerted effort to use LGBT rights as a state-level wedge issue across the country to motivate conservative—defined as antigay—voters. The Republican's success using LGBT rights issues as a wedge came in no small part due to the Republican base being more energized around the issue than the Democratic Party. Since the LGBT community was solidly voting Democratic at that time, the issue might not meaningfully boost turnout for Democrats.

American bisexuals began forming bi-specific regional and national communities in the United States during the late 1980s and early 1990s. The Bisexual Resource Center was founded in 1985. Originally known as the East Coast Bisexual Network, they were one of the first organizations in the United States specifically focused on the needs and interests of American bisexuals. Headquartered in Boston, Massachusetts, the Bisexual Resource Center continues to run a litany of local and national programming, including managing one of the most comprehensive archives of bisexuality in the United States. They also publish a biannual national resource guide that catalogs the country's bisexual clubs, organizations, research, and media. The Bay Area Bisexual Network was founded in 1987 in San Francisco, California, after succeeding the San Francisco Bisexual Center, and it continues to provide important social, informational, and wellness resources to the bisexual community. Reflecting the changing identity nomenclature, they have since been renamed as the Bay Area Bi+ and Pan Network. In 1987, San Francisco hosted the National Bisexual Conference shortly after the Second National March on Washington for Lesbian and Gay Rights. This is believed by many to be the first national forum on bisexuality. Also, recall that the national newsletter BiNet USA was created around this time. Activists and writers also led efforts to amplify the voices and perspectives of bisexual Americans to build better public and academic understandings of bisexuality.

Bisexual Americans have been increasingly well-known on their own right, especially since the landmark decision in *Obergefell v. Hodges* that upheld the constitutional right to same-sex marriage. In the public sphere, politicians are increasingly sharing that they are bisexual. Most are following in the footsteps of Governor Kate Brown of Oregon and Senator Kristen Sinema of Arizona, the first openly bisexual governor and member of Congress, respectively. Senator Kristen Sinema from Arizona, who previously served in the House of Representatives, holds the distinction of being the first bisexual member of both chambers of the legislature. While open bisexuals continue to be underrepresented in politics and have had slower gains in representation than openly gay and lesbian politicians, there has been an increasing number of openly bisexual candidates running for elected offices nationwide. Outside of political representation, classic characters of American media like Superman are being written as bisexual. We are fortunate to have conducted this research at a time of increased visibility of bisexuals and bisexual studies and during a time where the important point of understanding American bisexuals as a political force of their own has taken traction.

Data Collection

Our data on bisexuals consists of a consolidation of all the open-ended responses where the respondent self-identified as something other than gay, lesbian, or straight (or some equivalent). We have previously explained our data collection process for each group, so we will not repeat that here.

Results

We asked our survey participants how they described their sexuality in the open response series of questions. We anticipated that respondents would express a myriad of possible identities beyond just sexuality. While they did in fact report intersectional identities, like "white Catholic mother who is into BDSM," the most interesting aspect of the responses was that in each of our survey groups, the respondents expressed a wide range of sexual orientations. In order to effectively convey our findings, we have presented our data in two ways. First, we tabulated the frequency of each response based on the specific identities and orientations that they provided. We chose this approach because we were determined to allow these people to communicate their orientations as our respondents understand them because the differences between these labels, no matter how subtle, are meaningful to the respondents. Second, we took the raw tabulations and ascribed each response a master code, merging some orientations, for example bisexual and pansexual, into their conventional umbrella terms. We did so in order to compare the composition of these communities to the LGBT population in the United States and the overall American population. By presenting the data in these two ways, we hope that we avoid the appearance of erasure within some of the sexual minority groups while nonetheless being able to compare their representation in these groups with prevailing demographic analyses of LGBT Americans. Our respondents freely made identity claims that sometimes appear to be conflicting, which we observed as a reflection of deeply inclusive element to these communities that is not always present in the LGBT spaces or understood by heterosexual Americans.

There are a variety of terms that appear in our samples that may be helpful to explain at the outset. We present these definitions in no particular order. Asexual refers to the lack of or low level of sexual attraction to others, regardless of sex or gender. Demisexual refers to only feeling sexual attraction to someone after developing a deep emotional connection to a person and is also sometimes refered to as "gray-A" or gray-asexual. Androsexual refers to a sexual attraction to stereotypically masculine traits, irrespective of the sex or gender of the person exhibiting those traits. Gynosexual denotes a sexual attraction to stereotypically feminine traits, irrespective of the sex or gender of the person exhibiting those traits. Heteroflexible refers to someone with a predominately heterosexual orientation who also may on occasion have a sexual attraction to those of the same sex/gender but has this attraction or engages in sexual action far less frequently. Conversely, homoflexible refers to someone with a predominately gay or lesbian orientation who may have infrequent feelings of sexual attraction to or sexual activity with someone of the opposite sex/gender. Bicurious is also used to mean either homoflexible or heteroflexible or uncertainty about some aspect of sexual attraction. Omnisexuals have a sexual attraction that is not informed by another person's gender or gender presentation, but rather is gender blind sexuality. Pansexuality is the sexual attraction to people of all sex/gender identities. The technical distinction between pansexuality and bisexuality is that, for example, a bisexual person might be attracted to men and women and not attracted to nonbinary or trans people whereas a pansexual person would find people in all groups potentially sexually attractive. Queer is an umbrella term that can refer to a wide range of nonstraight sexual orientations and/or a sociopolitical position to not have one's sexual orientation ascribed a label. Sapiosexuality refers to people whose sexual attraction is derived from the intelligence of another person and is not informed by their sex/gender or physical presentation.

Bisexuals in Polyamory

The polyamory community that we sampled provided the most diverse list of sexual orientations in our study (table 6.1). Not only was there a rich display of nuanced, thoughtfully described sexual orientations, but there were several orientation configurations that help illustrate some aspects of sexual orientation that many people might overlook or be unfamiliar with. Several of the respondents who identified as bisexual and another orientation noted that they use bisexual as an understood umbrella term to others while finding a narrow sexual orientation to be more resonant with who they are. There was also one respondent who noted that they identify as bisexual, queer, gay, and lesbian. This may seem contradictory at first glance. Our respondent also shared that they are genderfluid which means that, because their gender identity is not

TABLE 6.1. Sexual Orientation of Polyamorists Raw Responses

Sexual Orientation of Polyamorists (Raw)

Orientation(s)	Number
Asexual	1
Androsexual	1
Bisexual	43
Bisexual and Pansexual	4
Bisexual and Queer	2
Bisexual, Queer, Gay, and Lesbian	1
Bisexual and Sapiosexual	1
Demisexual	1
Gynosexual	2
Heteroflexible	18
Homoflexible	1
Homosexual	5
Pansexual	20
Pansexual and Asexual	1
Pansexual and Demisexual	4
Pansexual and Homoflexible	1
Pansexual and Omnisexual	1
Pansexual and Queer	2
Queer	9
Queer and Gay/Lesbian	3
Queer and Omnisexual	1
Heterosexual	38
Heterosexual and Homosexual	1
Heterosexual and Heteroflexible	2
Sapiosexual and Pansexual	2
Bisexual and 2+ Bi-related identities	3
Did not answer	20
Total	188

fixed, the terms that they use to describe the kinds of sexual attractions they have also must, accordingly, be fluid. With the exception of one furry, polyamorists were the only group in our sample to use queer as a marker of their sexual orientation.

We then aggregated the responses into the most common sexual orientation terms: gay/lesbian, bisexual, queer, asexual, and heterosexual. You will note in table 6.2 that some of the totals changed while others remained the same. That is because demisexual (gray-asexual) was merged with asexuality just as pansexual, heteroflexible, and homoflexible were coded as bisexual. We kept androsexual and gynosexual unaggregated because those terms refer to an attraction to the behavior of others and not to appearance or sex organs. One in five of our respondents identified as heterosexual compared to nearly half (about 49 percent) who identified as bisexual. We were surprised to see that only about 3 percent of respondents identified solely as gay or lesbian. Only 7 of the 20 respondents who used more than one umbrella term identified, in part, as queer which may be used to refer to the bisexual umbrella or as a political position about sexual labels. That means that more than half of those who identified with more than one umbrella term were contesting boundaries because of how those identities resonated with who they are depending on the space, time, and the fluidity of who they are as dynamic individuals.

TABLE 6.2. Aggregated Sexual Orientation of Polyamorists

Sexual Orientation of Polyamorists (Aggregated)	
Orientation	Number
Lesbian or Gay	5
Bisexual	91
Queer	9
Asexual	2
Heterosexual	38
More than 1 Umbrella Term	20
Did not answer	20
Andro-/Gyno-sexual	3
Total	188

Bisexuals in BDSM

The members of the BDSM community in our sample used far fewer terms to describe their sexual identities than did the polyamorists in our study (table 6.3). However, about 60 percent of our respondents also shared their role within BDSM scenes as a key identity without our explicit prompting. Regarding their roles within BDSM scenes, 13 respondents shared that they were dominant, 12 submissive, and 10 switched roles. One respondent identified as "kinkysexual," which we were told later by an elite that this term refers to finding sexual attraction or arousal from specific kinds of sexual activities or fantasies, and without regard to the sex or gender of potential sexual partners.

After aggregating our survey response, we found that more than one-third of our respondents identified as bisexual (about 40 percent) (table 6.4). About a quarter of all respondents identified as either gay or lesbian. Only one person identified exclusively as queer and there were no asexual respondents. We found about 17 percent of our respondents identified solely as heterosexual. Finally, about 7 percent of our respondents identified with more than one of the more common umbrella terms.

TABLE 6.3. Sexual Orientation of BDSM Respondents Raw Responses

Sexual Orientation of BDSMPolyamorists (Raw)	
Orientation(s)	Number
Bisexual	16
Bisexual and Pansexual	1
Bisexual and Queer	1
Heteroflexible	1
Homosexual	14
Homosexual and Homoflexible	2
Kinkysexual	1
Pansexual	4
Queer	1
Heterosexual	10
Heterosexual and Heteroflexible	1
Did not answer	6
Total	58

TABLE 6.4. Aggregated Sexual Orientation of BDSM Respondents

Sexual Orientation of BDSM Respondents (Aggregated)

Orientation	Number
Lesbian or Gay	14
Bisexual	22
Queer	1
Asexual	0
Heterosexual	10
More than 1 Umbrella Term	4
Kink-based Orientation	1
Did not answer	6
Total	58

Bisexuals in Nudism

The sexual orientation responses of the nudists we surveyed were consistent with their stressing that they did not see nudism as having anything to do with sex. They also provided the fewest number of sexual orientation labels out of the four groups in our study. As detailed in table 6.5, one-third of our respondents (about 34 percent) did not provide an answer at all, with some saying that they did not believe that their sexual orientation was relevant to questions about nudism and their identity as a nudist.

When we aggregate the responses, we see the nudists look a bit more like the general population might if we ignore the 44 nonresponses (table 6.6).

About three-quarters of the respondents who answered the question, or 66 out of 86, identified as exclusively heterosexual which is significantly more than our other three communities. Heterosexual nudists constitute the only majority sexual orientation in any of our four sexual minoritized communities. That number combined with the large nonresponse rate resulted in only about 15 percent of the respondents sharing that they were not straight or a minority with respect to their sexual orientation. If the nonresponses are excluded, about 23 percent of the respondents were something other than heterosexual.

TABLE 6.5. Sexual Orientation of Nudists Raw Responses

Sexual Orientation of Nudists A(Raw)

Orientation(s)	Number
Asexual	2
Bisexual	9
Heteroflexible	1
Heterosexual	66
Homosexual	4
Homosexual and Bisexual	1
Homosexual and Demisexual	1
Homosexual and Homoflexible	1
Open	1
Did not answer	44
Total	130

TABLE 6.6. Aggregated Sexual Orientation of Nudists

Sexual Orientation of Nudists (Aggregated)

Orientation	Number
Lesbian or Gay	4
Bisexual	11
Queer	0
Asexual	2
Heterosexual	66
More than 1 Umbrella Term	3
Did not answer	44
Total	130

Bisexuals in the Furry Fandom

The furries in our sample provided a wide range of the previously mentioned identities. As documented in table 6.7, the asexual furries used language to communicate the gender or sex of individuals that they may become romantically attracted to and form an intimate bond with while not having a sexual attraction. In that sense, panromantic refers to the

TABLE 6.7. Sexual Orientation of Furries (Raw)

Orientation(s)	Number
Asexual	4
Asexual and Panromantic	1
Bisexual	30
Demisexual	3
Demisexual and Asexual	1
Demisexual and Heteroromantic	1
Heteroflexible	3
Heterosexual	34
Heterosexual and Asexual	1
Heterosexual and Open	1
Homosexual	31
Homosexual and Homoflexible	3
Pansexual	10
Queer and Homosexual	1
Did not answer	16
Total	140

forging of intimate, asexual bonds with individuals irrespective of one's sex or gender while heteroromantic refers to only finding those kinds of bonds with someone of a different sex or gender.

Furries responded with the most balanced distribution of responses (table 6.8). While only 30 respondents identified as "bisexual," once additional terms for something that might fall under an umbrella of bisexuality are combined, we see 53 out of 140 respondents could be generally referred to as bisexual. About a quarter each of the respondents identified as being either heterosexual or homosexual, with about 24 percent of responses each. While younger Americans are more likely to identify as nonheterosexual and the furries in our group were the youngest on average compared to the other three groups, our BDSM respondents had the lowest proportion of respondents identifying as heterosexual.

TABLE 6.8. Aggregated Sexual Orientation of Furries

Sexual Orientation of Furries (Aggregated)	
Orientation	Number
Lesbian or Gay	33
Bisexual	47
Queer	0
Asexual	5
Heterosexual	34
More than 1 Umbrella Term	5
Did not answer	16
Total	140

Why So Many Bi's?

Three of our four samples had more than one-third of respondents identifying within the umbrella of bisexual: about 49 percent of the polyamorists sample; about 38 percent of the BDSM sample; about 34 percent of the furries sample; and about 9 percent of the nudists sample. We suspect that the percent of nudists who identify as bisexuals actually to be higher, and that the relatively low 9 percent is an effect of the large proportion of those sampled who declined to answer. Because sex and sexuality are more taboo in the nudist community than in the others, suppression of expressions of bisexuality or any other type of nonheterosexuality may be subject to shame- and stigma-associated silence.

While all our communities had a robust distribution of sexual orientations, the consistently high proportion of sexual minority orientations greatly exceeds the estimated 3.5 percent of the overall American population that identifies as lesbian, gay, or bisexual. The large proportion of bisexuals in our samples may appear surprising but is, in fact, consistent with the broader, but underacknowledged, demographic studies that have found bisexuals to make up half of the LGB population in the United States (Gates 2011). There were dramatically more bisexuals in our study than gay or lesbian respondents, even though we maintained queerness as a separate category. As illustrated in table 6.9, there were at least 1.5 bisexual respondents

TABLE 6.9. Differences in the Number of Bisexual and Gay/Lesbian Respondents

	The Percentage of Bisexual and Gay/Lesbian Respondents*		
	Bisexual	Gay/Lesbian	Difference
Polyamorists	48.4%	2.7%	+1820%
BDSM	37.9%	24.1%	+157%
Nudists	8.5%	3.1%	+275%
Furries	33.6%	23.6%	+142%

*Difference was calculated using the full numbers, whereas numbers have been reported to the nearest tenth of one percent

for every gay or lesbian respondent. There were more than 17 times more bisexual polyamorists than there were gay and lesbian polyamorists.

It is remarkable that, even in the nudist community, which has the lowest proportion of bisexual and gay/lesbian respondents, there are still more than five times the bisexuals and twice as many gay/lesbians in our sample as there are in the overall population of the United States. The fact that bisexuals were represented far more than gay/lesbian respondents is consistent with the radical inclusivity of these communities. We did not observe anything in our data to suggest that the biphobia or bisexual erasure that exists in different LGBT communities would have any parallels or comparable fissures to latch onto in these four communities. Polyamory, by normalizing and embracing that it is natural for people to be sexually attracted to more than one person and to normalize entering multiple concurrent relationships, is underpinned by the acceptance of all kinds of possible consensual, adult relationships. The BDSM community is driven by different kinds of attractions, kinks and activities, where the roles in scenes are not determined by one's gender or sexuality but, instead, by individual preferences about power, domination, restraint, and pain. As discussed in chapter 4, the nudists in our study had a deeply libertarian sensibility toward sexuality, often adamantly saying that sexuality is and ought to be irrelevant to the life of the community. What makes furries special in this regard is that individuals in this community maintain nuanced, multifaceted personalities that draw from anthropomorphized ideals and who they are in the present moment. Furries cultivate fursonas that are genuine in a variety of social situations but that frequently have nothing to do with sex. Whereas the LGBT community has been constituted in large part on the basis of their oppression based on sexuality, we find that the BDSM, polyamory, nudists, and furry communities are created and maintained through a variety of interests and activities that, by not centering on sex, are particular inclusive for bisexuals.

7

A Passel of Perverts

A Comparison of These Non-Traditional Sexual Minorities

These four large groups are each viewed by the mainstream culture as comprised of sexually deviant people who embody perversity and spend their time with like-minded perverts who share their sexual pathologies. What the general public does not appreciate is that each group is a vibrant, nuanced, supportive community wherein individuals seek out their best lives among a cohort of the like-minded. Of course, for many of these people, their ideas about their best life and the community to which they belong include the sex and sexuality dimensions of their lives and identities. Each group also serves as a safe harbor community for those who identify as bisexual or otherwise not aligned with the gay-straight dichotomy which has been culturally constructed and embraced by much of the academic literature and society at large. The purpose of this chapter is to consider the groups together as a one consolidated group in order to discern how they are alike, how they are different, and how they have responded collectively as one outlier community to the mainstream culture that frames them as perverts. We are, as far as we know, the first researchers to pool these four groups together. We are not, however, the first to notice some connections or overlap among some of the groups. Recent scholarship has considered the role of kink in a feminist understanding of sex and sexuality and the navigation of relationships (Rehor and Schiffman 2021). Sex and sexuality in the virtual world have led to a plethora of research and some of those investigations consider the intersection of a few of our groups including, for instance, BDSM and furries (Brookey and Cannon 2009). Generally speaking, the "second life" literature—the nomenclature used by those who study and engage with the various virtual worlds, focuses on the activities and motivations behind those in the second world and not the "in real life" person behind the avatars. The most prevalent, if still scarce, literature that simultaneously engages more than one of these groups is to be found in psychology. For instance, a small but robust literature exists about how sex therapists might engage those patients who are in the kink community (see, e.g., Britton and Dunlap 2017). Additionally, as might be expected, the scholarly literature on deviance occasionally considers the intersection of two or more of these groups, including for example, nudism and BDSM (see, e.g., Giami 2019). We diverge from these scholarly treatments not only by including all four of our groups in the project, but also by avoiding the initial framing of the project as a study of pathology or deviance. Rather, we view these collectives as composed of people who are entitled to respect and dignity despite, and perhaps even because of, the non-traditional lifestyles they have chosen.

The four communities interact with their members and operate in very similar ways. The most obvious similarity among the way the groups interact with their members are the conferences in the BDSM and the furry fandom realms. By analogy, the nudist resorts can be thought of as standing conferences, so to speak, and the polyamory support groups, with their routinely scheduled meetings, serve the same purpose. The critically important group task of creating safe spaces, constructed for the express purpose of facilitating membership and mingling in and among the community of shared interests, has been an essential function for each of these communities. The main attraction at these events, whether the BDSM or furry conventions or the nudist resorts or the polyamory support groups, is the opportunity to openly associate with your tribe. Additionally, social media spaces take on similarly important functions across these groups. Indeed, according to many of the elites we interviewed, social media platforms have been the driver of membership expansion and maintenance for each of the groups. Although we spoke with many people in each group that grew up in a family enmeshed in the community in question, many other people identified themselves as what we might consider first generation kink. For those people who became members of these communities apart from any familial history, guidance, or tradition, social media platforms, movies or television shows, and good old-fashioned books were the first exposures to these groups. Of course, many of our interviewees were first made aware of the groups through a friend or acquaintance, but in general, even if their first contact happened in real life, they were directed to read a book or visit a website or chatroom to find out more. The opportunity to explore these communities in a solitary fashion from the safety of your own environment may make joining in the fun an easier and less risky proposition. The conferences always have specific programming for first time attendees and anyone who thinks of themselves as new to the group. The organizations affiliated with the groups frequently have formal mentoring structures for helping the new people, and they all have informal mentoring structures. Likewise, the nudist resorts have orientation tours and acclimation buddies who help raise the comfort levels of the newly nude while the entire concept of polyamory contemplates a support system within the relationship orbit. In sum, each one of these communities create specific institutional structures to ensure the newly engaged embrace the community at their own pace and in an approachable way.

In addition to the overt and unambiguous efforts at nurturing people new to the communities, they also hold safety and consent as a core value. Each of these groups suffers from a generalized caricature of sexual perversity and depravity as the defining, perhaps even dominant, characteristic of the identities affiliated with the groups. The most overtly sex-focused group is clearly the BDSM community, but even for them, membership in the community goes well beyond sex acts, and even the BDSM role playing itself sometimes entails intercourse and orgasm and sometimes does not. Each of these groups demands informed consent for any physical or even emotional contact as a normal aspect of interaction among members of the community. Equally important, each community is about a great deal more than sex even while each community celebrates a wide continuum of sexuality in a host of ways. Each community goes to great lengths to protect minors and demonstrate in overt and obvious ways that the groups are not predatory and do not tolerate predation toward minors or anyone else. One member of the BDSM community explained to us, "These spaces are the safest spaces that can be found. Our community would never tolerate rape, abuse, or bad behavior unless it is a scene. In other words, we only do what has been agreed to by everyone in advance–you don't get that kind of respect or safety out in the vanilla world!" Recall "vanilla" is the term often used by those in the BDSM lifestyle to describe those who do not engage in BDSM.

There are a few important differences among the groups. Nudists in our data were outliers in two very specific ways. First, they were less racially diverse than the other groups. We previously discussed this may be the result of some level of white privilege wherein nonwhites may simply be less willing to embrace the societal risks and costs of nudism than their white counterparts. This could also have been a function of where we collected data. Two of the nudist locations were inland in exurban Southern California in an area with a very low population of African Americans. The third location was several hours north of Philadelphia. These disproportionately white locations may have contributed to our smaller than expected sampling of African Americans and Latinos. We asked an African American male at the Olive Dell Ranch facility about minority communities and nudism and he suggested that nudism did not have the long history with Black and Brown communities that it did with whites. He explained further, "Prancing around the woods with your drawers off is something rich white people have been doing since before the Civil War. For communities of color, stripping down in front of other people is a newer concept." His explanation seems credible given the distinctly upper-class drivers of nudism as a historical movement. Still, it remains to be seen if we simply had a bad draw in our samples or if nudism actually is a more homogenous and white community than the others. Also, recall we observed much more racial diversity in the other groups than our survey responses revealed. In addition to the white privilege issue, we also attribute some of this to our virtual snowball technique as the closed online groups may be more racially homogenous (Bouchillan 2014).

Nudism is also an outlier community in another interesting dimension. During the conventions for the furry fandom and the BDSM community, we invariably saw a substantial amount of programming specifically for the trans community as well as gender nonconforming members of these communities. We also saw, talked with, and took surveys from trans members at each convention we attended. Our interactions with the polyamory community also encompassed members of the trans community as well as self-identified gender nonconforming people. We are not aware of a single encounter with a trans person in the nudist enclaves. To be completely clear, we may very well have interacted with members of the trans community and were simply unaware of it. However, we met no one who self-identified as trans and we saw no obvious physical manifestations—like chest reconstruction scars—on anyone we met. Likewise, given the inherent androgyny of many hairstyles, once clothes are taken away, nonconformity to gender becomes much harder to overtly signal. It may simply be that the nudist community is not felt to be particularly welcoming to those trans people who are constructing their presentation nonphysically. And again, we almost certainly suffered in this respect from our rural locations. Had we gone to more cosmopolitan venues, we may have met people who revealed their trans or gender nonconforming status to us. We think this raises a question that needs to be answered with additional research in the future. Specifically, are there groups that get marginalized by the groups that are already marginalized or is there broader solidarity among the nonmainstream. It is also possible that what might be thought of as subgroups—African American nudists, trans nudist, gender nonconforming nudists, and so forth—might have their own network of facilities and support structures that we simply did not uncover. We did have one man, Walter, at the Pennsylvania nudist resort tell us that sometimes groups rent out a significant portion of the facility at any given nudist resort. When we pressed him to expand on what he meant by groups, he said, "Oh, you know, like the Ohio State Alumni group or bikers or something." Accordingly, there may very well be subgroups that are smaller than the nudist population as a whole that have escaped our inquiry.

While the members of the groups were, at times, skeptical of us as outside interlopers, their skepticism manifested itself in different ways. The polyamorists frequently asked us if we were poly at the outset of our conversations and would shrug or show some other slight physical sign of disapproval when we told them we were not. However, even after the slight expression of disapproval, they then would also patiently explain things to us. None of the polyamorists just walked away from us once they found out we were not in polyamorous relationships. When we told one woman that none of us identified as polyamorous, she looked us up and down, and said, "Well, not yet anyway," and then laughed before giving us an interview. When the Furries asked us whether we were part of the community it seemed to be little more than polite conversation or small talk. The most common response to our revealing we were not Furries was akin to "Oh, okay." Not one single person seemed to be offended or more suspicious of us because we were not part of the community. The members of the BDSM likewise were nonplussed when we confessed we were not "in the life" and almost without exception they made suggestions for things we should try if we wanted to "have a taste of it" as one man in Dallas said. The nudists were more overtly judgmental but in a playful way. Invariably at some point, someone would nod their heads or point at our tan lines and say something like, "You aren't a nudist are you?," which was frequently followed by a gentle laugh or chuckle.

If we turn to the political attitudes and actions of these groups, we can see collectively they are politically aware and involved.

We begin by noting that the groups look very similar to the general population when they self-report whether they are registered to vote or not (figure 7.1). While nudist self-report a slightly higher level of voter registration, that might be more attributable to the whiter, older, and wealthier slant of our participants for that group rather than a nudist-specific preference for voting. One interesting point to be gleaned from

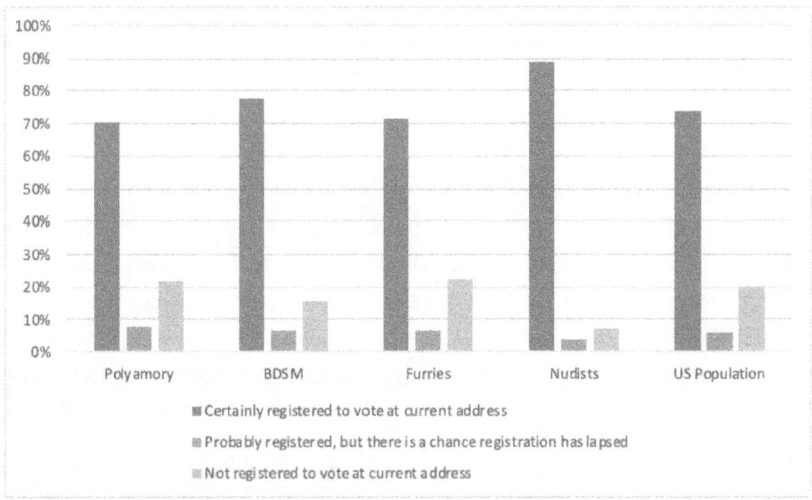

Figure 7.1. Voter Registration Comparison
*Source: Pew Research Center for the People & the Press, July 2013.

this data is that our respondents are not outliers from the rest of the citizenry. In other words, by this metric, our groups are not obviously less political than the rest of the country and should, perhaps, collectively be on the radar of the political parties as a potentially powerful voting bloc.

Of course, voting is a more important political act than simply registering to vote, and here, we see more variation (figure 7.2). We again see nudists as somewhat more active politically, and again, we attribute that to the demographics of our nudist respondents. We attribute the lower participation than the general public in the other groups to two factors. First, these groups trend a bit younger than the population as a whole and older people are more likely to vote, so these groups would be expected to vote at a lower rate. Second, while we found few political issues that unified the groups other than abortion and gay rights, these groups are all invisible to politicians and the political parties. In other words, no one is asking for their political support so it could simply be they are waiting to be inspired to vote by candidates who will give them a reason to vote.

If we compare the party affiliation of the groups, we can see they are all more Democratic leaning than the general public. Note that nudists had a significantly larger affiliation with the Republican Party than the population as a whole. Furries and polyamorists have a greater claim to political independence, and those who identify as BDSM and as nudists lack a majority in any one party (figure 7.3).

When we compare political ideology across the groups, the first thing to note is that each group has significantly larger clusters of people who identify "very liberal" or "liberal" than the population in general (figure 7.4). Perhaps reflective of the large numbers of liberals in these communities, other than nudists, those who identify as "very conservative" represent a much smaller share of the communities than among the general public. Again, the nudists are outliers in that they appear closer to the same distribution as the general population than the other three groups. Nonetheless, the nudists are still more liberal or very liberal than the general public.

Recall that combined, these groups encompass somewhere between 10 and 35 percent of the adult population in the United States. It might be time to rethink the conventional wisdom that the United States is a

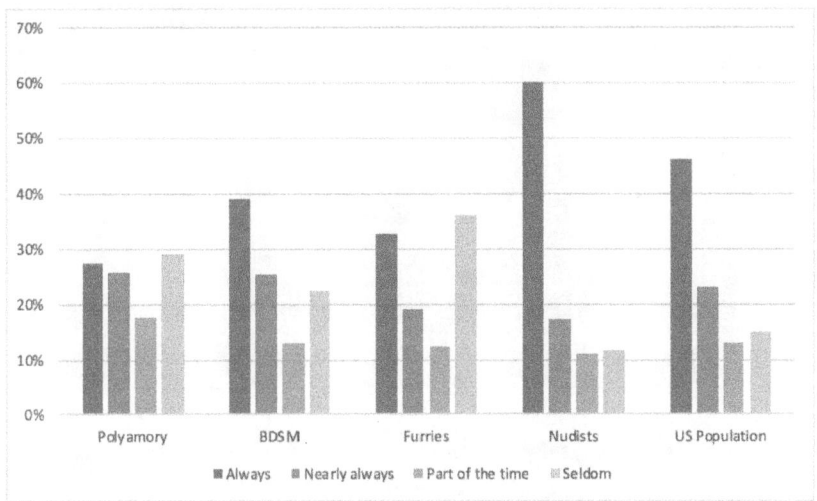

Figure 7.2. Voting Comparison
*Source: Pew Research Center for the People & the Press, July 2013.

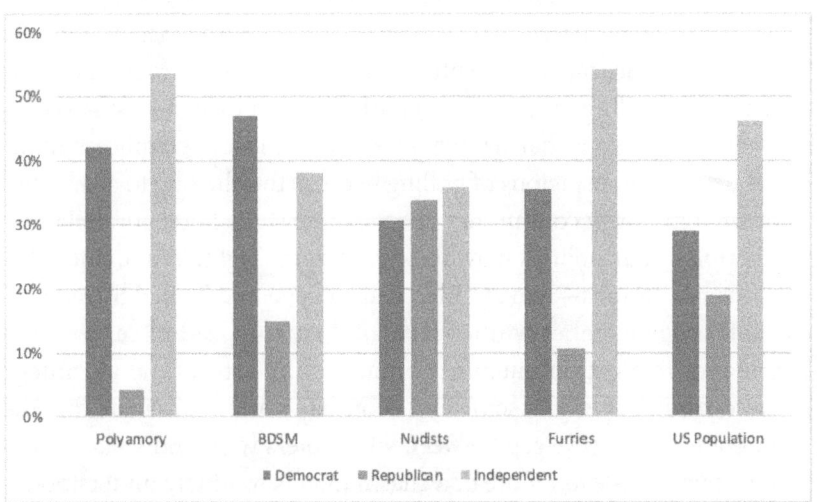

Figure 7.3. Party ID Comparison
*Source: Pew Research Center for the People & the Press, July 2013.

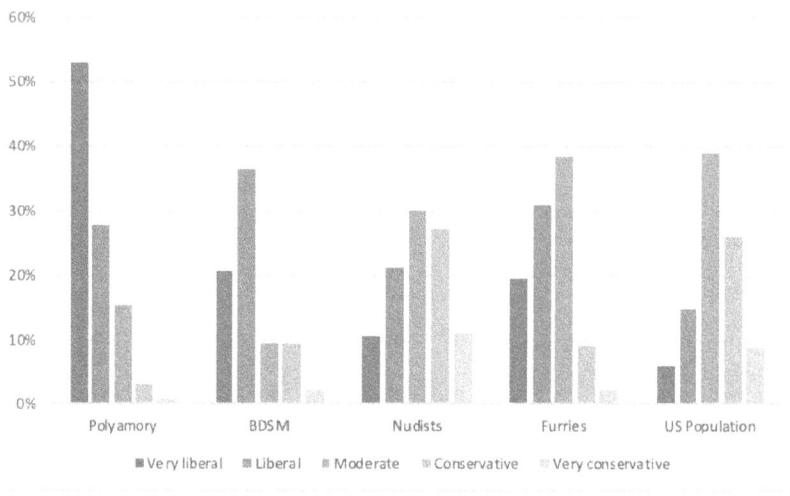

Figure 7.4 Ideology Comparison
*Source: Pew Research Center for the People & the Press, July 2013.

center-right country. Rather, it seems plausible that large swaths of the public have been missed by the measurement approaches of conventional polling. So-called shy voters may be more numerous than projected by the polling industry and may be reticent to answer surveys for very different reasons than are hypothesized. If in fact a significant number of people are suspicious of polling because they belong to a large but disfavored minority community like those we study here, our collective perception of our politics may be skewed to the right. While undoubtedly our institutions—like the Electoral College, the United States Senate, and single member winner-take-all districts—lead to center-right dominance in election outcomes because of the structural advantage given to rural and to a lesser extent suburban voters, it may be that the democratic deficit (the gap between what voters want and what policymakers pursue) is even more of a chasm than is routinely understood.

Beyond the broader questions about democracy and representation that this study raises, we note that these communities share a concern for privacy of intimacy and of association that may be shared by other sectors of the polity. Still, those who hold strong beliefs about the right to associate, or not, based on religion are often the same sectors of society that aggressively discount intimacy or association that seem unusual to them. It is difficult to imagine a scenario where a baker who objects to creating a wedding cake for a same-sex couple would be enthusiastic about creating a wedding cake for a "throuple," regardless of the genders involved. The right of privacy in intimacy and the right of association inherent in a right of privacy of intimacy may be inhibited in legal and cultural domains by the conservative legal voices with outsized power on the federal judiciary. That we have some Supreme Court justices that do not believe adults have the right to choose to use contraception suggests a conservative judiciary substantially out of step with the cultural realities and likely to be overtly hostile to each of these groups both individually and collectively. After all, Justice Antonin Scalia and Justice Clarence Thomas both claimed objection to equal rights for gays and lesbians in part because of the claimed fear of inevitable polygamy should marriage equality occur.

An additional dimension of this research that bears further consideration is the extent to which the groups have some overlapping members. We saw some polyamory adherents in all the groups. We also saw some aspect of social nudism in all the groups. Of course, it is possible that we observed the two behaviors that do not require special training for safety or special gear in all the locations because they are the simplest ones to export as it were. There were clearly BDSM adherents who simply kept a low profile at some of the non-BDSM locales. For instance, we interviewed a middle-aged man at Olive Dell Ranch who had dyed his pubic hair bright pink, he had several penis piercings, and he had a small whip tattoo on his hip just to the left of the pink shock of pubic hair. While he did not bring BDSM up in our conversation, the implications of genital gear, the whip tattoo, and his overall presentation suggests he is a member of the BDSM community as well as a nudist.

At Frolicon, we repeatedly saw one younger man, perhaps in his early twenties, walking around the venue completely nude with the exception of his shoes and a fanny pack that held the clothes he needed for the elevator and his wallet. Near the end of the convention, we talked with him briefly and he told us he identified as a nudist and that this was his first BDSM convention. He became interested in nudism after going to a nude beach in his teens and he became interested in BDSM after seeing pornography that depicted it. Recall we interviewed a furry in Pittsburgh who was also a nudist and grew up in a nudist family. Conceptually, once someone embraces breaking the rules of society one particular way, they may find it easier to break additional rules in new (to them) ways. Any of these groups could be a gateway to the others. For instance, someone who is already enmeshed in BDSM might be more open to becoming a member of the polyamory community than someone who does not identify as polyamorous. Additionally, the groups are perhaps also more readily accepting of others who do not conform, so the risk of disapproval when joining another group drops if you are already member of a nonconforming group.

Given the way that these groups welcome and are significantly populated with bisexuals, it is possible that people in these groups find judgment free experimentation or lifestyle sampling among the other groups as a matter of course. In other words, once some taboos are broken, safe space that offers an opportunity to break other taboos may be more inviting and less intimidating than for those people who are, in the words of the kink community, vanilla. Exploring one kink or alternative community may simply make people more comfortable exploring a different community as well. Moreover, whatever one may enjoy about any one of these specific communities can be found in abundance in some form in the other communities.

Another characteristic that these communities share is an ethic of body positivity and acceptance of all participants. For example, we observed very large people out and proud in each of these communities. These very large people, who the medical profession would refer to as morbidly obese, were in full regalia at the furry and BDSM conventions, fully nude at the nudist resorts, and fully comfortable in the polyamory groups. More importantly than their full participation was the appearance of complete and utter acceptance of them by the other members of the group with more standard physical builds. As an aside, this group of very large people deserve additional study. The very large may also be thought of as deviant via some societal norms. Their ubiquitous presence in the communities we studied and, equally important, their ubiquitous acceptance are phenomena worth exploring. While we did not construct our research to get at the politics and political activities of this particular population, the academy has begun to take sexuality and extreme obesity into account. For example, Conyers and Calhoun (2020) have a chapter in the recently published *Deviance Today* about obesity.

Indeed, it seemed that any sort of negativity or critical judgment of others based on appearance or extant characteristic was simply not tolerated or considered part of the normal discourse. Most of the conventions had "newbie" panels about acceptance and love for all who were in the orbit. We saw people who were confined to wheelchairs, amputees, and with visual and aural disabilities in each group and they were provided with all necessary accommodations and were part and parcel of the community in every sense of the word. Several of the conventions routinely had sign language interpreters. All of the conventions had special ambassadors or outreach assistants for anyone with special needs. Each group had specific programming for these often-marginalized communities. Conference events that might trigger reactions among the neurodivergent had ample warnings posted and there were several panels at the conferences about navigating neurodivergence in the community. In short, these groups accept and embrace their members as they are and welcome anyone who wants to join in the fun, so long as they follow the main rules of interaction by consent and ubiquitous respect for others.

8

Conclusions, Implications, Paths Forward

Kink Coalitions

This project led us to a clear understanding of many dimensions of the lives and loves of these marginalized communities. Of course, the irony is that the vanilla population and culture define those in the polyamory, BDSM, nudists, and furry communities by sexual deviance which is assumed to be the unifying parameter of these communities. That the vanilla among us obsess about the sex and sex lives of those in these communities while in fact, like the gay, lesbian, and trans communities, sex and sexuality make up only one part of a rich and complex identity, suggests there is an opportunity for education and enlightenment to bring about a greater understanding of the members of these groups. If these identities are core group identities—that is, these identities are the metric through which the individual identifies their group—then society writ large should understand and embrace that sex and sexuality are only small dimensions of these core identities.

In each of these four specific non-traditional sexual minorities—polyamory, BDSM (bondage and discipline, dominance and submission, sadism and masochism), furry, and nudist communities—members have well developed and sometimes overlapping sexual identities. And just like many others who are not in these communities, some have sexual identities that evolve and change over time even as their core group identity remains stable. Again, the sexual aspect of the core group identity is just one facet which varies between the communities and certainly varies among the individuals within each community. Sexuality, which is the factor of prurient interest to the larger culture outside the groups that frames these groups as perverts, is but a part of complex social identities that are equally or more important to those inside the group. The group members in each of these communities are well aware that they are joining, sometimes forming, and participating in disfavored, stigmatized, and ostracized social communities. Despite the well-known and considerable personal and professional risks and costs associated with membership in these groups, our respondents joined these communities to not only be true to who they are as individuals, but also because of the value they derive from their membership in the communities. Defining both the self-concept and the relational self are critical psychosocial processes for these individuals as they embrace these marginalized communities.

Our research revealed that a very large percentage of people in these four communities self-identify as bisexual. In hindsight, this is an obvious finding we should have expected. In polyamory, bisexuality could occur seamlessly where sexual and emotional relationships are not limited to one partner. With the BDSM community, the sexual and relationship dynamic revolves around power differentials and role playing rather than simple gendered norms and definitions. Furries can choose any gender or no gender and exist in a world constructed according to their preferences. There is no controlling canon that frames what is or is not authentic for furries. For nudists, the concept of personal freedom is such a primary motivator that societal barriers to bisexuality are easy to ignore. Moreover, once some level of cultural taboo has been broken, then lesser taboos, or even any taboo, may be more easily breached with less concern about personal or professional ramifications or societal disapproval. That is, to the extent that, for instance, BDSM can be thought of as more exotic or outrageous than bisexuality, BDSM adherents may be more comfortable considering a bisexual experience after having gone "further" than society deems appropriate through BDSM. Intersectionality, in this regard, may empower fuller self-expression.

One particular limitation in our data collection became clear as we saw the number of respondents identifying as bisexual, broadly understood, pile up in our open-ended questions. Specifically, we did not link the open-ended questions to the multiple-choice questionnaire that contained the demographic questions and the political attitude and political actions questions. We intentionally did not link the two questionnaires for several reasons. First, we were uncertain how long people would tolerate taking the survey and we were concerned we would have high response rates on the front end with severe drop off at the back end. Recall there are nine demographic questions, nineteen political attitudes and actions questions, and eleven open-ended questions. We decided that if there were two surveys, people who began the second survey would be more likely to finish it. In other words, the drop off could manifest itself simply as declining to take the second survey. Second, as we anticipated, not everyone wanted to take both surveys. Many respondents only answered the multiple-choice survey and some others only answered the open-ended one. Invariably, many of those who chose only the open-ended questionnaire did so because it was shorter even though they would have to type in their answers. Many of those who chose only the multiple-choice survey did so because they did not want to type out discursive answers and preferred clicking the answer from the multiple-choice roster. The third reason we did not link the two surveys was a concern about ensuring privacy. Our IRBs made several suggestions as to how to credibly present the promise of anonymity to the respondents and this was one of the strategies suggested by them that we embraced. Keep in mind that these populations may be particularly concerned about the risk of a lack of anonymity because of the animus toward the groups from the general population. While it would have been nice to isolate the political activities and political actions of those who identified as bisexual, we cannot be sure if we would have gotten the same enthusiasm and response rate had we taken another approach.

When we compared our data across these groups, we can see that, as a collective of social groups at the periphery of society, they share many of the same political attitudes, perhaps because they face many of the same challenges or perhaps because they share many of the same values. In particular, core values among these communities are tolerance, acceptance, and embrace of everyone else in the community. The exceptions to tolerance, acceptance, and embrace of others in the community were limited to those who violated the norms of tolerance, acceptance, and embrace or some other very important core principal like informed and full consent prior to sexual contact. This respect for the autonomy of others is also quite consistent with the unifying political concern about self-determination and autonomy. Specifically, these communities are much more pro-LGBT rights and pro-choice than the population as a whole.

We have made an initial foray into the scholarly and discursive gap in our knowledge about the political identities, communities, attitudes, and activities of these non-traditional sexual minorities. We believe our construction of the term non-traditional sexual minority has been useful not only for descriptive purposes, but also as a mechanism to differentiate these groups and their members and communities from the more thoroughly studied, and, in our parlance, traditional, minority groups of gay men, lesbians, and members of the trans community. Additional research should be conducted to ascertain whether members of the LGT community have distinctive experiences when enmeshed in these non-traditional sexual communities. That is, it is possible that being a furry or a nudist or in polyamory or BDSM may not be a fundamentally different experience for LGT members of those groups than it is for straight or bisexual members of these groups. Our expectation is that, in many cases and in many ways, the new chosen identity and community would dominate the LGT identity. In other words, at least for some people, we would expect to find that they describe themselves as "a furry who is gay" instead of "a gay who is a furry." Of course, research on the furry fandom is in its infancy and the parameters are still to be sorted out (see, e.g., chapter 22 in Conyers and Calhoun 2020).

As discussed at the beginning, we chose the term "perverts" for framing the project because the elites we interviewed for each group invariably, and without exception, at some point discussed at length the idea that society at large thought of their chosen community as a cluster of perverts that routinely engaged in deviant behavior but did little else. Beth, one of our elites at a BDSM convention, said, "Don't get me wrong. I AM a pervert and I do perverted things pretty routinely, or at least whenever I can. But I am a lot more than that and so is my tribe here." Following the lead of our elites, we use the term with affection and respect for these communities and their members and in the same aesthetic vein and intent as it is used by members of these communities. In other words, we use it to reappropriate the slur and to softly mock those who do not understand, and who still shame and ostracize these communities. We should also point out that we asked each elite we interviewed, as well as a substantial number of those rank-and-file members we interviewed, if they objected to the title of the project, and without exception they enthusiastically supported the perverts nomenclature. Jason, one elite from the polyamory community who is an academic, said "I really like the idea. I think the provocative aspect might help outsiders rethink their prior framing and those in the communities might also revisit whether they have shed shame in their own views of their groups."

The members of each of these groups hold a strong sense of community with other members. For instance, among the polyamorists, the community was very important for 65 percent of our respondents. The open-ended descriptions give us more insight to the power of the community; as one polyamorist said, "I feel we are a large and very close community but well-hidden, as it is still shamed. Having others like me to support me and understand me is a huge importance in my life and I doubt I would be able to function happily without the community."

Interestingly, while the outside world may see these groups as monolithic, within each group, our respondents taught us about the myriad of subsets within the groups that nonetheless shared the larger value system of the umbrella community. Each community had subsets defined by some activities or interests like gaming, arts and crafts, music or writing, golf or tennis, ping pong or billiards. Running clubs are common among all of these groups. Frolicon held a meet up session called "stitch and bitch" for sewing enthusiasts and "knit and bitch" for those who knit. The groups also create specific category names for many of these groups like "Galloping Furries" for a running group among the furry community and "Nerd Polys" for proudly geeky polyamorists. Sports, hobbies, cultural, and scientific interests all have orbits of smaller communities within the larger communities.

An aside, so-called nerds are celebrated in all of these communities. For example, also at Frolicon, there was a gameshow type event at midnight one night called "Um . . . actually" and it was described as "The game where geeks correct other geeks. Contestants will hear several pop culture facts read aloud with each statement having an incorrect piece of information. The player who best corrects their statement earns geek dominance among their peers as well as a chance at winning the game. But don't forget to precede your answer with *Um . . . actually*."

Perhaps not surprisingly, there are many subcommunities within polyamory that also provide a sense of community and belonging in a more task- or interest-specific fashion. We believe much could be learned by a closer examination of these subgroups. We also believe additional research needs to be done on demographic subgroups. In particular, we wish we were able to discover much more about the experience of nonwhites in these communities. We know these race and cultural enclaves within the groups exist, we simply need concerted strategies for getting at them. Additionally, we believe differences and similarities among age cohorts would also deliver a tranche of information that largely eluded us.

We would be remiss if we did not make some observations from this research about the challenges of field work among communities that are vulnerable, hidden, or prefer to not be the focus of attention. We were committed to demonstrating we were open-minded about the communities to maximize the trust we could build in a short period of time with our prospective respondents. This manifested itself in a variety of ways. With the polyamory groups, we made our first forays into the communities through elites with whom we already had a friendship. We entered the community with badges of credibility because of those relationships. We also were particularly aware of maintaining what might be termed a poker face no matter what we were told. The poker face was critical for all the groups.

At Beyond Vanilla, the first BDSM conference, we spent a tremendous amount of time before the conference and at the outset, speaking with Beth, the primary organizer and event manager. We wanted to ensure we did not break any unspoken etiquette rules and that we showed the community respect in every way possible. Of course, we also had an abundant supply of candy available at our table. We also spoke with and engaged the other people at the other tables and booths in the venders' space so that when attendees asked about us, the other venders might be inclined to say something positive about us. This interaction with the venders and artists also led us to many conversations that had an unintended consequence of enlightening us about the community and its members. We had many people tell us that we had been given a nod or word of approval by the other venders. We also were upfront and candid at all of the BDSM events about our lack of familiarity with the community and our desire to learn more about it. Generally speaking, those we interacted with seemed to genuinely enjoy talking about their way of life.

For our research among the nudists, we, perhaps obviously, signaled our trustworthiness by disrobing. We are convinced that a clothed researcher would be completely ignored. One elite, a woman who was one of the managers and owners of the facility in Pennsylvania, told us that while many people came to study the group—mostly psychology and sociology graduate students according to her—the ones who declined to disrobe always left with little to no cooperation from the members of the community. We signaled we could be trusted even if we were betrayed by our tan lines as not actually nudists. Ruth, another woman at Olive Dell Ranch, asked if the two of us who were there were nudists and then looked us up and down and answered her own question with a smile and little laugh "You maybe, but not you!" pointing at the stark tan lines. One of us had gone to several sessions at a tanning booth to minimize tan lines and the other had not.

For the furries, we had furry friendly props with us, including fox tails we wore at two events and a large plush Anteater, the mascot of the University of California–Irvine, at the events where we took surveys in the vender room. We also made sure to comment on the fursuits or partial fursuits whenever appropriate. For the furry conventions, many people participated without any outward manifestation such as a fursuit, so simply being friendly and open-minded and at a conference was a sufficiently strong signal.

For all of the virtual snowball solicitations, we were given permission to post by the moderators of the various sites, and that virtual introduction seems to have given us credibility in those venues. We dutifully answered any questions sent to us by any members of the closed social media groups and often looped the moderators in as an exercise in additional credibility building.

Perhaps the most important trust-building decision we made was to meet the people in their safe spaces. We were approachable precisely because the respondents trust the various elites, owners, and organizers of the various conferences (BDSM and furries), support groups (polyamory), and permanent facilities (nudists). Of course, our transparency about the project and overt commitment to anonymity were also critical to what we see as a successful data gathering effort in very challenging and diverse circumstances.

One interesting aspect of these communities that suggests an avenue for additional research is the potential for possible conflicts of interest between the elites who manage the events and places that are central to these communities and the best interests of the members of the communities. Specifically, at least in some dimensions, should these communities become widely accepted and mainstreamed, the need for these safe spaces that are narrowly tailored for the benefit and protection of these communities might diminish. Additionally, we were struck by an interesting generational dynamic. Frequently the elites were long-term members of the community who were often much older than the average member. Other than nudists, the communities had a significant proportion of younger and newer members who were not always aligned with the elders, so to speak, regarding where they wanted to see the community go. In particular, the younger cohorts seemed to desire greater political activity and engagement as a community, while the elders often seemed to want to continue to fly under the radar. The nudists were the exception because the people who frequent the facilities tended to range older than the other groups. We did talk with an acquaintance, young man in his midtwenties, Chas, who identifies as a nudist, but rarely if ever goes to the nudist facilities. He explained that his longtime girlfriend and their circle of friends prefer to go camping and be nude in an unstructured environment in places like Joshua Tree or Big Sur. They are more aligned with the traditional naturists than the nudist community that de-emphasizes sexuality. They avoid the structured nudist facilities in part because Chas and his friends are sexually fluid and see their social nudity in more overtly sexual terms than is embraced by formal nudist facilities. Accordingly, this dynamic might also be present among the nudists but was not as clear to us because the split between age cohorts is more complete. Further research might shed light on the generational distinctions among the groups including the diminution of the role of sex and sexuality in the community by established nudists.

An additional aspect of the dynamics of these communities that bears further research is the notion of "coming out"—or disclosure of identity—for these communities. We found the discussions about coming out to friends and family to sound comparable to the experience of coming out for members of the gay and lesbian communities as well as the trans community. One furry told us that coming out as a furry to his parents was more difficult than coming out as gay. His reasoning was they knew what a gay person was—and had no issues with his sexuality and told him they had thought he was gay since he was very young—but they were mystified by what a furry was. His parents did not know anything about the furry community and initially feared it was some sort of a cult. An elite in BDSM told us she would never come out to her parents as she knew they would not be able to process it and she feared they might try to take custody of her children away from her. While this was not the focus of our inquiry here, the navigation of the peripheral out-group, that is, family and friends that are not part of the specific community, is a facet of these lives that we hope to find out more about in future research.

Another observation we feel compelled to discuss involves the culture of the academy. We sailed through our Institutional Review Boards. While we were correctly determined to be not exempt from oversight because of the risk that these populations contain vulnerable subjects in some way, we found full support, quick responses, and serious and helpful consideration as we developed our empirical strategy. Likewise, when we sought reimbursement for our expenses as we gathered our data in the field, our local finance people were incredibly supportive. However, without fail, we had to write extraordinary justifications for the expenses. We bring this up at this juncture to reiterate that even in the enlightened environment of the academy, these groups face serious stigma.

Finally, we believe there are many communities among us that are invisible to the social sciences but still merit understanding, empathy, and acceptance. The many groups that compose our society and culture as a whole have much more in common than those who benefit from the in-group versus out-group of politics and power would have us all believe.

ACKNOWLEDGMENTS

Collectively, we owe a great debt to many people for their help as this project developed. In particular, Jason Wilby and Jaime Denison were incredibly helpful at the beginning of the project. The good folks at the Albuquerque Social Club and the Albuquerque LGBT Center were kind, patient, and very welcoming. The leaders of the polyamory support group there were also kind and generous with their time. We are especially grateful to "Sarge" at the Albuquerque Social Club for his in-depth explanation about the military origins of the leather and BDSM scenes. Brian Rasmussin's insights were very much appreciated. Beth from Beyond Vanilla was our BDSM spirit guide and we would not have been able to complete the project without her. Kameron Dunn has been an invaluable and irreplaceable source of knowledge and inspiration. Justin Killborn was instrumental at the outset in ensuring we were able to include one of the groups. We are very grateful for Sam Morgan's research assistance, and we also thank Eric Baldwin for his early assistance in data gathering.

We would be remiss if we did not take a moment to thank our institutions. We are so grateful to be located at institutions and in states that embrace and support academic freedom. There are any number of places where this project would not have been allowed or would not have been taken seriously by the academic administration. Our Institutional Review Boards were thorough, efficient, and most importantly, very helpful. Our finance teams consistently went to bat for us and we are so thankful for their insights and efforts.

Over time, we presented evolving versions of the various chapters at a host of annual conferences including those sponsored by the Midwest Political Science Association, the American Political Science Association, the Western Political Science Association, the Southern Political Science Association, and the Law & Society Association. We thank those conferences as well as the discussants, chairs, copanelists, and audience members. Without fail, the project improved after we processed the feedback we received at each conference. No doubt we will inadvertently omit some people, but among those who gave us wonderful feedback, we thank, in no particular order: Angie Wilson, Andrew Flores, Ben Bishin, Heather Smith-Cannoy, Jason Pierceson, Jody Perry, Kelli Johnson, Jami Taylor, Susan Burgess, Heath Fogg Davis, Cynthia Burack, Zein Murib, Tom Keck, Ken Sherrill, Alan Darpini, Alex Keena, Mike Latner, Tony McGann, Russ Dalton, Scott Barclay, Chris Shortell, Charlemagne Chateau, Gabriel Rodenborn, David Lublin, Gabriele Magni, Gary Segura, Jeff Yates, David Leitch, Jeremiah Garretson, Jeremy Serna, Logan Casey, Mateo Espinosa, Matt Dempsey, Phillip Ayoub, Royce Carroll, Scott Swagerty, Alan Darpini, Moopies, Ivan, Lola, Buddy, and Val Jenness. We are profoundly sorry to anyone we may have omitted.

Of course, we are especially grateful to all those people who chose to take our surveys, share their stories, and help guide us through their private terrains and sanctuaries. We were received with more kindness, generosity, good humor, and love than we could have ever hoped for. These communities made this project what it is.

Individually, Tony thanks his husband Julio Rodriguez for putting up with the craziness of the academic life (and this project in particular) and for his constant support and encouragement. Tony is also very grateful for Shawn and Connor and their enthusiastic willingness to jump into this project without reservation.

Shawn thanks his husband Ariel "Buchi" Barcenas for his support and humor and Nomada Bakery for all the coffee and croissants. Shawn also is thankful for the collaboration with Tony and Connor.

Connor would like to thank his wife, Misbah Hyder, for her unyielding support and enthusiasm for telling the stories of those who are overlooked and to Tony and Shawn for their partnership, endurance, and pluck.

REFERENCES

Achen, Christopher H., and Larry Bartels. 2016. *Democracy for Realists: Why Elections Do Not Produce Responsive Government*. Princeton, NJ: Princeton University Press.
Anapol, Deborah. 2010. *Polyamory in the Twenty-First Century*. New York: Roman and Littlefield.
Anderson, Eric. 2010. "'At Least with Cheating There Is an Attempt at Monogamy': Cheating and Monogamism among Undergraduate Heterosexual Men." *Journal of Social and Personal Relationships* 27 (7): 851–72.
Angelides, Steven. 2001. *A History of Bisexuality*. Chicago: The University of Chicago Press.
Annett, Sandra. 2014. *Anime Fan Communities: Transcultural Flows and Frictions*. New York, NY: Palgrave Macmillan.
Arndt, William B., John C. Foehl, F. Elaine Good. 1985. "Specific Sexual Fantasies Themes: A Multidimensional Study." *Journal of Personality and Social Psychology* 48 (2): 472–80.
Aspegren, Elinor. 2020. "A US First? Massachusetts City Votes to Recognize Polyamorous Relationships in Domestic Partnership Policy." *USA Today*, July 3, 2020.
Associated Press. 2012. "Berkeley Lawmakers Recognize Bisexual Pride Day." *Press Democrat*, September 18, 2012.
Aviram, Hadar. 2010. "Geeks, Goddesses, and Green Eggs: Political Mobilization and the Cultural Locus of the Polyamorous Community in the San Francisco Bay Area." In *Understanding Non-Monogamies*, edited by Meg Barker and Darren Langdridge, 87–93. New York: Routledge.
Aviriam, Hadar, and Gwendolyn M. Leachman. 2015. "The Future of Polyamorous Marriage: Lessons from the Marriage Equality Struggle." *Harvard Journal of Law & Gender* 38 (1): 296–336.
Baird, Joel Banner. 2018. "Burlington Naked Man: Police Explain When Public Nudity Crosses Line." *Burlington Free Press*, July 6, 2018. www.burlingtonfreepress.com.
Baldwin, Guy. 1991. "A Second Coming Out." In *Leatherfolk: Radical Sex, People, Politics, and Practice*, edited by Mark Thompson, 169–78. Boston, MA: Alyson Publications.
Baltar, Fabiola, and Ignasi Brunet. 2012. "Social Research 2.0: Virtual Snowball Sampling Method Using Facebook." *Internet Research* 22 (1): 57–74.
Barcan, Ruth. 2004. *Nudity: A Cultural Anatomy*. New York: Oxford University Press.

Barker, Meg. 2005. "This Is My Partner, and This Is My . . . Partner's Partner: Constructing a Polyamorous Identity in a Monogamous World." *Journal of Constructivist Psychology* 18 (1): 75–88.

Barker, Meg, and Darren Langdridge. 2010. "Whatever Happened to Nonmonogamies? Critical Reflections on Recent Research and Theory." *Sexualities* 13 (6): 748–72.

Barnett, Jessica P. 2014. "Polyamory and Criminalization of Plural Conjugal Unions in Canada: Competing Narratives in the s.293 Reference." *Sexuality Research and Social Policy* 11 (1): 63–75.

Barreto, Matt A., and Francisco I. Pedraza. 2009. "The Renewal and Persistence of Group Identification in American Politics." *Electoral Studies* 28 (4): 595–605.

Barringer Gordon, Sarah. 1996a. "'Our National Hearthstone': Anti-Polygamy Fiction and the Sentimental Campaign against Moral Diversity in Antebellum America." *Faculty Scholarship at Penn Law* 1429.

Barringer Gordon, Sarah. 1996b. "The Liberty of Self-Degradation: Polygamy, Women's Suffrage, and Consent in Nineteenth-Century America." *Journal of American History* 83 (3): 815–47.

Bauer, Robin. 2008. "Transgressive and Transformative Gendered Sexual Practices and White Privileges: The Case of the Dyke/Trans BDSM Communities." *WSQ: Women's Studies Quarterly* 36 (3): 233–53.

Bauer, Robin. 2010. "Non-monogamy in Queer BDSM Communities: Putting the Sex Back into Alternative Relationship Practices and Discourse." In *Understanding Non-Monogamies*, edited by Meg Barker and Darren Langdridge, 142. New York: Routledge.

Beckmann, Andrea. 2007. "The 'Bodily Practices' of Consensual 'SM,' Spirituality and Transcendence." In *Safe, Sane, and Consensual: Contemporary Perspectives on Sadomasochism*, edited by Darren Langdridge and Meg Barker, 98–118. Buffalo, NY: Prometheus Books.

Berelson, Bernard, Paul F. Lazarsfeld, and William N. McPhee. 1954. *Voting: A Study of Opinion Formation in a Presidential Campaign. Midway reprint edition*. Chicago: University of Chicago Press.

Bienvenu, Robert V., II. 1998. "The Development of Sadomasochism as a Cultural Style in the Twentieth-Century United States." PhD diss., Indiana University.

Bishin, Benjamin G. 2009. *Tyranny of the Minority: The Subconstituency Politics Theory of Representation*. Philadelphia, PA: Temple University Press.

Bishin, Benjamin G., Thomas J. Hayes, Matthew B. Incantalupo, and Charles Anthony Smith. 2015. "Opinion Backlash and Public Attitudes: Are Political Advances in Gay Rights Counterproductive?" *American Journal of Political Science* 60 (3): 625–48.

Bishin, Benjamin G., Thomas J. Hayes, Matthew B. Incantalupo, and Charles Anthony Smith. 2020. "Elite Mobilization: A Theory Explaining Opposition to Gay Rights." *Law & Society Review* 54 (1): 233–64.

Bishin, Benjamin G., Thomas J. Hayes, Matthew B. Incantalupo, and Charles Anthony Smith. 2021. *Elite-Led Mobilization and Gay Rights, Dispelling the Myth of Mass Opinion Backlash*. Ann Arbor: University of Michigan Press.

Bishin, Benjamin G., and Charles A. Smith. 2013. "When Do Legislators Defy Popular Sovereignty? Testing Theories of Minority Representation." *Political Research Quarterly* 66 (4): 794–803.

Blumstein, Phillip W., and Pepper Schwartz. 1993. "Bisexuality: Some Social Psychology Issues." In *Psychological Perspectives on Lesbian and Gay Male Experience*, edited by Linda D. Garnets, Douglas C. Kimmel, 168–83. New York: Columbia University Press.

Blumstein, Philip W., and Pepper Schwartz. (1977) 2000. "Bisexuality: Some Social Psychological Issues." *Journal of Social Issues* 33 (2): 30–45. Reprinted in *Bisexuality in the United States: A Social Sciences Reader* edited by Paula C. Rodriguez Rust, 339–52. New York: Columbia University Press.

Bobo, Lawrence, and Franklin D. Gilliam Jr. 1990. "Race, Sociopolitical Participation, and Blank Empowerment." *American Political Science Review* 84 (2): 377–93.

Bode, Janet. 1976. *View from Another Closet: Exploring Bisexuality in Women*. New York: Hawthorne.

Brady, Henry E. 2003. "An Analytical Perspective on Participatory Inequality and Economic Inequality." A paper for the Russell Sage Foundation Project on the "Social Dimensions of Inequality." January 28, 2003.

Brooks, Thomas R., Tara N. Bennett, Ashley Myhre, Courtney N. Plante, Stephen Reysen, Sharon E. Roberts, and Kathleen C. Gerbasi. 2022. "'Chasing Tail': Testing the Relative Strength of Sexual Interest and Social Interaction as Predictors of Furry Identity." *Journal of Sex Research*. Last accessed December 5, 2022.

Brown, Courtney, and Michael MacKeun. 1987. "Political Context and Attitude Change." *American Political Science Review* 81 (2): 471–90.

Brown, Meghan Ann. 2015. "Animal People." MA thesis, Iowa State University.

Brumann, Christoph. 2000. "The Dominance of One and its Perils: Charismatic Leadership and Branch Structures in Utopian Communes." *Journal of Anthropological Research*, 56 (4): 425–51.

Bryant, Clifton D., and Craig J. Forsyth. 2012. "The Complexity of Deviant Lifestyles." *Deviant Behavior* 33 (7): 525–49.

Butler, Judith. 1990. *Gender Trouble: Feminism and the Subversion of Identity*. New York: Routledge.

Callis, Abigail S. 2009. "Playing with Butler and Foucault: Bisexuality and Queer Theory." *Journal of Bisexuality*, 9 (3–4): 213–33.

Campbell, Angus, Philip E. Converse, Warren E. Miller, and Donald E. Stokes. 1960. *The American Voter*. New York: John Wiley.

Cardoso, Daniel. 2019. "The Political is Personal: The Importance of Affective Narratives in the Rise of Poly-activism." *Sociological Research Online* 24 (4): 691–708.

Cardoso, Daniel, Ana Rosa, and Marisa Torres da Silva. 2021. "(De) Politicizing Polyamory: Social Media Comments on Media Representations of Consensual Non-Monogamies." *Archives of Sexual Behavior* 50 (2): 1325–40.

Carey, Benedict. 2005. "Straight, Gay, or Lying? Bisexuality Revisited." *New York Times*, July 5, 2005.

Carr-Gomm, Philip. 2010. *A Brief History of Nakedness*. Chicago: Reaktion Books.

Casler, Lawrence. 1971. "Nudist Camps." *Medical Aspects of Human Sexuality* 5 (5): 92–98.

Chandra, Kanchan. 2006. "What is Ethnic Identity and Does It Matter?" *Annual Review of Political Science* 9 (1): 397–424.

Chandra, Kanchan. 2012. Introduction to *Constructivist Theories of Ethnic Politics*, edited by Kanchan Chandra, 1–47. New York: Oxford University Press.

Chauncey, George. *Gay New York: Gender, Culture, and the Making of the Gay Male World, 1890–1940*. New York: Basic Books.

Chmielewski, Wendy E., Louis J. Kern, and Marlyn Klee-Hartzell, eds. 1993. *Women in Spiritual and Communitarian Societies in the United States*. New York: Syracuse University Press.

Coleman, Eli. 1987. "Assessment of Sexual Orientation." *Journal of Homosexuality* 1 (1–2): 9–24.

Colker, Ruth. 1996. *Hybrid: Bisexuals, Multiracials, and Other Misfits under American Law*. New York: New York University Press.

Collins, Patricia Hill. 1990. *Black Feminist Thought: Knowledge, Consciousness and the Politics of Empowerment*. New York: Hyman.

Collis, Clark. 2002. "Dear Superstar: David Bowie; The Thin White Duke is Happy to Answer Your Questions about Cocaine, Ziggy Stardust and Iman. He'd Even Be Happy to Talk about the Mid-'70s—If Only He Could Remember Them." *Blender*, August 2002.

Conley, Terri D., Amy C. Moors, Jes L. Matsick, and Ali Zeigler. 2013. "The Fewer the Merrier?: Assessing Stigma Surrounding Consensually Non-monogamous Romantic Relationships." *Analyses of Social Issues and Public Policy* 13 (1): 1–30.

Conley, Terri D., Ali Zeigler, Amy C. Moors, Jes L. Matsick, and Brandon Valentine. 2012. "A Critical Examination of Popular Assumptions about the Benefits and Outcomes of Monogamous Relationships." *Personality and Social Psychology Review* 17 (2): 124–41.

Connolly, Pamela H. 2006. "Psychological Functioning of Bondage/Domination/Sadomasochism (BDSM) Practitioners." *Journal of Psychology & Human Sexuality* 18 (1): 79–120.

Conyers, Addrain, and Thomas C. Calhoun, eds. 2020. *Deviance Today*. 2nd ed. New York: Routledge.

Cornell University Library. N.d. "Sandstone Retreat Records, Circa 1968–1981." Division of Rare and Manuscript Collections. https://rmc.library.cornell.edu/.

Coyote, Ash. 2020. "The Fandom: A Furry Documentary FULL MOVIE" YouTube. Video 1:28:47. https://youtube.com.

Crowe, Cameron. 1976. "David Bowie: Playboy Interview." *Playboy*. www.playboy.com.

Cummings, Rebekah, and Jeff Turner. 2019. "Response to Anti-Polygamy Legislation." *Women's Exponent Project*. https://exhibits.lib.utah.edu.

Currey, Mason. 2013. "Benjamin Franklin Loved to Compose in the Nude: Naked Calisthenics, Air Baths, Head Stands, and Other Strange Artistic Habits." *Slate*, May 3, 2013. www.slate.com.

Damm, Cassandra, Michael P. Dentato, and Nikki Busch. 2018. "Unravelling Intersecting Identities: Understanding the Lives of People Who Practice BDSM." *Psychology & Sexuality* 9 (1): 21–37.

Darwin, Helena. 2017. "Doing Gender Beyond the Binary: A Virtual Ethnography." *Symbolic Interaction* 40 (3): 317–34.

Davis, Heath Fogg. 2018. *Beyond Trans: Does Gender Matter?* New York: New York University Press.

DeMaria, Richard. 1978. *Communal Love at Oneida: A Perfectionist Vision of Authority, Property, and Sexual Order.* Lewiston, NY: Edwin Mellen.

Deshotels, Tina Hebert, and Craig J. Forsyth. 2020. "Conjuring, Expanding, and Blurring Boundaries of Sexual Subcultures: The Grounding of the Fluid." *Deviant Behavior*, 41 (6): 814–23.

Devine, Christopher J. 2015. "Ideological Social Identity: Psychological Attachment to Ideological In-Groups as a Behavioral Influence." *Political Behavior* 37 (3): 509–35.

Devon, Molly, and Phillip Miller. 2003. *Screw the Roses, Send Me the Thorns: The Romance and Sexual Sorcery of Sadomasochism.* Fairfield, CT: Mystic Rose Books.

Dirda, Michael. 2012. "Library of Congress Issues List of 'Books That Shaped America.'" *Washington Post*, June 21, 2012. www.washingtonpost.com.

Djupe, Paul A., Jacob R. Neiheisel, and Anand E. Sokhey. 2018. "Reconsidering the Role of Politics in Leaving Religion: The Importance of Affiliation." *American Journal of Political Science* 62 (1): 161–75.

Donaldson, Kayleigh. 2018. "Foxy: Why Everyone Has a Crush on Disney's Robin Hood." *SYFY Fangrrls* (blog), May 8, 2018. www.syfy.com/.

Donaldson, Stephen. 1995. "The Bisexual Movement's Beginnings in the 70s: A Personal Retrospective." In *Bisexual Politics: Theories, Queries, & Visions* edited by Naomi Tucker, 31–45. New York: Harrington Park Press.

Douglas, Jack D., Paul K. Rasmussen, and Carol Ann Flanagan. 1977. *The Nude Beach.* Beverly Hills, CA: Sage.

Dunn, Kameron. 2022. "Furry Fandom, Aesthetics, and the Potential in New Objects of Fannish Interest." *Transformative Works and Cultures* 37.

Egan, Patrick J. 2020. "Identity as Dependent Variable: How Americans Shift Their Identity to Align with Their Politics." *American Journal of Political Science*, 65 (3): 699–716.

Eisney, Shiri. 2013. *Bi: Notes for a Bisexual Revolution.* New York: Seal Press.

Ellis, Lee, Donald Burke, and M. Ashley Ames. 1987. "Sexual Orientation as a Continuous Variable: A Comparison Between the Sexes." *Archives in Sexual Behavior* 16 (6): 523–29.

Erickson, Jennifer M., Anna M. Slayton, Joseph G. Petersen, Hannah M. Hyams, Lori J. Howard, Shane Sharp, and Brad J. Sagrin. 2021. "Challenge at the Intersection of Race and Kink: Racial Discrimination, Fetishization, and Inclusivity Within the BDSM (Bondage-Discipline, Dominance-Submission, and Sadism-Masochism) Community." *Archives of Sexual Behavior* 51 (2): 1063–74.

Ernulf, Kurt E., and Sune M. Innala. 1995. "Sexual Bondage: A Review and Unobtrusive Investigation." *Archives of Sexual Behavior* 24 (6): 631–54.

Evans, Kyle. 2008. "The Furry Sociology Survey." *Furry Sociology Survey*. Accessed August 10, 2016. www.cannedgeek.com.

Eve, Even. 1985. "Glossary of Keristan English (Abridged)." *Kerista: Scientific Utopianism and the Humanities* 1 (4). http://kerista.com.

Ferrer, Jorge N. 2018. "Mononormativity, Polypride, and the 'Mono-poly Wars.'" *Sexuality and Culture* 22 (1): 817–36.

Foster, Kimberly. 2015. "Wrestling with Responsibility in the Age of #Blacklivesmatter: A Dialogue." *For Harriet* (blog), October 13, 2015. www.forharriet.com/.

Foucault, Michel. 1990. *The History of Sexuality, Volume I: An Introduction*. New York: Vintage.

Fourier, Charles. (1808) 1996. "The Theory of the Four Movements." In *Cambridge Texts in the History of Political Thought*, edited by Gareth Steadman Jones and Ian Patterson. New York: Cambridge University Press.

Fox, Margalit. 2006. "Nena O'Neill, 82, an Author of 'Open Marriage,' is Dead." *New York Times*, March 26, 2006. https://www.nytimes.com.

Fritscher, Jack. 1991. "Artist Chuck Arnett: His Life/Our Times." In *Leatherfolk: Radical Sex, People, Politics, and Practice*, edited by Mark Thompson, 106–18. Boston, MA: Alyson Publications.

Gates, Gary. 2011. "How Many People are Lesbian, Gay, Bisexual, and Transgender?" Williams Institute, UCLA School of Law. https://williamsinstitute.law.ucla.edu.

Gerbasi, Kathleen C., Penny L. Bernstein, Samuel Conway, Laura L. Scaletta, Adam Privitera, Nicholas Paolone, and Justin Higner. 2008. "Furries from A to Z (Anthropomorphism to Zoomorphism)." *Society and Animals* 16: 197–222.

Gerbasi, Kathleen C., Laura L. Scaletta, Courtney N. Plante, and Penny L. Bernstein. 2011. "Why so FURious? Rebuttal of Dr. Fiona Probyn-Rapsey's Response to Gerbasi et al.'s Furries from A to Z (Anthropomorphism to Zoomorphism)." *Society and Animals* 19 (3): 302–4.

Goffman, Erving. 1963. *Stigma: Notes on the Management of Spoiled Identity*. Englewood Cliffs, NJ: Prentice-Hall.

Goodman, Leo A. 1961. "Snowball Sampling." *Annals of Mathematical Statistics* 32 (1): 148–70.

Gould, Deborah B. 2009. *Moving Politics: Emotion and ACT UP's Fight against AIDS*. Chicago: University of Chicago Press.

Gross, Paul. 1973. "The Ethics of Polygamy." *Reason*, July 1973. https://reason.com.

Gurley, George. 2001. "Pleasures of the Fur." *Vanity Fair*, March 2001. www.vanityfair.com/.

Hamelin, Larry. 2013. "And to No More Settle for Less Purity." *Praxis: A Journal of Politics*, 1 (1): 58–73.

Hamilton, Laura, and Elizabeth. A. Armstrong. 2009. "Gendered Sexuality in Young Adulthood: Double Binds and Flawed Options." *Gender and Society* 23 (5): 589–616.

Hardy, Janet W., and Dossie Easton. 2017. *The Ethical Slut*. 3rd ed. New York: Ten Speed.

Haritaworn, Jin, Chin-ju Lin, Christian Klesse. 2006. "Poly/logue: A Critical Introduction to Polyamory." *Sexualities* 9 (5): 515–29.

Harvard Law Review. 2022. "Three's Company, Too: The Emergence of Polyamorous Partnership Ordinances." *Harvard Law Review* 135 (5): 1441–63.

Haupert, Margaret L., Amanda N. Gesselman, Amy C. Moors, Helen E. Fisher, and Justin R. Garcia. 2016. "Prevalence of Experiences with Consensual Nonmonogamous Relationships: Findings from Two National Samples of Single Americans." *Journal of Sex & Marital Therapy* 43 (5): 434–40.

Healy, Michael John, and Michael B. Beverland. 2013. "Unleashing the Animal Within: Exploring Consumers' Zoomorphic Identity Motives." *Journal of Marketing Management* 29 (1–2): 225–48.

Heckathorn, Douglas D. 1997. "Respondent-Driven Sampling: A New Approach to the Study of Hidden Populations." *Social Problems* 44 (2): 174–99.

Herbert, Ali, and Angela Weaver. 2015. "Perks, Problems, and People Who Play: A Qualitative Exploration of Dominant and Submissive BDSM Roles." *Canadian Journal of Human Sexuality* 24 (1): 49–62.

Herold Junior, Carlos, Bruna Solera, Eliane Regina Crestani Tortola, André Dalben, and Larissa Michele Lara. 2021."Women and Nudity in the Brazilian Naturist Movement in the 1950's." *Revista Estuos Feministas* 29 (3).

Hertzog, Mark. 1996. *The Lavender Vote: Lesbians, Gay Men, and Bisexuals in American Electoral Politics*. New York: New York University Press.

Higginbotham, Evelyn Brooks. 1993. *Righteous Discontent: The Women's Movement in the Black Baptist Church, 1880–1920*. Cambridge, MA: Harvard University Press.

Hoffman, Brian. 2015. *Naked: A Cultural History of American Nudism*. New York: New York University Press.

Hogg, Michael A., Deborah J. Terry. 2000. "Social Identity and Self-Categorization Processes in Organizational Contexts." *American Management Review* 25 (1): 121–40.

Holmes, J. Shormaker. 2006. "Bare Bodies, Beaches, and Boundaries: Abjected Outsiders and Rearticulation at the Nude Beach." *Sexuality and Culture* 10 (4): 29–53.

Holt, Karen. 2016. "Blacklisted: Boundaries, Violations, and Retaliatory Behavior in the BDSM Community." *Deviant Behavior* 37 (8): 917–30.

Hout, Michael, and Claude S. Fischer. 2002. "Why More Americans Have No Religious Preference: Politics and Generations." *American Sociological Review* 67 (2): 165–90.

Howl, Thurston. 2015. "Yiff? Muff? Sex in the Furry Fandom." In *Furries among Us: Essays on Furries by the Most Prominent Members of the Fandom*, edited by Thurston Howl, 48–53. Lansing, MI: Thurston Howl Publications.

Hsu, Kevin J., and J. Micahel Bailey. 2019. "The 'Furry' Phenomenon: Characterizing Sexual Orientation, Sexual Motivation, and Erotic Target Identity Inversions in Male Furries." *Archives of Sexual Behavior* 48: 1349–69.

Huckfeldt, R. Robert, and John D. Sprague. 1995. *Citizens, Politics, and Social Communication: Information and Influence in an Election Campaign.* Cambridge: Cambridge University Press.

Huddy, Leonie, Lilliana Mason, and Lene Aaroe. 2015. "Expressive Partisanship: Campaign Involvement, Political Emotion, and Partisan Identity." *American Political Science Review* 109 (1): 1–17.

Hutchins, Loraine, and Lani Ka'ahumanu. 1991. *Bi by Any Other Name: Bisexual People Speak Out.* New York: Alyson Books.

Ilfeld, Fred, Jr., and Roger Laver. 1964. *Social Nudism in America.* New Haven, CT: College and University Press.

IMDb. 2022. "*Speed Racer.*" Accessed November 30, 2022. www.imdb.com.

Jakobsen, Janet R. 2020. *The Sex Obsession, Perversity and Possibility in American Politics.* New York: New York University Press.

Janus, Samuel S., and Cynthia L. Janus. 1993. *The Janus Report on Sexual Behavior.* New York, NY: Wiley.

Jeansonne, Sherry A. 2012. "Breaking Down Stereotypes: A Look at the Performance of Self Identity with the Furry Community." MA thesis, Texas State University.

Jones, Philip Edward. 2021. "Respectability Politics and Straight Support for LGB Rights." *Political Research Quarterly* 75 (4): 935–49.

Katz, Jonathan. 1976. *Gay American History: Lesbians and Gay Men in the USA; A Documentary History.* New York: Crowell.

Kern, Louis J. 1981. *An Ordered Love: Sex Roles and Sexuality in Victoria Utopias—The Shakers, the Mormons, and the Oneida Community.* Chapel Hill: University of North Carolina Press.

Kernell, Samuel, Jacobson, Gary C., and Lynn Vavreck. 2018. *The Logic of American Politics.* 8th ed. New York, NY: CQ Press.

Key, Vladimer O., Jr. 1984. *Southern Politics in State and Nation.* New York: Alfred A. Knopf.

Kidwell, Claudia Brush. *Women's Bathing and Swimming Costume in the United States.* Project Gutenberg. October 1, 2011. www.gutenberg.org.

Kinder, Donald R., and Nathan P. Kalmoe. 2017. *Neither Liberal nor Conservative: Ideological Innocence in the American Public.* Chicago: University of Chicago Press.

Kingkade, Tyler, Ben Goggin, Ben Collins, and Brandy Zadrozny. 2022. "How an Urban Myth about Litter Boxes Became a GOP Talking Point." *NBC News,* October 14, 2022. www.nbcnews.com.

Kinsey, Alfred C., Wardell B. Pomeroy, and Clyde E. Martin. 1998. *Sexual Behavior in the Human Male.* Bloomington: Indiana University Press.

Kinsey, Alfred C., Wardell B. Pomeroy, Clyde E. Martin, and Paul H. Gebhard. 1998. *Sexual Behavior in the Human Female.* Bloomington: Indiana University Press.

Klee-Hartzell, Marlyn. 1993. "Family Love, True Womanliness, Motherhood, and the Socialization of Girls in the Oneida Community, 1848–1880." In *Women in Spiritual and Communitarian Societies in the United States,* edited by Wendy E. Chmielewski, Louis J. Kern, and Marlyn Klee-Hartzell. New York: Syracuse University Press.

Klein, Marty, and Charles Moser. 2006. "SM (Sadomasochistic) Interests as an Issue in a Child Custody Proceeding." *Journal of Homosexuality* 50 (2–3): 233–42.

Kleinplatz, Peggy J., and Charles Moser, eds. 2006. *Sadomasochism: Powerful Pleasures.* New York: Routledge.

Klesse, Christian. 2014. "Polyamory: Intimate Practice, Identity, or Sexual Orientation?" *Sexualities* 17 (1–2): 81–99.

Kramer, Stephanie. 2020. "Polygamy is Rare Around the World and Mostly Confined to a Few Regions." Pew Research Center, December 7, 2020. www.pewresearch.org.

Langdridge, Darren. 2006. "Voices from the Margins: Sadomasochism and Sexual Citizenship." *Citizenship Studies* 10 (4): 373–89.

Langdridge, Darren, and Trevor Butt. 2005. "The Erotic Construction of Power Exchange." *Journal of Constructivist Psychology* 18 (1): 65–73.

Laroque, J. P. 2014. "A Brief History of BDSM." *Xtra Magazine*, November 13, 2014.

Levine, Ethan Czuy, Debby Herbenick, Omar Martinez, Tsung-Chieh Fu, and Brian Dodge. 2018. "Open Relationships, Nonconsensual Nonmonogamy, and Monogamy among U.S. Adults: Findings from the 2012 National Survey of Sexual Health and Behavior." *Archives of Sexual Health and Behavior* 47 (5): 1439–50.

Lewis, Andy. 2014. "*Fifty Shades of Grey* Sales Hit 100 million." *Hollywood Reporter*, February 16, 2014. www.hollywoodreporter.com.

Lewis, Richard, dir. 2003. *CSI: Crime Scene Investigation.* Season 4, episode 5, "Fur and Loathing." Aired October 30, 2003. Written by Jerry Stahl. California: CBS Paramount.

Loder, Kurt. 1982. "David Bowie: Straight Time. No more Masks or Poses. The Singer Finally Comes Up from Down Under." *Rolling Stone Magazine*, March 12, 1982.

M., Alan. N.d. "A History of Loving More." Loving More. www.lovingmorenonprofit.org.

M., Alan. 2007. "'Polyamory' Enters the Oxford English Dictionary, and Tracking the Word's Origins." *Polyamory in the News!*, January 6, 2007. https://polyinthemedia.blogspot.com.

Maase, Jacob W. 2015. "Keeping the Magic: Fursona Identity and Performance in the Furry Fandom." MA thesis, Western Kentucky University.

MacDonald, A. P., Jr. 1981. "Bisexuality: Some Comments on Research and Theory." *Journal of Homosexuality* 6 (3): 21–36.

MacDonald, A. P., Jr. 1982. "Research on Sexual Orientation: A Bridge that Touches Both Shores but Doesn't Meet in the Middle." *Journal of Sex Education and Therapy* 8 (1): 9–13.

MacDonald, A. P., Jr. (1983) 2000. "A Little Bit of Lavender Goes a Long Way: A Critique of Research on Sexual Orientation." *Journal of Sex Research* 19 (1): 94–100. Reprinted in *Bisexuality in the United States: A Social Sciences Reader*, edited by Paula C. Rodriguez Rust, 24–30. New York: Columbia University Press.

Magister, Thom. 1991. "One among Many: The Seduction and Training of a Leatherman." In *Leatherfolk: Radical Sex, People, Politics, and Practice*, edited by Mark Thompson, 91–105. Boston, MA: Alyson Publications.

Margolis, Michele. 2018. "How Politics Affects Religion: Partisanship, Socialization, and Religiosity in America." *Journal of Politics* 80 (1): 30–43.

Marquis, Kathy. 1993. "Diamond Cut Diamond: The Mormon Wife vs. the True Woman, 1840‑1890." In *Women in Spiritual and Communitarian Societies in the United States*, edited by Wendy E. Chmielewski, Louis J. Kern, and Marlyn Klee-Hartzell. New York: Syracuse University Press.

Martin, Lisa. 2021. "A New Bisexual Tradition." *Bi Women Quarterly*, December 2, 2021. www.biwomenquarterly.com.

Martinez, A. 1985. "Moralists Crusade Takes Toll on Elysium Fields." *American Sunbathing Association Bulletin*, February 1985.

Mays, Dorothy A. 2004. *Women in Early America: Struggle, Survival, and Freedom in a New World*. Santa Barbara, CA: ABC-CLIO.

McConaghy, Nathaniel. 1987. "Heterosexuality/Homosexuality: Dichotomy or Continuum." *Archives of Sexual Behavior* 16: 411–24.

McDonald, Dee. 2010. "Swinging: Pushing the Boundaries of Monogamy?" In *Understanding Non-Monogamies*, edited by Meg Barker and Darren Langdridge, 72–73. New York: Routledge.

Meacham, Jon. 2007. *American Gospel: God, the Founding Fathers, and the Making of a Nation*. New York: Random House Publishing Group.

Midori. 2005. *Wild Side Sex: The Book of Kink*. Los Angeles, CA: Daedalus Publishing.

Milford, Nancy. 2001. *Savage Beauty: The Life of Edna St. Vincent Millay*. New York: Random House.

Miller, Phillip, and Molly Devon. 2003. *Screw the Roses, Send Me the Thorns: The Romance and Sexual Sorcery of Sadomasochism*. Fairfield, CT: Mystic Rose Books.

Mint, Pepper. 2004. "The Power Dynamics of Cheating: Effects on Polyamory and Bisexuality." *Journal of Bisexuality* 4 (3): 55–76.

Monterrubio, Carlos. 2019. "Hosts and Guests' Social Representations of Nudism: A Mutual Gaze Approach." *Annals of Tourism Research* 75: 18–28.

Morgan, Matt. 2008. "Creature Comfort: Anthropomorphism, Sexuality, and Revitalization in the Furry Fandom." MA thesis, Mississippi State University.

Moser, Charles, and Peggy Kleinplatz. 2006. "Introduction to the State of Our Knowledge on SM." *Journal of Homosexuality* 50 (2–3): 1–15.

Nast, Heidi J. 2006. "Loving Whatever: Alienation, Neoliberalism, and Pet-Love in the Twenty-First Century." *International E-Journal for Critical Geographies* 5 (2): 300–327.

Negy, Charles, and Samantha Winton. 2008. "A Comparison of Pro- and Anti-Nudity College Students on Acceptance of Self and of Culturally Diverse Others." *Journal of Sex Research*, 45 (3): 287–94.

New, Christine M., L. Chandler Batchelor, Allison Shimmel-Bristow, Michael Schaeffer-Smith, Erica Magsam, Sara Bridges, Emily L. Brown, and Tristan McKenzie. 2021. "In Their Own Words: Getting It Right for Kink Clients." *Sexual and Relationship Therapy*, August 18, 2021.

Newmahr, Staci. 2010. "Power Struggles: Pain and Authenticity in SM Play." *Symbolic Interaction* 33 (3): 389–411.

Newmahr, Staci. 2011. *Playing on the Edge: Sadomasochism, Risk, and Intimacy*. Bloomington: Indiana University Press.

Ngai, Sianne. 2012. *Our Aesthetic Categories: Zany, Cute, Interesting*. Cambridge, MA: Harvard University Press.

Olsen, Marvin E. 1970. "Social and Political Participation of Blacks." *American Sociological Review* 35 (4): 682–97.

Ortmann, David M., and Richard A. Sprott. 2013. *Sexual Outsiders: Understanding BDSM Sexualities and Communities*. Lanham, MD: Rowman and Littlefield.

Osaki, Alex. 2008. "State of Fandom." *Furry Research Center*, June 27, 2008. http://www.furcenter.org.

Page, Michael. 1998. "The History of the Bi Pride Flag." BiFlag.com, December 5, 1998. Archived from the original on August 1, 2001.

Passet, Joanne E. 2003. *Sex Radicals and the Quest for Women's Equality*. Urbana: University of Illinois Press.

Patten, Fred. 2017. *Furry Fandom Conventions, 1989–2015*. Jefferson, NC: McFarland.

Pedraza, Francisco I., and Matt Barreto. 2009. "The Renewal and Persistence of Group Identification in American Politics." *Electoral Studies* 28 (4): 595–605.

Pew Research Center. 2013. "For the People & the Press Poll." July 2013.

Plante, Courtney N., Stephen Reysen, Sharon E. Roberts, and Kathleen C. Gerbasi. 2013. "Furry Fiesta 2013 Summary." *International Anthropomorphic Research Project*. Accessed August 12, 2016.

Plante, Courtney N., Stephen Reysen, Sharon E. Roberts, and Kathleen C. Gerbasi. 2016. *FurScience! A Summary of Five Years of Research of the International Anthropomorphic Research Project*. Waterloo, ON: FurScience.

Plante, Rebecca F. 2006. "Sexual Spanking, the Self, and the Construction of Deviance." *Journal of Homosexuality* 50 (2–3): 59–79.

Pollen, Annebella. 2017. "Utopian Bodies and Anti-fashion Futures: The Dress Theories and Practices of English Interwar Nudists." Special issue, *Utopian Studies* 28 (3): 451–81.

Polyamory Legal Advocacy Coalition. 2021. "Cambridge Becomes 2nd US City to Legalize Polyamorous Domestic Partnerships." Press release, "Our Mission," March 9, 2021. https://polyamorylegal.org.

Powls, Jonathan, and Jason Davies. 2012. "A Descriptive Review of Research Relating to Sadomasochism: Considerations for Clinical Practice." *Deviant Behavior* 33 (3): 223–34.

Probyn-Rapsey, Fiona. 2011. "Furries and the Limits of Species Identity Disorder: A Response to Gerbasi et al." *Society and Animals* 19 (3): 294–301.

Reid, Luc. 2006. *Talk the Talk: The Slang of 65 American Subcultures*. Cincinnati, OH: Writer's Digest Books.

Reysen, Stephen, Courtney N. Plante, Sharon E. Roberts, and Kathleen Gerbasi. 2020. "Psychology and Fursonas in the Furry Fandom." In *Furries among Us 3: Essays by Furries about Furries*, edited by Thurston Howl, 86–104. Lansing, MI: Thurston Howl Publications.

Rubel, Alicia N., and Tyler J. Burleigh. 2020. "Counting Polyamorists Who Count: Prevalence and Definitions of an Under-Researched Form of Consensual Nonmonogamy." *Sexualities* 23 (1–2): 3–27.

Rubin, Gayle. 1991. "The Catacombs: A Temple of Butthole." In *Leatherfolk: Radical Sex, People, Politics, and Practice* edited by M. Thompson, 119–41. Boston, MA: Alyson.

Rubin, Gayle. 1998. "The Miracle Mile: South of Market and Gay Male Leather 1962–1997." In *Reclaiming San Francisco: History, Politics, Culture*, edited by James Brook, Chris Carlsson, and Nancy J. Peters, 247–72. San Francisco, CA: City Lights.

Rubin, Jennifer D., Amy C. Moors, Jes L. Matsick, Ali Ziegler, and Terri D. Conley. 2014. "On the Margins: Considering Diversity among Consensually Nonmonogamous Relationships." *Journal für Psychologie* 22 (1): 1–23.

Samuel, Lawrence R. 2013. "The American Way of Swinging." *Psychology Today*, August 11, 2013. www.psychologytoday.com.

Sandnabba, N. Kenneth, Pekka Santtila, and Niklas Nordling. 1999. "Sexual Behavior and Social Adaptation among Sadomasochistically Oriented Males." *Journal of Sex Research* 36 (3): 273–82.

Santtila, Pekka, N. Kenneth Sandnabba, Niklas Nordling, and Alison Laurence. 2002. "Investigating the Underling Structure in Sadomasochistically Oriented Behavior." *Archives of Sexual Behavior* 31 (2): 607–27.

Scheff, Elisabeth. 2013. *The Polyamorists Next Door: Inside Multiple-Partner Relationships and Families*. Lanham, MD: Rowman and Littlefield.

Schildkraut, Deborah. 2014. "Boundaries of American Identity: Evolving Understandings of 'Us.'" *Annual Review of Political Science* 17: 441–60.

Schilt, Kristen and Laurel Westbrook. 2009. "Doing Gender, Doing Heteronormativity: 'Gender Normals,' Transgender People, and the Social Maintenance of Heterosexuality." *Gender and Society* 23 (4): 440–64.

Schrank, Sarah. 2019. *Free and Natural: Nudity and the American Cult of the Body; Nature and Culture in America*. Philadelphia: University of Pennsylvania Press.

Schroer, Sandra Ellen. 2005 *State of the "Union": Marriage and Free Love in the Late 1800s* New York: Routledge.

Schulenberg, Shawn. 2013. "Essentially Contested Subjects: Some Ontological and Epistemological Considerations When Studying Homosexuals and Terrorists." *New Political Science* 35 (3): 449–62.

Scott, Gini Graham. 1980. *Erotic Power: An Exploration of Dominance and Submission*. Secaucus, NJ: Citadel Press.

Seabrook, Jason. 2010. "'It Gives Me Thunder': Reflections on 'Becoming Fur.'" MA thesis, Carleton University.

Sedgwick, Eve Kosofsky. 1990. *Epistemology of the Closet*. Berkeley: University of California Press.

Seguin, Lea J. 2019. "The Good, the Bad, and the Ugly: Lay Attitudes and Perceptions of Polyamory." *Sexualities* 22 (4): 669–90.

Sheff, Elisabeth A. 2012. "Three Waves of Non-monogamy: A Select History of Polyamory in the United States." Sheff Consulting (blog), October 23, 2012. https://elisabethsheff.com.

Sheff, Elisabeth A. 2022. "The Second Wave of Consensual Non-monogamy in the U.S." *Psychology Today*, April 27, 2022. www.psychologytoday.com.

Sheff, Elisabeth, and Corie Hammers. 2011. "The Privilege of Perversities: Race, Class, and Education among Polyamorists and Kinksters." *Psychology & Sexuality* 2 (3): 198–223.

Simula, Brandy. 2015. "Exploring Women's, Trans*, and Queer BDSM Subcultures." *Sex Roles* 73 (9–10): 456–58.

Smith, Charles A. 2007. "The Electoral Capture of Gay and Lesbian Americans: Evidence and Implications from the 2004 Election." *Studies in Law, Politics, and Society* 40: 103–21.

Smith, Charles A. 2011. "Gay, Straight, or Questioning? Sexuality and Political Science." *Political Science & Politics* 44 (1): 35–38.

Smith, Charles A., Shawn R. Schulenberg, and Eric Baldwin. 2017. "The 'B' Isn't Silent: Bisexual Communities and Political Activism." In *LGBTQ Politics: A Critical Reader* edited by Marla Brettschneider, Susan Burgess, and Christine Keating, 89–109. New York: New York University Press.

Smith, Glenn, and Michael King. 2009. "Naturism and Sexuality: Broadening Our Approach to Sexual Wellbeing." *Health and Place* 15 (2): 439–46.

Smith, H.W. 1980. "A modest test of cross-cultural differences in sexual modesty, embarrassment and self-disclosure." *Qualitative Sociology* 3, 223–241.

Sprott, Richard, and Anna Randall. 2017. "Health Disparities among Kinky Sex Practitioners." *Current Sexual Health Reports* 9 (3): 104–8.

Spurlock, John C. 1988. *Free Love: Marriage and Middle-Class Radicalism in America, 1825–1860*. New York: New York University Press.

Stansell, Christine. 2000. *American Moderns: Bohemian New York and the Creation of a New Century*. New York: Henry Holt and Company.

States News Services. 1989. "Lobbying for Nudists' Rights." *New York Times*, December 24, 1989. www.nytimes.com.

Statista.com. 2021. "Total Population of the United States by Gender 2010–2025." Accessed November 4, 2021.www.statista.com.

Steadman Jones, Gareth, and Ian Patterson, eds. 1996. *The Theory of the Four Movements, Cambridge Texts in the History of Political Thought*. New York: Cambridge University Press.

Stein, David. 1991. "S/M Copernican Revolution: From a closed world to the infinite universe." In *Leatherfolk: Radical Sex, People, Politics, and Practice* edited by M. Thompson, 142–56. Boston, MA: Alyson.

Stoehr, Taylor. 1979. *Free Love in America: A Documentary History*. New York: AMS Press.

Story, Marilyn D. 1987. "A Comparison of Social Nudists and Non-nudists on Experience with Various Sexual Outlets." *Journal of Sex Research* 23 (2): 197–211.

Strike, Joe. 2017. *Furry Nation: The True Story of America's Most Misunderstood Subculture*. Jersey City, NJ: Cleis Press.
Strobel, Connor B. S. 2022a. "Devising Deviance: Class, Race, and the Making of the Sexual Underclass." PhD diss., University of California Irvine.
Strobel, Connor B. S. 2022b. "The Shadow that Hovered Over: Gender Salience in Eating Disorder Recovery." *Gender Issues* 39: 368–86.
Sunday Times. 2014. "Morning Glory Zell Ravenheart." July 27, 2014. www.thetimes.co.uk.
Taylor, Jami K., Daniel C. Lewis, and Donald Haider-Markel. 2018. *The Remarkable Rise of Transgender Rights*. Ann Arbor: University of Michigan Press.
Theroux, Louis. 2018. *Louis Theroux: Altered States*. Season 1, episode 1, "Love Without Limits." Aired November 4, 2018, on BBC Two. Produced and directed by Aaron Fellows.
Thompson, Bill. 1994. *Sadomasochism: Painful Perversion or Pleasurable Play?* London: Cassell.
Thompson, Mark. 1991. *Leatherfolk: Radical Sex, People, Politics, and Practice*. Boston, MA: Alyson.
Travis, John. 1997. "Sea-Bathing from 1730 to 1900." In *Recreation and the Sea* edited by Stephen Fisher. Exeter: University of Exeter Press.
Uslaner, Eric, and Mitchell Brown. 2005. "Inequality, Trust, and Civic Engagement." *American Politics Research* 33 (6): 868–94.
Vaid, Urvashi. 1995. *Virtual Equality: The Mainstreaming of Gay and Lesbian Liberation*. New York: Anchor Books.
Van Wyk, Paul H., and Chrissan. S. Geist. 1984. "Psychosocial Development of Heterosexual, Bisexual, and Homosexual Behavior." *Archives of Sexual Behavior* 13 (6): 505–44.
Vazquez Richard A. 2001. "The Practice of Polygamy: Legitimate Free Exercise of Religion or Legitimate Public Menace? Revisiting Reynolds in Light of Modern Constitutional Jurisprudence." *New York University Journal of Legislation and Public Policy* 5 (1): 225–54.
Verba, Sidney, Kay Lehman Schlozman, and Henry Brady. 1995. *Voice and Equality: Civic Voluntarism in American Politics*. Cambridge, MA: Harvard University Press.
Vidal, Gore. 1969. "A Distasteful Encounter with William F. Buckley Jr." *Esquire*, September 1, 1969.
Vignoles, Vivian L., Camillo Regalia, Claudia Manzi, Jen Golledge, and Eugenia Scabini. 2006. "Beyond Self-Esteem: Influence of Multiple Moties on Identity Construction." *Journal of Personality and Social Psychology* 90 (2): 308–33.
Vonnegut, Kurt. 1990. "Heinlein Gets the Last Word." *New York Times*, December 9, 1990. www.nytimes.com.
Warner, Michael. 1999. *The Trouble with Normal: Sex, Politics, and the Ethics of Queer Life*. New York: Free Press.
Weinberg, Jill D. 2016. *Consensual Violence: Sex, Sports, and the Politics of Injury*. Oakland: University of California Press.
Weinberg, Martin S. 1971. "Nudists." *Sexual Behavior* 1 (5): 51–55.

Weinberg, Martin S., Colin J. Williams, and Charles Moser. 1984. "The Social Constituents of Sadomasochism." *Social Problems* 31 (4): 379–89.

Weiss, Margot. 2006. "Mainstreaming Kink." *Journal of Homosexuality* 50 (2–3): 103–32.

Weiss, Margot. 2011. *Techniques of Pleasure: BDSM and the Circuits of Sexuality*. Durham, NC: Duke University Press.

Weiss, Margot. 2015. "BDSM (Bondage, Discipline, Domination, Submission, Sadomasochism)." In *The International Encyclopedia of Human Sexuality* edited by Patricia Whelehan and Anne Bolin, 113–16. New York, NY: John Wiley.

Weitzman, Geri. 2006. "Therapy with Clients Who Are Bisexual and Polyamorous." *Journal of Bisexuality* 6 (1–2): 137–64.

West, Candace, and Don H. Zimmerman. 1987. "Doing Gender." *Gender and Society* 1 (2): 125–51.

West, Keon. 2018. "Naked and Unashamed: Investigations and Applications of the Effects of Naturist Activities on Body Image, Self-Esteem, and Life Satisfaction." *Journal of Happiness Studies* 19: 677–97.

Wheeler, Leigh Ann. 2013. *How Sex Became a Civil Liberty*. New York: Oxford University Press.

Williams, John Alexander. 2007. *Turning to Nature in Germany: Hiking, Nudism, and Conservation 1900–1940*. Palo Alto: Stanford University Press.

Wonderley, Anthony. 2017. *Oneida Utopia: A Community Searching for Happiness & Prosperity*. Ithaca, NY: Cornell University Press.

Wright, Susan. 2006. "Discrimination of SM-Identified Individuals." *Journal of Homosexuality* 50 (2): 217–31.

Yardley, William. 2013. "John Williamson, Co-Founder of the Sandstone Retreat, Dies at 80." *New York Times*, May 4, 2013. www.nytimes.com.

Yost, Megan R. 2010. "Consensual Sexual Sadomasochism and Sexual Aggression Perpetration: Exploring the Erotic Value of Power." PhD diss, University of California Santa Cruz.

Yost, Megan R., and Lindsay E. Hunter. 2012. "BDSM Practitioners' Understanding of Their Initial Attraction to BDSM Sexuality: Essentialists and Constructivist Narratives." *Psychology & Sexuality* 3 (3): 244–59.

Young, Jessica M. 2014. "We Are Pioneers: Polyamorists' Stigma Management Strategies." MA thesis, Southern Illinois University.

Zhang, Weiwu, Thomas Johnson, Trent Seltzer, and Shannon Richard. 2010. "The Revolution Will Be Networked: The Influence of Social Networking Sites on Political Attitudes and Behavior." *Social Science Computer Review* 28 (1): 75–92.

INDEX

abortion rights, 61
Adams, John Quincy, 114–15
aesthetic, xi, 8, 72, 74, 149–50, 152, 168, 171
agism, 93, 173–74
AIDS epidemic. *See* HIV/AIDS
Algos, Queen Ana, 89–90
American Association for Nude Recreation, 125
American Civil Liberties Union (ACLU), 78, 118–20, 121
American Gymnosophical Society, 125
American Institute of Bisexuality, 200
Andrews, Stephen Pearl, 36
anime, 158, 172
anthropomorphism, 150–51, 157
Anti-Polygamy Society, 32
Arnett, Chuck, 77–78
asexuality, 21, 182–83, 205, 208, 211
assimilation, 198
Aviram, Hadar, 43

Bartell, Gilbert D., 39
Barthel, Kurt, 125
bathing, 114–15
BDSM, definition, 8–9, 68, 70–71; furry fandom and, 72, 153, 169; legality of, 68, 83–84, 101; nonmonogamy and, 42
Berkman, Alexander, 36
bestiality, 12
Beyond Vanilla, 51–52
Bi Any Other Name: Bisexual People Speak Out (Hutchins and Ka'ahumanu), 195–96
Bienvenu, Robert V. II, 74

bimodal model of sexuality, 1, 6, 11, 186, 216
biphobia, 187
Bisexual Empowerment Conference: A Uniting, Supportive Experience (BECAUSE), 198
bisexuality, 1, 64–65, BDSM and, 209–10, 214; furry fandom and, 211–12, 214–15; legality of, 196; nudism and, 210–11, 213; political activity, 11, 196–98; polyamory and, 206, 208, 214; stereotypes, 190–91, 195
Bisexuality Awareness Week, 199–200
Bisexuality (plus) Day, 198–99
Bisexual Network of the USA, Inc (Bi/Net USA), 198, 199
The Bisexual Option (Klein), 193
Bisexual Political Action Committee (BiPAC), 197–98
Blumstein, Phillip W., 192
Bode, Janet, 192
body image, 105, 109–10, 226
Bowie, David, 202
Brisbane, Albert, 34
Brzezinski, Mika, 161
Bush, George W., 202–3
Butler, Judith, 193–194

Calhoun, Thomas C., 226–27
cartoons, 157–58
Casler, Lawrence, 108
Catholic Church, 117–18
Catholic Legion of Decency, 119–20
Chaddock, Charles Gilbert, 189

255

Chauncey, George, 77
chosen communities, 5–7
Church of All Worlds, 40–41
Citizens United v. FEC, 142–43
The City and the Pillar (Vidal), 201
Coleman, Eli, 193
Colker, Ruth, 196
Collins, Patricia Hill, 196
colonial America, 112–13
Comfort, Alex, 38
coming out, 22–23, 235–36
Communications Decency Act, 83
compersion, 38–39
complex marriage, 33
Comstock Act, 78
consensual nonmonogamy, 7, 27–28
consent, 7, 12, 70, 84, 101, 218, 230
Conway, Samuel, 163–64
Conyers, Addrain, 226–27
cosplay, 9–10, 149
CSI: Crime Scene Investigation, 160–61

Darwin, Helena, 194
DeBlasse, Tony, 83
Defense of Marriage Act, 125
de Sade, Marquis, 73
deviance, 2, 79, 106, 159–60, 161, 216–17, 231
Deviant Behavior (journal), 161
Deviance Today (journal). *See* Calhoun, Conyers
Diagnostic and Statistical Manual of Mental Disorders (DSM), 162–63
"doing gender." *See* West, Candace; Zimmerman
Donaldson, Stephen, 197
Douglas, Jack, 108
Dr. Phil, 160
Drummer, 78
Durkheim, Emile, 108

Edmunds Act, 32
Edmunds-Tucker Act, 32

electoral capture, 203
Ellis, Lee, 193
environmental movement, 144
essentially contested identity, 5, 155–56
The Ethical Slut (Hardy and Easton), 65
Eulenspiegel Society, 81
Evans, Kyle, 166

family, 108, 116–17, 128, 146
fandom, 9–10, 150, 152
fascism, 110
feminism, 37, 81, 192, 194
FetLife, 83
Fifty Shades of Grey (James), 69, 79
flag, bisexuality pride, 200
foot fetish, 71
Foucault, Michel, 192
Fourier, Charles, 33–35
Francoeur, Anna, 38
Francoeur, Robert, 38
Franklin, Benjamin, 113–14
free love, 35–39
free speech, 118
Freud, Sigmund, 189
furaffinity.net, 156
furry fandom, 157–58, 163, art and, 166–67, 183; children and, 10; definition, 9–10; media and, 160–61, 163–74; political engagement, 184–85
furry parade, 170–71
fursona, 10, 149–50, 156
fursuits, 10, 149–50, 171

gay men, 93, 94
gendered norms, 229
Gender Trouble (Butler), 193–94
Gerbasi, Kathleen C., 162–63
The Gold Coast (leather bar), 79
Goldman, Emma, 36
Griswold v. Connecticut, 120

Hannequin, Victor, 35
Hapgood, Hutchins, 36

The Harrad Experiment (Rimmer), 40
Heinlein, Robert, 40
Her (film), 45–46
Hertzog, Mark, 196
heteronormativity, 1, 27–28, 108, 145, 148
heterosexuality, 210
hippy culture, 121–22
The History of Sexuality Vol. 1 (Foucault), 192
HIV/AIDS, 41, 82, 197
Hoffman, Brian, 110
Holmes, Schormaker J., 108, 109
homophobia, 29
Hot and Cool Sex, 38
Howard, Brenda, 197
Hutchins, Loraine, 195–96

identity, 3–4, 5–6, 188, 189
identity politics, 1, 3, 152–53
immigration, 116–17, 189–90
individual sovereignty, 36–37
International Anthropomorphic Research Project, 150, 155, 162, 167
International Mr. Leather, 80
internet, 31, 41–42, 158, 183
intersectionality, 196, 229
Ithaca Statement, 197

James, Henry Sr., 35
Jeansonne, Sherry, 4
The Joy of Sex, 38

Ka'ahumanu, Lani, 195–96
Kerista community, 38
King, Michael, 108
kink, 73–74, 216–17
Kinsey Reports, 191–92
Klein, Fritz, 198
Klein, Marty, 195

Laroque, J.P., 78
latent illegality, 12–13
Lavender Menace, 200

Lavender Scare, 190
Lawrence v. Texas, 147
leather, 71, 75–76
leather community, 8
Leather Pride Flag, 83
legal protections, 5, 6, 12
lesbians, 48, 50, 81
liberty, 120–21
Love in the Phalanstery, 35
Loving More, 42

MacDonald, 192–93
March on Washington for Gay and Lesbian Rights, 82
marriage equality, x, 61–62, 202–3
matrix of domination, 196
Mattachine Society, 197
McCarthyism, 79–80, 190
McConaghy, Nathaniel, 193
media, 45–46, 183
MeToo Era, 83
Meyer v. State of Nebraska, 120
military, 75–76
Modern Times Community, 36
monogamy, 27–28
mononormativity, 27–28
More Joy of Sex, 38
Mormonism, 31–32, 42
Morning Joe, 161
Morrill Anti-Bigamy Act, 32, 42–43
motorcycle club, 75, 76

Naked: A Cultural History of American Nudism (Hoffman), 110
naturists, 9, 105, 111–12, 122, 125, 143–44, 235
Negy, Charles, 110, 146
nerds, 232
New York v. Burke, 119
non-traditional sexual minorities, 2, 231
North, Gary, 198
Noyes, John Humphrey, 32–33, 34, 35–36, 39

Nude & Natural, 126
nudism, 9, 116, 119–20, 123–24, 145
Nudist magazine, 117, 119

Obergefell v. Hodges, x, 84, 125, 204
Oneida Community, 32–33, 35
O'Neill, George, 39
O'Neill, Nena, 39
Open Marriage (O'Neill), 39
Orejudos, Dom, 79–80
Osaki, Alex, 166

Parmelee, Maurice, 146
Parmelee v. United States, 120
patriarchy, 7, 29, 31, 50
Patten, Fred, 158
performative turn, 193–95
Physique Pictoral, 78
Pierce v. Society of Sisters, 120
pinups, 77
political engagement, 95–99, 134–38, 154, 176–79
politics of respectability, 163–65
polyamory, 7–8, 28–29, 41–42, 43
Polyamory Legal Advocacy Coalition (PLAC), 43
polygamy, 7, 12, 30, 31–32, 40
pornography, 167–68
power, fetishization of, 69, 70, 73, 91
Presmont, John, 38
privacy of intimacy, 224–25
Probyn-Rapsey, Fiona, 162–63
Proposition 31 (Rimmer), 40
Psychpathia Sexualis (von Krafft-Ebing), 189
puppy play, 8, 71–72
Puritans, 114

Quakers, 114
queer studies, 194–95

race, 88–89, 219, 233
racialized play, 89–90
religion, 29, 32

religious play, 90–91
Renslow, Chuck, 79–80
representation, 200–201, 204
respectability, 10, 163–65
Reynolds v. United States, 42
right of association, 224–25
Rimmer, Robert, 40
Robin Hood (Disney), 157, 171
Roe v. Wade, 147
roleplaying, 167–68, 218
Rove, Karl, 203

safety, 88, 218
same-sex marriage. *See* marriage equality
Sandstone Retreat, 37
scenes, 70
Schilt, Kristen, 194
Schoonmaker, L. Craig, 197
Schrank, Sarah, 110
Schulenberg, Shawn, 155
Schwartz, Pepper, 192
scripts, 108–9, 128
Seabrook, Jason, 150
"second life," 216–17
Sedgwick, Eve, 194–95
sexual revolution, 39
sex wars, 81–82
Sheff, Elisabeth, 41
shy voters, 224
Sky Farm, 125
Smith, Charles A., 203
Smith, Glenn, 108
Smith, H.W., 108
social construction, 5, 155
social media, 70, 147–48, 217–18
Society of Janus, 81
Stein, David, 82–83
stigma, 4, 6, 12–13, 22, 28, 29, 65, 159
Story, Marilyn D., 109
Stranger in a Strange Land (Heinlein), 40
Swedenborg, Emanuel, 35
swinging, 39–40, 41, 80

Talese, Gay, 38, 40
The Theory of the Four Movements and of General Destinies (Fourier), 33–34
therianthropy, 151
Thompson, Mark, 76
Thy Neighbor's Wife (Talese), 38, 40
traditional sexual minorities, ix
transgender, 1, 186–87, 194

United States v. Windsor, x, 125
utopian communities, 30, 31–35, 36, 37, 123

Van Buren, Martin, 113
vanilla, 228
Vanity Fair, 160
veterans, 75–76
Vidal, Gore, 201-2
View from Another Closet: Exploring Bisexuality in Women (Bode), 192

virtual snowball sampling, 13, 15–16
von Krafft-Ebing, Richard, 189

Weinberg, Martin S., 107–8
Wesp, Jennifer L., 41
Westbrook, Laurel, 194
West, Candace, 193
West, Keon, 109
Wheeler, Leigh Ann, 119
white privilege, 20, 21, 130, 219
Wilde, Oscar, 188, 189–90
Williamson, Barbara, 37–38
Williamson, John, 37–38
Winton, Samantha, 110, 146
Women's Christian Temperance Union, 32

yiff, 156
youth, 50–51

Zell, Oberon, 40
Zimmerman, Don H., 193

ABOUT THE AUTHORS

CHARLES ANTHONY "TONY" SMITH is Professor of Political Science and Law at the University of California–Irvine. He is author and co-author of seven books including *Gerrymandering in America: The House of Representatives, the Supreme Court, and the Future of Popular Sovereignty*; *Gerrymandering the States: Partisanship, Race, and the Transformation of American Federalism*; *Elite-Led Mobilization and Gay Rights: Dispelling the Myth of Mass Opinion Backlash*; and *The Rise and Fall of War Crimes Trials: From Charles I to Bush II*. He is currently the Editor in Chief of *Political Research Quarterly*.

SHAWN R. SCHULENBERG is Professor of Political Science and Chair of the Faculty Senate at Marshall University. He is the co-editor of *Same-Sex Marriage in Latin America* and *Same-Sex Marriage in the Americas* well as several articles and book chapters on sexuality and politics. His research includes work on same-sex marriage in Latin America.

CONNOR B. S. STROBEL is Collegiate Assistant Professor and a Harper-Schmidt Fellow in the Society of Fellows and at the University of Chicago.

www.ingramcontent.com/pod-product-compliance
Lightning Source LLC
Chambersburg PA
CBHW031144020426
42333CB00013B/501